America's Heritage Trail

South Carolina

North Carolina

Virginia

*A Tour Guide to Historical
Sites of the Colonial and
Revolutionary War Period*
BY M. VICTOR ALPER

America's Heritage Trail

COLLIER BOOKS
A Division of Macmillan Publishing Co., Inc.
New York

COLLIER MACMILLAN PUBLISHERS
London

Macmillan Publishing Co., Inc.
866 Third Avenue, New York, N. Y. 10022
Collier Macmillan Canada, Ltd.

Library of Congress Cataloging in Publication Data
Alper, M   Victor.
    America's heritage trail.
    Includes index.
    1.   South Carolina—Description and travel—1951-
—Guide-books.   2.   North Carolina—Description and
travel—1951-   —Guide-books.   3.   Virginia—
Description and travel—1951-   —Guide-books.
I.   Title.
F267.3.A46   1976   917.5   75-45114
ISBN 0-02-097160-5   pbk.

First Collier Books Edition 1976

America's Heritage Trail is also published in a hardcover
edition by Macmillan Publishing Co., Inc.

Designed by Jack Meserole

Maps by Clarice Borio, New York City, New York

Printed in the United States of America

For J. Sokol

Contents

LIST OF MAPS   xi

ACKNOWLEDGMENTS   xiii

TO THE READER   xv

CHRONOLOGY OF THE AMERICAN
REVOLUTION   xvii

South Carolina

CHARLESTON   3

Revolutionary War History, 3
Colonial and Revolutionary War Sites, 7
Important Colonial Houses, 24
Non-Revolutionary Sites of Interest, 28
Recommended Side Trips, 33

GEORGETOWN   43

Revolutionary War History, 43
Colonial and Revolutionary War Sites, 44
Important Colonial Houses, 46

SANTEE   48

Revolutionary War History, 48
Colonial and Revolutionary War Sites, 49
Non-Revolutionary Site of Interest, 51

CAMDEN   52
    Revolutionary War History, 52
    Colonial and Revolutionary War Sites, 54
    Other Revolutionary War Sites and
       Important Colonial Houses, 61
    Non-Revolutionary Sites of Interest, 62
    Recommended Side Trips, 64

SPARTANBURG AREA   69
    King's Mountain—Revolutionary War History, 69
    King's Mountain National Military Park, 71
    Cowpens—Revolutionary War History, 75
    Cowpens National Battlefield Site, 77
    Downtown Spartanburg, 78
    Recommended Side Trip, 81

North Carolina

GREENSBORO AREA   87
    Guilford Courthouse—Revolutionary War History, 87
    Guilford Courthouse National Military Park, 89
    Alamance—Revolutionary War History, 98
    Alamance Battleground State Historic Site, 100

WINSTON-SALEM (OLD SALEM)   104
    Revolutionary War History, 104
    Old Salem Sites, 108

HILLSBOROUGH   115
    Revolutionary War History, 115
    Hillsborough Sites, 116

WILMINGTON AREA   119
    Revolutionary War History, 119
    Colonial and Revolutionary War Sites, 121

Important Colonial Houses, 123
Non-Revolutionary Sites of Interest, 125
Brunswick Town—Revolutionary War History, 126
Brunswick Town State Historic Site, 127
Orton Plantation—Revolutionary War History, 131
Currie (Moore's Creek)—Revolutionary War History, 132
Moore's Creek National Military Park, 134

NEW BERN   138
  Revolutionary War History, 138
  Colonial and Revolutionary War Sites, 139
  Important Colonial Houses, 146

EDENTON   148
  Revolutionary War History, 148
  Colonial and Revolutionary War Sites, 150
  Important Colonial Houses, 157

Virginia

WILLIAMSBURG   161
  Revolutionary War History, 161
  Williamsburg Sites, 165
  Recommended Side Trip, 178

YORKTOWN   180
  Revolutionary War History, 180
  Yorktown Battlefield Site, 184
  Yorktown—"Town of York," 188
  Recommended Side Trip, 192

RICHMOND   198
  Revolutionary War History, 198
  Colonial and Revolutionary War Sites, 201
  Important Colonial Houses, 205

Non-Revolutionary Sites of Interest, 206
Recommended Side Trips, 209

CHARLOTTESVILLE   212
Revolutionary War History, 212
Monticello, 213
Other Sites near Monticello, 217
Downtown Charlottesville, 219

FREDERICKSBURG   221
Revolutionary War History, 221
Colonial and Revolutionary War Sites, 223
Important Colonial Houses, 232
Non-Revolutionary Sites of Interest, 233
Recommended Side Trip, 235

ALEXANDRIA   239
Revolutionary War History, 239
Colonial and Revolutionary War Sites, 241
Important Colonial Houses, 251
Recommended Side Trips, 252

MOUNT VERNON   258
Revolutionary War History, 258
Mount Vernon Mansion, 260

Useful Facts

STATE FACTS   267
MOTELS AND HOTELS   270
CAR RENTALS   292
INFORMATION FOR INTERNATIONAL
VISITORS   293
INDEX   303

List of Maps

South Carolina   2

North Carolina   86

Virginia   160

Acknowledgments

I am grateful for the courteous assistance of the staffs of the New York Public Library, Charleston County Library, Wilmington Public Library, Charlottesville Public Library, and the libraries of the University of South Carolina and the University of Virginia. The following institutions also have been most helpful: Charleston Museum; Georgetown Chamber of Commerce; Hillsborough Chamber of Commerce; Richmond Chamber of Commerce; New Bern Historical Society; Historic Edenton, Inc.; North Carolina Department of Archives; Virginia State Travel Service; and the National Park Service of the U.S. Department of the Interior.

I am indebted to the following people, who have been generous in their aid: Mrs. Edward Ball, Charleston; James Buchanan, Director, Walnut Grove Plantation; David Sanders, Director, Alamance Battleground State Historic Site; William Hubbard, Director, Guilford Courthouse National Military Park; Michael W. Brantley, Director, Tryon Palace Complex; Professor W. K. Dorsey, Cape Fear Technical Institute; Ann Jordan, Moore's Creek National Military Park; Laura Feller, Moore House, Yorktown Battlefield Site; Thomas Whitford, Press Bureau, Colonial Williamsburg; and Margaret B. Sinclair, Tourist Council, Alexandria. Thanks is due to J. Sokol for many stimulating discussions and to F. Roffman for an astute reading of sections of the manuscript.

I also wish to acknowledge my debt to these excellent books: Beverly Da Costa, ed., *Historic Houses of America* (New York, 1971); Marshall Davidson, *Colonial Antiques* (New York, 1967); *Historical Handbook* Series, National Park Service (Washington, D.C., dates vary); Frank Sarles and Charles Shedd, *Colonials and Patriots* (Washington, D.C., 1964); George Scheer and Hugh Rankin, *Rebels and Redcoats* (New York, 1957); and Christopher Ward, *The War of the Revolution* (New York, 1952).

To the Reader

This book describes major events and battles of the American Revolution and presents practical information for travelers who wish to explore America's Heritage Trail. Although Colonial and Revolutionary War Sites are emphasized in the text, subordinate sections—"Non-Revolutionary Sites of Interest" and "Recommended Side Trips"— are included to permit travelers to experience other aspects of a region's history. The suggested Walking and Driving Tours list the individual sites in the order encountered by sightseers. Afterward, these sites, arranged *alphabetically* according to category, are described in detail.

The narrative, which begins with the British siege of Charleston and ends with the death of George Washington at Mount Vernon, takes the reader on a northward journey —from South Carolina into North Carolina and then Virginia. Since the narrative units are self-contained, however, one may start at any point.

Visitors to sites are advised to verify schedules and admission fees, which are subject to change. Because many historic houses are being restored for the Bicentennial, their contents may differ slightly from the descriptions herein. If recommended roads are under construction, alternate routes may be followed with the aid of a good road map. Every effort has been made to print the most recent data, but the author and the publisher cannot be responsible for any changes of information or omissions.

As you read these pages, it is hoped that the fascinating drama of the American Revolution may excite your imagination and stir your spirit.

Chronology of the American Revolution

1770

MARCH 5	The Boston Massacre: British soldiers fire on a crowd in Boston, resulting in the death of five persons.
APRIL 12	Parliament repeals duties (imposed by the Townshend Revenue Act, November 20, 1767) on paper, glass, lead, and dyestuff but retains the tax on tea.

1771

MAY 16	Royal Governor Tryon's forces crush a Regulator uprising at Alamance, North Carolina.
JUNE 19	Six Regulators are executed at Hillsborough, North Carolina.

1772

JUNE 9	Rhode Islanders attack and burn the British ship *Gaspée*.
NOVEMBER 2	Samuel Adams organizes the first Committee of Correspondence in Boston.

1773

MAY 10   To save the mismanaged East India
                Company from bankruptcy, Parliament
                partially refunds taxes the company had
                paid and permits shipment of tea directly
                to retailers in the American colonies.
                Established importers and citizens pro-
                test.

DECEMBER 16   Boston Tea Party: Men disguised as
                Indians board three ships in Boston Har-
                bor and heave 342 chests of tea into the
                water.

1774

MAY–JUNE   The Coercive Acts ("Intolerable Acts")
                passed by Parliament go into effect. The
                Massachusetts Government Act (May 20)
                modifies the provincial government by
                providing a new council under a military
                governor, who also has authority over
                town meetings. The Administration of
                Justice Act (May 20) protects officials
                of the Crown accused of capital offenses
                by permitting them to be tried elsewhere.
                The Boston Port Bill (June 1) closes
                Boston to commerce. The extension of the
                Quartering Act (June 2) provides for the
                housing of British troops in America.

JUNE 22   The Quebec Act grants the territory be-
                tween the Ohio and Mississippi Rivers to
                the province of Quebec, thereby estab-
                lishing Roman Catholicism and French
                civil law in the area.

SEPTEMBER 5   The First Continental Congress (fifty-six delegates from twelve colonies) meets in Philadelphia.

SEPTEMBER 9   Delegates from towns in Suffolk County, Massachusetts, adopt the Suffolk Resolves, which denounce the Coercive Acts as unconstitutional and recommend economic sanctions against England.

OCTOBER 25   Angry women of Edenton, North Carolina, sign a resolution protesting the tax on tea and the harsh policies of the British government.

1775

MARCH 23   Patrick Henry delivers his "Give me Liberty or give me Death" speech in Richmond, Virginia.

APRIL 19   At Lexington, Massachusetts, British soldiers fire on the Patriots, then march to Concord where the Redcoats are forced to retreat.

APRIL 19   The siege of Boston begins: Patriot forces surround the British garrisoned in the city.

APRIL 20   Royal Governor Dunmore of Virginia orders powder and munitions secretly removed from the Williamsburg Magazine, causing Patriots to march on the town.

MAY 10   The Second Continental Congress convenes in Philadelphia.

MAY 10   Fort Ticonderoga, New York, is captured by a detachment of Green Mountain Boys under Ethan Allen and troops commanded by Benedict Arnold.

MAY 24 — John Hancock is elected president of the Continental Congress.

JUNE 11–12 — The first naval battle of the American Revolution occurs near Machias, Maine, resulting in the capture of two British ships, the *Margaretta* and the *Unity*.

JUNE 15 — The Second Continental Congress elects George Washington Commander-in-Chief of the Continental Army.

JUNE 17 — At the Battle of Bunker Hill (Breed's Hill) the British rout the Patriots but sustain high casualties.

JULY 3 — In Cambridge, Massachusetts, Washington assumes command of the army.

DECEMBER 22 — Esek Hopkins is appointed Commander-in-Chief of the Continental Navy.

1776

JANUARY 1 — The American assault on Quebec fails.

JANUARY 9 — Thomas Paine publishes *Common Sense*, urging Americans to declare their independence of Great Britain.

FEBRUARY 27 — The Patriots are victorious at the Battle of Moore's Creek, North Carolina.

MARCH 17 — The British evacuate Boston.

APRIL 17 — John Barry is the first commissioned officer of the American Navy to capture a British warship, the *Edward*.

JUNE 28   Patriot forces on Sullivan's Island, South Carolina, repulse the British fleet, preventing its entry into Charleston Harbor.

JULY 4   The Continental Congress adopts the Declaration of Independence.

AUGUST 27   The British overpower the Americans during the Battle of Long Island.

AUGUST 29   Washington's defeated troops retreat to Manhattan.

SEPTEMBER 15 British warships move into the East River and force the Americans to withdraw from mid-Manhattan.

SEPTEMBER 16 At Harlem Heights, New York, the Americans prove their ability to drive back the enemy.

SEPTEMBER 21 Nathan Hale is captured.

SEPTEMBER 26 Congress appoints Benjamin Franklin a Commissioner to Paris.

OCTOBER 28   The Patriots are defeated at White Plains, New York.

NOVEMBER 16 Fort Washington on Manhattan is captured by British and German troops.

NOVEMBER 20 Americans abandon Fort Lee, New Jersey.

DECEMBER 8   The British occupy Newport, Rhode Island.

DECEMBER 26 After crossing the Delaware River, Washington and his men surprise the Hessians quartered at Trenton.

1777

JANUARY 3	At the Battle of Princeton Washington's counteroffensive compels the British to withdraw.
JANUARY 6	Washington establishes his winter headquarters at Morristown, New Jersey.
JUNE 13	The Marquis de Lafayette arrives in America to join the Patriot cause.
JUNE 14	The Continental Congress passes a resolution authorizing the design of the American flag.
AUGUST 16	Americans overpower their enemy during the Battle of Bennington.
SEPTEMBER 11	General William Howe's troops defeat Washington's army at the Battle of Brandywine, Pennsylvania.
SEPTEMBER 18	The Continental Congress flees Philadelphia.
SEPTEMBER 19	Patriots clash with General John Burgoyne's soldiers at Freeman's Farm (Saratoga Campaign).
SEPTEMBER 20	General Anthony Wayne's men are caught in a surprise attack, the "Paoli Massacre."
SEPTEMBER 26	General Howe occupies Philadelphia.
OCTOBER 4	American strategy fails at the Battle of Germantown.
OCTOBER 7	Americans defeat Burgoyne's troops at Bemis Heights (Saratoga Campaign).

OCTOBER 17	General Burgoyne surrenders his army at Saratoga, a serious defeat for the British.
NOVEMBER 15	Congress adopts the Articles of Confederation.
NOVEMBER 16	Fort Mifflin, Pennsylvania, is abandoned by the Patriots.
DECEMBER 19	The Continental Army establishes its camp at Valley Forge (until June 18–19, 1778).

1778

FEBRUARY 6	France signs a Treaty of Alliance with America.
MAY 18	General Howe turns over command of British forces in America to Henry Clinton.
JUNE 18	Clinton evacuates Philadelphia and marches toward New York City.
JUNE 28	A series of confused assaults occurs at Monmouth, New Jersey.
JULY 3–5	Indians and Loyalists destroy houses and massacre residents of Wyoming Valley, Pennsylvania.
DECEMBER 29	The British capture Savannah, Georgia.

1779

JUNE 16	Spain declares war on Great Britain.
JULY 5	New Haven, Connecticut, is attacked by a British expedition.

JULY 16   General Anthony Wayne's men capture the British-held fortification at Stony Point, New York.

SEPTEMBER 23   In an important naval battle John Paul Jones forces the surrender of the British ship *Serapis*.

SEPTEMBER 27   John Jay is named Minister to Spain.

OCTOBER 9   A Franco-American attempt to retake Savannah fails.

OCTOBER 25   The British evacuate Newport, Rhode Island.

1780

MARCH 15   Congress devalues American currency.

MAY 12   Charleston, South Carolina, is occupied by the British.

JULY 10   French troops under Rochambeau arrive at Newport.

AUGUST 16   Americans suffer a serious defeat at Camden, South Carolina.

SEPTEMBER 23   Benedict Arnold's treachery is discovered.

OCTOBER 2   Major John André, a British spy who negotiated with Arnold for the betrayal of West Point, is executed.

OCTOBER 7   Patriot forces crush their adversary at King's Mountain, South Carolina.

OCTOBER 14   General Nathanael Greene assumes command of the American forces in the South.

1781

JANUARY 5–7   British forces plunder Richmond, Virginia.

JANUARY 17   The Patriots are victorious at Cowpens, South Carolina.

FEBRUARY 20   Henry ("Light-Horse Harry") Lee routs a detachment of Loyalists marching to join Cornwallis' army at Hillsborough, North Carolina.

FEBRUARY 20   Congress appoints Robert Morris Superintendent of Finance.

MARCH 1   The last state formally ratifies the Articles of Confederation.

MARCH 15   Cornwallis wins the Battle of Guilford Courthouse, North Carolina, but approximately a quarter of his soldiers are casualties.

APRIL 23   Americans capture Fort Watson, South Carolina.

APRIL 25   The Americans are defeated at Hobkirk's Hill, South Carolina.

JULY 6   Cornwallis repulses Lafayette near Jamestown, Virginia.

AUGUST 22   Cornwallis garrisons his troops at Yorktown, Virginia.

SEPTEMBER 5   In a naval engagement off Virginia the French fleet inflicts heavy damage on British vessels.

SEPTEMBER 8 — At Eutaw Springs, South Carolina, the British take control of the battlefield after Patriot troops are thrown into disorder.

SEPTEMBER 28 — The American and French siege of Yorktown begins.

OCTOBER 19 — Cornwallis surrenders his army.

1782

MARCH 20 — England's Prime Minister, Lord North, resigns.

NOVEMBER 30 — American and English Commissioners sign the Preliminary Articles of Peace.

DECEMBER 14 — British troops evacuate Charleston.

1783

JUNE 24 — Congress flees Philadelphia after troops in the city revolt.

SEPTEMBER 3 — The Treaty of Paris officially ending the war and acknowledging America's independence is signed.

NOVEMBER 25 — The British evacuate New York City.

DECEMBER 23 — Washington resigns his commission as Commander-in-Chief of the Continental Army and returns to Mount Vernon.

South Carolina

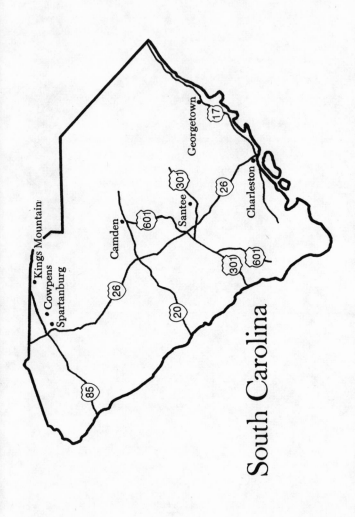

South Carolina

Charleston

In 1779 British war strategists decided to attempt to capture the Southern colonies through a campaign beginning in South Carolina and moving into Virginia. Sir Henry Clinton, Commander-in-Chief of the British forces in America, determined to first establish a base at Charleston, then advance northward to rally the numerous Loyalists in aid of his military operations. (A previous effort in 1776 had been repulsed when the British fleet was unable to pass the guns of the fort on Sullivan's Island at the entrance to Charleston Harbor.)

The siege of Charleston began in late March 1780. On the upper end of Charleston Neck, the British constructed three sets of parallel entrenchments connected to one another by a series of transecting trenches. Batteries were erected at strategic positions. From the opposite side of the city, at the entrance to Charleston Harbor, eight warships under the command of Admiral Marriot Arbuthnot loomed menacingly.

The defense of the city was entrusted to General Benjamin Lincoln, who commanded a woefully inadequate force of 4,000 men against the adversary's well-trained 14,000 troops. Undaunted, he ordered the building of a small canal to repel a foot attack and issued instructions for the construction of several breastworks and redoubts. Across the mouth of the Cooper River a log-and-chain boom was extended as a buffer for the already blockaded American ships.

But these maneuvers were in vain. After a summons to

3

surrender was rejected by General Lincoln on April 10, the British assault commenced. On April 13 the batteries rained red-hot shells and fireballs on Charleston, which set countless buildings aflame. As the bombardment continued, word came that the northern defense at Monk's Cross had fallen to the British. When Clinton's troops approached nearer to the city, Governor Rutledge and three members of the City Council fled.

On May 6 Fort Moultrie surrendered to the British fleet without firing a shot. The merciless assault of 200 artillery pieces on May 9 finally broke the spirit of the townspeople.

Three days later the American troops laid down their arms. The soldiers became prisoners of war, and the militia and armed residents were released on their promise not bear arms again.

Losses were light—76 men killed and 189 injured on the British side, and 89 men killed and 138 wounded on the American side. But the surrender of Charleston was one of the major American defeats of the Revolutionary War.

The British occupied the city until December 14, 1782.

VISITORS' CENTER   85 Calhoun Street (in front of the Municipal Auditorium), phone 722–8338. Information, pamphlets, and books are available here. Also contact the Chamber of Commerce, Lockwood Drive at the Marina, phone 577–2510.

GUIDED TOURS   Gray Line Tours, phone 722–4444 or 722–1112. Daily 10 A.M. and 2 P.M., March to September 1; remainder of the year, Monday through Saturday, 10 A.M. Tours originate at the Francis Marion Hotel. Adults $3.50; children under 12, $2.00.

Charleston Guide Service, phone 722–8338. Licensed guides, who furnish their own cars, provide private tours of the city. Tours for three to five persons cost approximately $7.00 per hour.

Gray Line Harbor Tours, phone 722–4444 or 722–1112. Daily 9:30 A.M., noon, 2:30 P.M. and 4 P.M. during the summer; remainder of the year, daily, 2:30 P.M. The boat departs from the Gray Line Pier, off the Battery. Adults $3.00; children under 12, $1.50.

All the above tours, schedules, and fees are subject to change.

PUBLIC TRANSPORTATION   The South Carolina Electric and Gas Company Transportation Department provides daily bus service to most of the metropolitan area. Phone 722–2226.

TAXI SERVICE   Yellow Cab, phone 577–6565; Veterans Cab, phone 577–5577; Ever-Ready Cab, phone 722–8383.

WALKING TOURS   Most of Charleston's major points of interest can be seen in three walking tours. The listing below consists primarily of Revolutionary War sites. (NR signifies an important *Non-Revolutionary site*; P indicates a historic Colonial house which is now a *private residence*.)

Tour A	Tour B
Area bounded by Cumberland Street on the north, Tradd Street on the south, East Bay Street on the east, and Meeting Street on the west.	Area bounded by Tradd Street on the north, South Battery on the south, East Bay Street on the east, and Meeting Street on the west.
Start at East Bay and Broad Streets:	Start at Tradd and Meeting Streets:
Exchange Building	Nathaniel Russell House (NR)
Old Slave Market (NR)	Royal Governor's Residence (P)
Pink House	
Huguenot Church (NR)	

Dock Street Theater

St. Philip's Church

Powder Magazine

Market Hall (NR)

Gibbes Art Gallery (NR)

City Hall (NR)

Washington Square

St. Michael's Church

Hunley Museum (NR)

Cabbage Row (NR)

Heyward-Washington
House

Bee House (P)

End at Tradd and
Church Streets.

William Washington
House (P)

Gibbes House (P)

White Point Gardens
(Harbor Tour)

Rainbow Row

End at Tradd and East
Bay Streets.

Tour C

Area bounded by Broad Street on the north,
Lamboll Street on the south, King Street
on the east, and Legare Street on the west.

Start at Broad and King Streets:

Ramsay House (P)

Izard House (P)

Rutledge House (P)

British Staff Quarters (P)

Brewton House (P)

End at King and Ladson Streets.

Colonial and Revolutionary War Sites

DOCK STREET THEATER *Corner of Church and Queen Streets. Open Monday, Wednesday, and Friday 10 A.M. to 1 P.M. during July and August. Remainder of the year, Monday through Friday 10 A.M. to 5 P.M.; Saturday 10 A.M. to 1 P.M. Free.* The Dock Street Theater—the first building in America designed exclusively for theatrical productions—opened on February 12, 1736, with George Farquhar's well-known comedy *The Recruiting Officer* (1706). Fire destroyed the structure in 1740, and a new theater was built on the site in 1754. Townspeople thronged to the opening night to see Nicholas Rowe's *The Fair Penitent* (1703). The well-known acting companies of Lewis Hallam and David Douglass frequently appeared at the Dock Street Theater.

Charlestonians so enjoyed dramatic productions that in 1773 a larger building had to be constructed on the site to accommodate the theatergoing crowds. One historian observed that the theater's first season was "the most brilliant of Colonial America." That year 118 productions were staged, including comedies, Shakespearean tragedies, and operas.

Few performances were given during the Revolutionary War. The building on Dock Street (present-day Queen Street) escaped destruction during the British bombardment and occupation. After the war the theater was closed because public officials considered the performances too frivolous. By 1791 all legal strictures were removed and entertainment was again permitted here—in time for George Washington's visit to Charleston.

In the early 1800s the Planter's Hotel, which offered lavish accommodations for planters and travelers, was built on this site, and it included an auditorium. According to tradition, actor Junius Brutus Booth (father of Edwin Booth), who occupied a room here in 1838, became so enraged during an argument with his manager that he tried to kill him with a hotel andiron!

By the late nineteenth century the building had deteriorated to a pale shadow of its former elegance. In the early 1930s the federal government granted funds for a project to restore the Planter's Hotel and to create a reconstruction of the Dock Street Theater.

The present building, which opened on November 26, 1937, is noted for its fine Adam-style woodwork in the hotel rooms and its faithfully reproduced interior of a Georgian playhouse. (Today, the theater is operated by the Footlight Players, Charleston's community theater group.) The restored facade is graced by a delicate cast-iron balcony that was part of the original building.

ELFE HOUSE   *54 Queen Street. Open Tuesday to Friday 10 A.M. to 5 P.M. Fee $1.00.*   This was the home of Thomas Elfe (1719–1775), one of Charleston's most important cabinetmakers, who came to the colony from England in 1747 and built this house thirteen years later. All the original cypress paneling has been preserved in this four-room structure, and reproductions of Elfe's furniture are on display. The small building in the rear was a workshop.

Elfe's furniture was highly prized by residents of the area, and his account books reflect a profitable enterprise.

EXCHANGE BUILDING AND PROVOST DUNGEON
East end of Broad Street. The Provost Dungeon is open Monday through Saturday 10 A.M. to 5 P.M., Sunday 1

*Dock Street
Theater, Charleston*
(ALPER)

P.M. *to 5* P.M., *from March 1 to Labor Day. In October,
November, and February the schedule is Monday
through Friday 10* A.M. *to 2* P.M., *Saturday 10* A.M. *to
5* P.M., *Sunday 1* P.M. *to 5* P.M. *The dungeon is closed
December and January. Adults $1.00, children 50¢.*
Before the present building was constructed, a guardhouse—standing behind the protective walls of the
Half Moon Battery—was located on this site, which
then fronted on the water. Completed about 1704, the
two-story structure served as the military center of
Charleston.

It was here that the notorious pirate Stede Bonnet and
his crew were confined prior to their execution in 1718.
Stede, an educated man of good family and a retired
British army major, had joined Edward Teach ("Blackbeard") in his raids on South Carolina coastal towns. In

June 1718 the pirate fleet captured nine vessels, one of which carried Samuel Wragg, a member of the Grand Council, who was held for ransom. When the pirates' demands were met, Wragg and the other captives were freed, but the citizens of Charleston had become outraged. They empowered Colonel William Rhett, commanding two sloops and 160 men, to track down the buccaneers. A month later Rhett captured Bonnet and his crew off the North Carolina coast and returned to Charleston in triumph.

In 1771 the guardhouse was replaced by the present building, which was designed by a local archiect, William Rigby Naylor, and built by John and Peter Horlbeck. The structure, which cost £44,000, was financed by a duty on rum, wine, bread, and biscuits.

In 1773 Charlestonians rebelled against the British tax on tea by interfering with the unloading of ship cargoes. Hundreds of chests of East India tea were seized from Captain Carling's ship on December 22, 1773, and were placed in the underground chambers of the Exchange Building. Several shipments seized from other vessels were stored here as well.

Representatives from all parts of South Carolina assembled in the Exchange Building in 1774 to elect delegates to the First Continental Congress. Christopher Gadsden, Henry Middleton, John Rutledge, Thomas Lynch, and Edward Rutledge were chosen for the assembly that would decide the issue of independence from England. (Middleton served as the second president of the Congress from October 22, 1774, to May 10, 1775.)

On November 15, 1774, Charleston had its own "Tea Party." After Captain Samuel Ball had refused an ultimatum to return to England or to destroy his tea, several merchants came aboard and dumped the tea into the harbor. A crowd of spectators gathered near this site.

In March 1776 the South Carolina Provincial Congress

met here to establish the first independent government in America. John Rutledge was chosen president and Henry Laurens vice president.

When the British occupied Charleston in 1780, they chose the Exchange Building for their military headquarters. From the steps of this building Lord William Campbell, the newly appointed royal governor, heard his commission read to him, but the hostility of the local citizenry was embarrassingly obvious as only fifteen persons attended the ceremonies. In view of the incendiary political situation, the usual rounds of cannon fire that accompanied such events were dispensed with.

Several days before the British captured Charleston General William Moultrie (who, commanding the fort on Sullivan's Island, had defeated the British forces in June 1776) and his comrades carried 10,000 pounds of powder from the magazine to the Exchange cellar. It remained there—hidden behind a bricked-up wall—

Mannequins arranged in a tableau in the Provost Dungeon of the Exchange Building, Charleston (CHARLESTON TRIDENT CHAMBER OF COMMERCE)

until the city was returned to Patriot control. Through-out the occupation the British were sitting on a virtual powder keg without knowing it!

The cellar of the Exchange Building was converted into a prison—the Provost Dungeon—where outspoken Patriot men and women were shackled. Political activists from all parts of South Carolina were driven in chains in a forced march to Charleston and incarcerated here. Crowded together in the dark, vermin-infested dungeon, many of the weakened prisoners fell prey to "jail fever" and died.

After the Revolutionary War, the Exchange Building was the scene of many gay events, such as the cele-bration honoring President George Washington in May 1791. To the President's delight, the ladies gave him an unusual welcome. Many women wore sashes across their bosoms with the words "Long Life to the Presi-dent." Others, hoping to flatter their distinguished guest when he greeted them with a hand kiss, commissioned local artists to paint Washington's image on the back of their hands.

In 1818 the Exchange Building was sold to the federal government for use as a custom house. At the end of the century it served as a post office. It was later deeded to the South Carolina Society of the Daughters of the American Revolution.

HEYWARD-WASHINGTON HOUSE   *87 Church Street. Open Monday through Saturday 10 A.M. to 4:30 P.M.; Sunday 2 P.M. to 5 P.M. Adults $1.00, children 50¢.* Daniel Heyward, a wealthy rice planter from St. Luke's Parish, built this house in 1770. After his death, it passed to his son Thomas, who was a member of the South Carolina House of Commons (1772), served on the Committee of Safety (1775), and as a delegate to the Continental Congress (1776) signed the Declara-tion of Independence.

A captain of artillery, he took part in the defense of

Savannah (1779) and the siege of Charleston (1780).
After the British captured Charleston, Heyward was
sent, along with about sixty other prominent Charlestonians, to be incarcerated at Fort San Marcos in St.
Augustine, Florida (then under British control). According to legend, on July 4, 1781—the fifth anniversary
of the adoption of the Declaration of Independence—
these political prisoners determined to demonstrate their
patriotism. Heyward is credited with writing a rousing
ballad which was sung by his compatriots until their
British guards silenced them.

During Thomas Heyward's imprisonment his wife
and her sister, Mrs. George Abbott Hall, continued to
occupy this house. When, on the evening of May 12,
1781, the British ordered Charleston residents to commemorate the first anniversary of the fall of their city
by placing lighted candles in their windows, Mrs. Heyward boldly disobeyed. Enraged by this act of defiance,
loyal Tories mobbed the house, and during the melee
Mrs. Hall suffered a stroke and died. Mrs. Heyward
spent her final days in exile in Philadelphia.

During George Washington's visit to Charleston in
1791 he lodged in the Heyward house. As Thomas Heyward was then residing at his plantation, White Hall
(in St. Luke's Parish), the City Council rented his fine
Georgian mansion for a week and installed a housekeeper and servants to care for the distinguished visitor.

Washington arrived on May 2 at Hadrell's Point (on
the north side of the Cooper River opposite Charleston)
where he was met by a delegation of prominent citizens,
including John Bee Holmes (the City Recorder), Charles
Cotesworth Pinckney (a former representative to the
Constitutional Convention), and Edward Rutledge (a
former delegate to the Continental Congress). The
President was then rowed across the river in a flat-bottom
boat, accompanied by scores of small crafts filled with
cheering citizens.

Heyward-Washington House, Charleston (ALPER)

Washington was welcomed at Prioleau's Wharf (at the end of Queen Street) by Governor Charles Pinckney, Lieutenant-Governor Isaac Holmes, and members of the City Council. The President was then conducted to the Exchange Building, where he reviewed a parade. That evening he attended a state dinner at the governor's residence.

During the remainder of the week he was feted by prominent Charlestonians, made official visits to the city's sites, and was honored at a ball at the Exchange Building. He also received visitors at the Heyward house.

The furnishings of the Heyward-Washington House are truly elegant. In the **Reception Room,** to the right of the entrance hallway, stands an impressive library case. Made in Charleston (possibly at the shop of cabinet-maker Robert Walker), this piece is monumental in proportions. A hole in the upper section of the right side was made by a small shell in 1865, when federal troops occupied the city.

Above the mid-eighteenth-century slant-top desk, of kingswood imported from Brazil, hangs a portrait of George Washington painted on the reverse side of the glass. It is a copy after Gilbert Stuart.

To the left of the fireplace is a case containing memorabilia of the Heyward family. Among the cherished items is a sash worn by Eliza Lucas Pinckney at the Charleston reception for the first President. Washington and Mrs. Pinckney had become such close friends that when she died he asked to be one of her pallbearers.

Like guardian spirits, Daniel Heyward (builder of this house) and his first wife (Mary Miles)—austerely portrayed in the Stolle portraits (after Theus)—look down at the **Dining Room** furnishings: the Chippendale-style chairs clustered around the dining room table; the "cellarette," a container for chilling wines; the Crown Derby dinner set; and the Vieux Paris porcelain dessert service once owned by Thomas Heyward, Jr.

During his visit Washington occupied the second-floor **Bedroom** to the right of the stairway. The Charleston-made four-poster bed here belonged to the Heyward family. The fine bow-front chest of drawers is distinguished by fluted quarter-columns on the corners and ogee-bracket feet. Nearby stands a corner chair with removable seat, becoming a convenience or "pot chair." The Hepplewhite-design washstand, decorated with eagles and thirteen stars, is highly treasured because it is said to have been used by Washington when he resided in Philadelphia as President.

The handsome **Drawing Room**, which is fully paneled, contains delicate fretwork mantel trim, two beautifully carved doors mounted by broken pediments, and decorative ceiling molding. In the center of the room stands a tea table in the Chinese Chippendale style and two chairs attributed to Thomas Elfe, the famous Charleston cabinetmaker.

On the fine marbletop table (*c.* 1760)—below the round English Chippendale mirror—rests a mahogany clock made by John James Himley, a Huguenot clock-maker who worked in Charleston near the end of the eighteenth century. (The misspelling of "Charleston" makes this a curiosity piece.)

A marble bust of George Washington on the slant-top desk once belonged to the family of Colonel William Washington, the President's cousin.

Among the furnishings in the blue-and-white **With-drawing Room** is a mahogany library case with a broken-arch top, bracket feet, and elaborate satinwood-and-ivory inlay. Considered one of the finest cases of its kind made in America, it was owned by John Bee Holmes, recorder of Charleston. Holmes' portrait, hang-ing nearby, was painted by Samuel F. B. Morse (1791–1872), famed for his invention of the telegraph, who lived in Charleston for several years while working as a portraitist.

The ceramic figure on the mantel is a representation of Benjamin Franklin, even though it is mislabeled "Washington" on the base. Above the mantel is a portrait (after Theus) of Thomas Heyward, Jr.

MARION SQUARE *Calhoun Street between King and Meeting Streets* This public mall was named for Gen-eral Francis Marion (1732–1795, born near George-town, S.C.), who became known as the "Swamp Fox" because of his ability to elude the British by escaping to safety through the swamps.

On the west side of the square stands the only re-maining section of the Tabby Horn Work—the fortifica-tion walls of the Colonial defense system that extended across the city from river to river.

Dominating the square is a statue of John C. Calhoun (1782–1850), a South Carolina statesman who served

as Secretary of War (1817–1825), Vice President
(1825–1832) under John Quincy Adams, Senator (1833–
1844), and Secretary of State (1844–1845).

POWDER MAGAZINE   *79 Cumberland Street. Open
Tuesday through Saturday 9:30 A.M. to 4 P.M. Adults
50¢, students 25¢.*   Built in 1713, the Powder Magazine
was originally part of the Carteret Bastion, which protected the northwest corner of Colonial Charleston. The
squat, eight-gabled structure, with walls thirty-two
inches thick, has groined vaulting of brick and tabby
(a mortar made from oyster shells). In this building
was stored the colony's gunpowder supply.

On display in the museum are several eighteenth-
century brocade dresses—one of them from the family

*Section of a wall of a Colonial fortification, Marion Square,
Charleston* (ALPER)

of Eliza Lucas Pinckney, who introduced the indigo plant into South Carolina. One can also see clothes worn by Charlestonian Henry Laurens (1724–1792), president of the Continental Congress (1777–1778), who was taken prisoner by the British, transported to England where he was incarcerated in the Tower of London, and later returned in a prisoner exchange (1782) for General Charles Cornwallis.

Engravings of South Carolina's four signers of the Declaration of Independence—Edward Rutledge, Arthur Middleton, Thomas Lynch, and Thomas Heyward, Jr.— hang on the austere brick walls. Nearby, cases contain dainty Rockingham cups and saucers, handsome jewel boxes brought to Charleston by French Huguenots, ornate Dresden candlestick holders, and fine pieces of Staffordshire china (owned by Robert Marion, nephew of Francis Marion, the "Swamp Fox").

The two cannon in front of the Powder Magazine, which bear the seal of King George III, were originally placed along the waterfront.

ST. MICHAEL'S CHURCH *80 Meeting Street. Open daily* 9 A.M. *to* 5 P.M. St. Michael's was completed in 1762 and the building remains unchanged except for the addition of a sacristy (in 1883). Designed by local architect Samuel Cardy, the church has a Doric portico and a 190-foot segmented steeple. In Colonial times, as a fire-warning device, a lighted lantern was hung from the spire on a long pole pointing in the direction of the conflagration.

During the Revolutionary War Major Traille of the Royal Artillery took down St. Michael's bells and sent them to England as a prize of war. After the war they were purchased by a Mr. Ryhiner, a merchant of Charleston, who returned them to their home.

In June 1862 the bells were sent for safekeeping to Columbia, South Carolina, where they were destroyed by Sherman's wanton army. Fragments of metal were recovered, however, and sent to Mears and Steinbank of London—the original founders—who, using the original molds, were able to recast the bells. They were installed in St. Michael's in March 1867.

The original chancel window, shattered by shells in 1865, has been replaced by a beautiful Tiffany window *St. Michael Slaying the Dragon*, from a painting by Raphael.

In the southeast corner of the middle aisle stands the original pulpit, with a sounding board supported by two Corinthian columns. The impressive organ was imported from England in 1768 and is thought to be one of the oldest of its type in this country.

The pew known as the "Governor's Pew" has been occupied by many prominent worshippers, including George Washington and Robert E. Lee.

Visitors to St. Michael's churchyard may be surprised to see the headboard of a bed used as a grave marker. It was placed there in 1770 by William Luyten, who was too poor to buy a stone to mark the grave of his wife, Ann.

Buried also in the churchyard are two of the four South Carolina signers of the Federal Constitution (1787)—John Rutledge (1739–1800) and Charles Cotesworth Pinckney (1746–1825).

ST. PHILIP'S CHURCH *146 Church Street. Open daily 9 A.M. to 5 P.M.* St. Philip's is the oldest Episcopal congregation in the Carolinas. The first church, a small black cypress structure on a brick foundation, was built in 1681–1682 on the site now occupied by St. Michael's (southeast corner of Meeting and Broad Streets).

The second St. Philip's—built on the present Church Street site in 1723—was a brick building with three porticoes and an octagonal domed tower. It was here, in 1736, that the British theologian-evangelist John Wesley preached during his visit to America. George Washington attended Sunday morning services here on

May 8, 1791, and President Monroe visited on May 2, 1819. The Right Reverend Robert Smith, the first Bishop of the Episcopal Diocese of South Carolina, administered policy and officiated at services at the second St. Philip's.

The church caught fire in 1796 and was saved from destruction by a black boatman, who was rewarded with his freedom. But in February 1835 a conflagration raged out of control, razing St. Philip's and nearby structures.

The third and present edifice, which opened for services May 3, 1838, is similar in design to the second church, although a chancel was added and a 200-foot-high steeple replaced the tower. During the War between the States ten Union shells penetrated St. Philip's, wrecking the chancel and demolishing the organ. The bells were removed to be melted down and recast into cannon.

Among the prominent persons buried in the church-yard are Robert Johnson (the first royal governor of South Carolina), Edward Rutledge (a signer of the Declaration of Independence), Colonel William Rhett (captor of the infamous pirate Stede Bonnet), Christopher Gadsden (a delegate to the Continental Congress and later a lieutenant-governor of South Carolina), and John C. Calhoun (Vice President under John Quincy Adams).

UNITARIAN CHURCH   8 *Archdale Street. Open daily 9 A.M. to 5 P.M.*   This is the home of the oldest Unitarian congregation in the South. The church was under construction at the beginning of the War of Independence. During the occupation of Charleston British soldiers were quartered here; later the building was used as a stable. After the war, the church was completed and dedicated in 1787. The entire interior was remodeled during the 1850s under the supervision of architect Francis D. Lee. The interior, with its fan-tracery vault-

St Philip's Church, Charleston (ALPER)

ing, was patterned after that of the Chapel of Henry VII at Westminster Abbey, England.

The stained-glass chancel window, dating from the 1780s, is one of the finest in Charleston. The upper panes depict the four Evangelists—Matthew, Mark, Luke, and John. The lower panel shows Aaron and Moses standing beside the Ark of the Covenant.

WASHINGTON SQUARE *Broad, Meeting, and Chalmers Streets* In this pleasant park, which adjoins City Hall, stand three noteworthy monuments.

The first, a statue of British statesman William Pitt (1708–1778), was erected by the grateful citizens of Charleston for his speeches in Parliament against the Stamp Act, speeches that ultimately led to the repeal of that hated legislation. In 1766 the Commons House of Assembly voted a £1,000 commission to sculptor Joseph Wilton to create an appropriate work. Dedicated in 1770, the Pitt statue was first placed at the intersection of Broad and Meeting Streets. After an arm was destroyed during the British bombardment of 1780, the statue was moved to the yard of the old Orphan House on Calhoun Street, where it remained until placed in its present location.

A second statue honors native South Carolina poet Henry Timrod (1828–1867); it was designed by E. Valentine and erected in 1901.

A third monument, dedicated to the Washington Light Infantry (a nineteenth-century military unit named for George Washington), was erected in the 1890s.

WHITE POINT GARDENS (THE BATTERY) *At Murray Boulevard and East Battery (Confluence of the Ashley and Cooper Rivers)* A small fortification occupied this site during the War of Independence, when the British fleet and the bombardment of the city forced Charleston's surrender.

In 1838 the area was transformed into a promenade

with gardens, which became a popular place for stylishly dressed Charlestonians to spend a Sunday afternoon. During the Civil War earthworks were built and batteries were erected once again to command the harbor.

REVOLUTIONARY WAR CANNON *Opposite Church Street* This four-pounder is said to have been used in the defense of Charleston in 1780.

SERGEANT JASPER STATUE *Center walkway* During the Battle of Sullivan's Island on June 28, 1776, Sergeant William Jasper leaped outside the walls to recover the flag from the battered flagstaff and, fastening it to a pole, raised it again above Fort Sullivan (Moultrie).

PIRATE MARKER *South Battery* In the second decade of the eighteenth century Charleston shipping was preyed upon by marauding buccaneers. It was on this spot that gallows were erected to execute and display for warning captured pirates. The notorious Stede Bonnet, ally of Blackbeard, and his crew met their end here in 1718.

SIMMS MONUMENT *Center walkway* This monument honors William Gilmore Simms (1806–1870), native poet, novelist, and historian. His romances of Revolutionary times include *The Partisan* (1835), *The Forayers* (1855), and *Eutaw* (1856). His biographies of Revolutionary War leaders Francis Marion (1844) and Nathanael Greene (1849) remain valuable reference sources.

BROOKE RIFLE CANNON *Murray Boulevard* This is an example of the powerful artillery pieces developed during the Civil War by John Mercer Brooke, a scientist and naval officer.

UNION CANNON *Facing Murray Boulevard* These four cannon were brought from Fort Pitt, Pennsylvania, by Union troops for the bombardment of Fort Sumter, which began in October 1863.

Important Colonial Houses

During March and April some of these houses may be open to the public through a series of tours. Information can be obtained from the Historic Charleston Foundation, 51 Meeting Street, or phone 723–1623 for details.

BEE HOUSE   *94 Church Street*   This brick town house was built in the 1730s by Thomas Bee, a delegate to two Continental Congresses and a member from 1776 to 1782 of the South Carolina House of Representatives. He also participated in several military campaigns during the Revolutionary War. In 1790 George Washington appointed him United States District Judge for South Carolina in gratitude for his service to state and nation.

The property was later purchased by Governor Joseph Alston, whose wife was Theodosia Burr, celebrated daughter of Aaron Burr, Vice President under Thomas Jefferson.

In this house John C. Calhoun, Robert Hayne, and several other political leaders wrote the first draft of the Ordinance of Nullification. This ordinance, passed by the South Carolina legislature in defiance of the federal Tariff Act of 1832, was an affirmation of the principle of states' rights. Its adoption precipitated a constitutional crisis, and President Andrew Jackson responded with a strongly worded proclamation threatening to send troops to the port of Charleston and asserting the power of the federal government over individual states.

BREWTON HOUSE *27 King Street* This magnificent Georgian mansion was built between 1765 and 1769 by Miles Brewton, a prosperous Charleston merchant. The design is attributed to architect Ezra Waite. Brewton had for ten years been a member of the Commons House of the Colonial legislature. After he and his family were lost at sea on their way to Philadelphia in 1775, the house was inherited by his sisters. One of the sisters, Mrs. Rebecca Motte, was residing here at the time of the British occupation.

General Henry Clinton and Lieutenant Colonel Francis Rawdon selected this house for their headquarters. At the insistence of the British, Mrs. Motte reluctantly presided at the table but is said to have kept her three daughters sequestered in the garret. During the Civil War Union Generals Meade and Hatch occupied the house (1864–1865).

BRITISH STAFF QUARTERS *15 Legare Street* Built by John Fullerton in the early 1770s, the house was commandeered by the British from 1780 to 1782. Officers on the staffs of Generals Cornwallis and Clinton were quartered here. (The generals lodged at the Brewton House, 27 King Street. At that time, a pathway led from the Brewton House through a posterngate to 15 Legare.)

GIBBES HOUSE *64 South Battery* This handsome Georgian house was built in 1772–1773 by William Gibbes, a wealthy shipowner and merchant, who fought in the War of Independence. In 1800 the new owner, Mrs. Sarah Moore Smith, added to the exterior a marble staircase and ornamented the interior in the fashionable Adam style. (Mrs. Washington A. Roebling, widow of the builder of the Brooklyn Bridge, resided here in the 1930s.)

IZARD HOUSE *110 Broad Street* His Excellency James Glen, governor of the province, occupied this early Georgian house in 1750. Since 1756 it has been occupied by the descendants of the distinguished Izard family. Walter and Ralph Izard were Patriots during the Revolutionary War. (Ralph Izard later served in Congress, 1782–1783.) Their sister Sally was the wife of the royal governor, Lord William Campbell. Another sister, Polly, married Arthur Middleton, a signer of the Declaration of Independence.

THE PINK HOUSE *17 Chalmers Street* This structure (c. 1695–1710), built of West Indian coral stone, served as a pre-Revolutionary War tavern. In the 1750s Thomas Coker was the proprietor of the tavern, which was a popular haunt of sailors from the nearby harbor. The building faced what was then called Mulatto Alley, a street lined with bordellos. Soon after 1800, when the Charleston City Council launched a campaign to rid the area of undesirable elements, the Pink House was bought for use as a private home.

RAINBOW ROW *83–107 East Bay Street* These brightly colored row houses, built in the mid-eighteenth century, were occupied by merchants during the Revolutionary War. The first floor was used for business and the upper floor for living quarters. Since no interior stairways were constructed, the second floor had to be reached by an outside staircase.

RAMSAY HOUSE *92 Broad Street* In this three-story house lived Dr. David Ramsay (1749–1815), a surgeon who selflessly cared for the wounded during the Revolutionary War. A member of the South Carolina legislature, he was incarcerated when the British captured the city in 1780 and later was sent with other political prisoners to be held at Fort San Marcos in St. Augustine. After his release, he wrote *A History of the Revolution of South Carolina from a British Colony to an Independent State*. Dr. Ramsay served as a member of the Congress (1782–1786) and as president of the South Carolina Senate (1792, 1794, 1796). This distinguished leader, who was assassinated in the spring of 1815, was deeply mourned by the people of his state.

ROYAL GOVERNOR'S RESIDENCE (DANIEL HUGER HOUSE) *34 Meeting Street* This imposing brick house, owned by Daniel Blake, served as the residence of the last royal governor of South Carolina. It is believed that on September 13, 1776, Captain Adam McDonald, a soldier in the Patriot army, disguised himself as a British soldier, deceived Royal Governor William Campbell, and obtained plans concerning the deployment of Loyalist forces.

The next night Patriot forces assembled at Gadsden's Wharf (at the foot of present-day Calhoun Street) to launch a secret attack on Fort Johnson, the British fortification commanding the southern approach to Charleston Harbor. Campbell, realizing he was in danger and understanding his authority had been significantly diminished, stealthily slipped out of this house and, escaping to a ship anchored in the harbor, took with him the great seal of the province.

RUTLEDGE HOUSE *116 Broad Street* This dwelling was originally owned by John Rutledge, who served as president of South Carolina during the period of the Revolutionary War (1776–1783). He also was a delegate (1765) to the Stamp Act Congress, served as a member of the Continental Congress (1774–1775) and played an important role in drafting the United States Constitution, afterward attending the state ratifying convention (1788). Rutledge was appointed an Associate Justice of the United States Supreme Court (1789–1791).

WASHINGTON HOUSE *8 South Battery* This house was owned by William Washington (1752–1810), a cousin of George Washington. Born in Virginia, William Washington had distinguished himself in battle at Trenton and Princeton before he was sent to South Carolina as a lieutenant colonel. He led his regiments to victory over the British at Cowpens but was captured at Eutaw Springs.

After the war, he and his wife, Jane Elliott, moved into this fine two-story house (built in 1768 by Thomas Savage). According to legend, Jane made the flag that William Washington's cavalry unit carried into battle at Eutaw Springs (September 8, 1781).

Non-Revolutionary Sites of Interest

CABBAGE ROW   *89–91 Church Street*   This group of buildings was once populated by poor black families who called it "Cabbage Row." Charleston-born DuBose Heyward (1885–1940) used this setting (calling it "Catfish Row") for his novel *Porgy* (1925), which was adapted into a play and then by George Gershwin into an opera, *Porgy and Bess* (1935).

THE CHARLESTON MUSEUM   *121–125 Rutledge Avenue. Open Monday through Saturday, 10 A.M. to 5 P.M., Sunday and holidays 2 P.M. to 5 P.M. Closed December 25. Free.*   Founded in 1773, this is one of the oldest museums in the nation. It displays a fine collection of the early arts and crafts of South Carolina as well as splendid pieces of furniture, unusual examples of textiles, and woodwork paneling salvaged from old houses. Also worth visiting is the natural history section featuring birds, mammals, fossils, minerals, and reptiles.

CITY HALL   *80 Broad Street. The Council Chamber is open Monday through Friday 10 A.M. to 5 P.M. Free.*   This is the second oldest city hall in the United States. It was designed by Charlestonian Gabriel Manigault and was erected in 1801 on the site of the marketplace, a large square where produce from nearby plantations was offered for sale.

On December 14, 1782, when the British evacuated Charleston, Patriot troops assembled here as they prepared to take control once again of the city.

Today, visitors to the Council Chamber can see the following paintings: John Trumbull's *George Washington* (1792), Edward Savage's *John Huger* (1787), Rembrandt Peale's *Christopher Gadsden* (*c.* 1795), Samuel F. B. Morse's *James Monroe* (1819–1820), John Vanderlyn's *Andrew Jackson* (1824), and Charles Fraser's *The Marquis de Lafayette* (1825).

City Hall stands on one of the "Corners of the Four Laws" named by Ripley, author of *Believe It or Not*. On each of the four corners of the intersection of Broad and Meeting Streets is a structure representing an aspect of law: St. Michael's Church, ecclesiastical law; the United States Post Office and the Federal Court, federal law; the courthouse, state law; and the City Hall, city law.

GIBBES ART GALLERY *135 Meeting Street. Open Tuesday through Saturday 10 A.M. to 5 P.M., Sunday 2 P.M. to 5 P.M. Closed national holidays. Free.* This imposing structure, built in 1904, houses an excellent collection of American paintings, including works by Benjamin West, Samuel F. B. Morse, Washington Allston, Charles Willson Peale, and Gilbert Stuart. The museum is also noted for its outstanding collection of Japanese prints and Oriental art objects. It is the headquarters of the Carolina Art Association.

HUGUENOT CHURCH *136 Church Street. Open Monday through Friday 10 A.M. to 1 P.M., Saturday and Sunday 10 A.M. to noon. Organ concerts April and May at noon on Fridays.* The present Gothic church, the fourth structure on this site since 1687, was designed by E. B. White. Completed in 1845, it was the place of worship for many persons of French descent who had

settled in the surrounding countryside. At one time,
church services were scheduled so that the parishioners
could sail down the Cooper River on the ebb tide and
return home on the flood tide. Services were held in
French until 1828.

HUNLEY MUSEUM *50 Broad Street. Open Monday
through Saturday 10 A.M. to 5 P.M., Sunday 1 P.M. to
5 P.M. Closed Thanksgiving, December 25, and January
1. Free.* In the basement of a building erected in
1798 for the Bank of South Carolina is a museum of
Confederate naval history. One of the most arresting
exhibits is a replica of the *Hunley,* the first military sub-
marine to sink an enemy ship—the federal sloop *Housa-
tonic* on February 17, 1864.

KAHAL KADOSH BETH ELOHIM *90 Hasell Street.
Open daily 9 A.M. to 1 P.M.* This is one of the oldest
synagogues in the country. The first synagogue built on
this site in 1792 was destroyed by fire in 1838. The present structure, in the Greek Doric style, was finished two
years later.

In 1824 the congregation of Beth Elohim became the
first Jewish Reform congregation in the United States.

MANIGAULT HOUSE *350 Meeting Street. Open daily
except Monday 10 A.M. to 5 P.M. Adults $1.00, students
50¢.* An outstanding example of Adam architecture, this
mansion was built in 1803 by Joseph Manigault and designed by his brother Gabriel, a planter and amateur
architect. The east end of the dining room terminates in
a segmental concave, and the curvature is echoed at the
west end of the building by a bowed piazza, thus giving
the structure rigid symmetry.

The interior is noted for its decorative cornices and
ceilings, elaborately carved mantels, and an impressive
unsupported circular staircase.

The furnishings include a fine chest on chest (in the
bedroom) made by Charleston cabinetmaker Thomas
Elfe, a twelve-panel coromandel screen (in the entrance

Drawing room of the Manigault House, Charleston (CHARLESTON TRIDENT CHAMBER OF COMMERCE)

hall), a Beauvais tapestry (in the card room), an eighteenth-century boulle clock (in the dining room), two Louis XV commodes with ormolu mounts and marble tops (in the upstairs drawing room), and a portrait (in the drawing room) of Mrs. Peter Manigault, mother of Joseph and Gabriel, painted in 1757 by Jeremiah Theus.

MARKET HALL *Market and Meeting Streets. Open Tuesday through Saturday 10 A.M. to 1 P.M. March through May 1 and during July and August. Closed holidays. Adults 50¢, children 25¢.* Constructed in 1841 on land originally owned by Charles Cotesworth Pinckney (an important political leader of the Revolutionary period), this building—with its four imposing Doric columns and decorative frieze—is now used by the United Daughters of the Confederacy as a chapter hall. It also houses a museum exhibiting memorabilia of the Confederacy.

OLD SLAVE MARKET *6 Chalmers Street. Open Monday through Saturday 10 A.M. to 5 P.M., Sunday 2 P.M.*

to 5 P.M. *Closed January 1, Thanksgiving, and December 25. Adults 75¢, children 25¢.* In 1856 Thomas Ryan and Son, brokers, purchased this building for an auction mart. About thirty brokers sold slaves, livestock, and furniture here. Slaves were housed in nearby buildings before the sale. Some historians estimate that as many as 80,000 Africans had been imported into the colonies by the time of the Revolution. When the British evacuated Charleston, they confiscated 5,000 slaves to be sold in Florida and Jamaica.

Since 1938 the Old Slave Market has been a museum dedicated to the cultural history of the American Negro.

RUSSELL HOUSE   *51 Meeting Street. Open Monday through Saturday 10 A.M. to 1 P.M. and 2 P.M. to 5 P.M., Sunday 2 P.M. to 5 P.M. Closed December 25. Adults $1.00, children 50¢.* Nathaniel Russell, a native of Rhode Island who settled in Charleston in the late 1760s and became a prosperous merchant, built this luxurious house (designed by architect Russell Warren) in 1809 at a cost of $80,000.

This magnificent mansion is distinguished by the two unusual elliptical rooms, the spiral free-flying staircase, the beautifully carved woodwork and the exquisite furniture. Among the important furnishings are an Aubusson rug (*c.* 1800), an early-nineteenth-century Italian table with a scagliola top, a harp made by Sébastien Erard in 1803, a pair of lyre-back chairs made in Baltimore, a Chamberlain Worcester tea service (*c.* 1800), and a Regency bronze and ormolu clock.

The Russell family resided here until 1857 when the house was sold to the governor of South Carolina, Robert F. W. Alston. Since 1955 it has been the headquarters of the Historic Charleston Foundation.

UNITED STATES NAVAL BASE   *Travel north along East Bay Street*   This is the third largest naval complex in the country, with 14,000 naval personnel and 10,000 civilian personnel. The public may visit submarines, mine sweepers, and destroyers here.

Ships are open to visitors each Saturday and Sunday from 1 P.M. to 4 P.M. Contact the Naval Base Public Affairs Office, United States Naval Base, Charleston, or phone 743–3940 for information.

Recommended Side Trips

Boone Hall Plantation

From Charleston proceed 8 miles north on Route 17. Directly opposite Christ Church is the road leading to Boone Hall Plantation.

The plantation is open Monday through Saturday 9 A.M. to 5 P.M., Sundays 1 P.M. to 5 P.M. Closed Thanksgiving and December 25. Adults $1.75, children 50¢.

Boone Hall Plantation was the property of John Boone, one of the earliest settlers in South Carolina, who received this land as a grant in 1681 from the Lords Proprietors. It became a thriving cotton plantation of 17,000 acres.

A magnificent three-quarter-mile avenue of huge moss-draped oaks leads to the main house, which was renovated in 1935. Visitors can also see nine small structures that were used as slave quarters. The formal gardens and pecan groves add to the beauty of this estate, which was used in the filming of *Gone with the Wind*.

Charles Towne Landing Park

Take Route 17 South out of Charleston, then pick up Route 171. Follow the signs to Charles Towne Landing.

Open daily 10 A.M. to 6 P.M. Closed December 24 and 25. Adults $1.00, youngsters (6–14), 50¢, children (under 5) free.

In this park is the site of the first settlement of Charleston. In 1670 three small ships with 140 English men and women landed here—on the western bank of the Ashley River—and built a settlement which they named Albemarle Point (for the Lord Proprietor, George Monk, the first Duke of Albemarle). Soon afterward, the settlement was renamed Charles Towne in honor of the king.

During the spring of 1680 the government and many colonists moved across the river to a new site, on which the present-day city of Charleston grew.

Charles Towne Landing is part of a 184-acre park administered by the state of South Carolina.

VISITORS' CENTER   A snack bar, gift shop, rest rooms, and a bicycle rental booth are located here.

GUIDED TOURS   A train tour around the area is available for 50¢.

CHARLES TOWNE LANDING   The major points of interest include:

    Reconstructed Palisade Walls marking the approximate location of the early settlement.

    Full-Scale Replica of the Adventure, a seventeenth-

Pavilion, Charles Towne Landing (ALPER)

century trading vessel used by the colonists. Visitors may board the ketch, now moored in the lagoon.

Crop Garden with the same variety of plants that the settlers grew.

Pavilion with exhibitions describing the development of Colonial South Carolina. Artifacts discovered here are on display.

Wildlife Sanctuary with various types of animals indigenous to this region in the seventeenth and eighteenth centuries. Some species are now almost extinct.

Sullivan's Island

Leave Charleston by Route 17 North, crossing over the Cooper River Bridge. Proceed on Route 703 for several miles. After you cross the causeway and small drawbridge on Sullivan's Island, turn right at the first stop sign onto

Middle Street. Fort Moultrie is about 1½ miles down the road.

Open 8 A.M. to 5 P.M. in winter and 8 A.M. to 6 P.M. in summer. Closed Christmas Day. Free.

The original fort on this island (Fort Sullivan), was in the shape of a square with a bastion at each corner. Built of palmetto logs placed in two parallel rows sixteen feet apart—the space between being filled with sand—the fort was armed with thirty-one guns (ranging from nine- to twenty-six-pounders).

On June 28, 1776, the British fleet under Admiral Peter Parker attacked the Patriot-held fort, commanded by Colonel William Moultrie. Instead of shattering the fort's walls, the shells from the British ships buried themselves in the fibrous palmetto logs. Moultrie's cannon damaged several ships and forced one man-of-war to run aground. Under the cover of night the British withdrew, and five weeks later the entire fleet sailed north. A grateful South Carolina Assembly passed a resolution giving old Fort Sullivan a new name—Fort Moultrie.

But early in 1780 the enemy fleet, commanded by Admiral Marriot Arbuthnot, reappeared off Charleston. At daybreak on May 3, two hundred men, led by Captain Charles Hudson of His Majesty's frigate *Richmond*, made an unopposed landing on Sullivan's Island and the besieged fort was forced to surrender. This was a major defeat leading to the British occupation of Charleston.

Fort Moultrie was reoccupied by the Americans on December 14, 1782. When President George Washington visited Charleston in 1791, he toured Sullivan's Island accompanied by General Moultrie and other distinguished citizens. By that time, Fort Moultrie had been abandoned and had fallen into disrepair.

The present brick fort was built between 1807 and 1811. The original walls and the magazines are still intact, although the barracks were destroyed during the Civil War.

On December 26, 1860, Major Robert Anderson—fearing attack from the Confederate forces who lay claim to federal property in the area—moved the small garrison he commanded at Fort Moultrie to Fort Sumter out in the harbor.

Fort Moultrie had served as an army post until 1947, when it was deactivated.

FORT MOULTRIE   The main points of interest are:

Outside the **Entrance Gate** visitors may see the grave of Osceola (*c.* 1800–1838), Seminole leader who was confined here in 1838 because he had opposed the United States government's plans to relocate the Indians. Several months after his imprisonment he died.

The **Guardrooms** flanking the main entrance.

The **Munitions Magazine** and **Battery Bingham** (a two-gun battery built in 1899), **Battery McCorkie** (a 1901 battery with three guns), and **Battery Lord** (with several rapid-fire guns mounted in 1903 to protect the harbor).

The **Main Storage Magazine** of two rooms, built in 1837.

The **1809 Powder Magazine,** the oldest structure in the fort.

The **Twelve-Pounder Field Cannon** used during the Civil War.

Fort Sumter National Monument

Fort Sumter is on an island in the Charleston Harbor and can be reached only by boat. Open 8 A.M. to 5 P.M. in winter, 8 A.M. to 6 P.M. in summer. Closed Christmas Day.

This five-sided brick-and-stone fortification was con-

structed between 1829 and 1860. Named for South Carolina's Revolutionary War hero Thomas Sumter (1734–
1832), it was armed with 135 guns and garrisoned 650
men.

After the Ordinance of Secession was passed (December
20, 1860), South Carolina demanded all federal property
within its borders, particularly the forts in Charleston
Harbor. On December 26 Major Robert Anderson re-
moved his United States Army command from Fort
Moultrie to the stronger defensive site of Fort Sumter.
When President James Buchanan refused to order Ander-
son's evacuation, the governor of South Carolina, F. W.
Pickens, ordered guns from nearby forts aimed directly at
Fort Sumter.

On January 9, 1861, an unarmed merchant vessel, *Star
of the West*, which was sent to reinforce the Fort Sumter
garrison, was driven back by the fire of South Carolina
guns. Three months later, while newly inaugurated President Abraham Lincoln was considering action to provision
the beleaguered fort, it was fired upon by Confederate
guns (April 12). After a thirty-four-hour bombardment,
Anderson and his men agreed to withdraw. The next day

Exterior walls of Fort Moultrie Sullivan's Island (ALPER)

Fort Sumter, Charleston Harbor (CHARLESTON TRIDENT CHAMBER OF COMMERCE)

President Lincoln called for 75,000 men, and the Civil War had begun.

In 1863 Union naval attacks on the fort were repulsed. Not until 1865, when Sherman forced the evacuation of Charleston, was the United States flag raised above the fort.

GUIDED TOURS Two-hour tours usually leave at 9:30 A.M., 12 noon, and 2:30 P.M. March through June at 9:30 A.M., 10:45 A.M., 12 noon, 1:30 P.M., 2:30 P.M., and 4 P.M. July through September. Tour boats depart from the pier located at the foot of Calhoun Street on Lockwood Drive. Adults $3.00, children $1.50. For information, phone Fort Sumter Tours, 722–1691.

FORT SUMTER

LEFT FLANK GUN ROOMS In the gun rooms of the lower tier are mounted two guns on casemate carriages: one is a rifled and banded forty-two-pounder; the other is a forty-two-pound smooth bore.

ENLISTED MEN'S BARRACKS   This three-story building had a kitchen and mess facilities on the ground floor and sleeping quarters on the upper stories.

OFFICERS' QUARTERS   Besides serving as a lodging for the officers, this structure contained storerooms, administrative offices, powder magazines, and a guardhouse.

LEFT FACE   Only the ruins remain of the left-face brick casemates that were destroyed by Union guns during the Civil War.

RIGHT FACE   Guns mounted on the lower tier were involved in the initial exchange of fire with Fort Moultrie on April 12–14, 1861.

RIGHT GORGE ANGLE   On April 12, 1861, Captain Abner Doubleday, using a gun mounted on the first tier, was the first from Fort Sumter to return fire.

UNION GARRISON MONUMENT   The United States government erected this monument in 1932 in memory of the garrison defending Fort Sumter. The names of the soldiers manning the fort are listed on a tablet.

MUSEUM   Exhibits dramatically re-create the historical events associated with Fort Sumter.

Magnolia Gardens

Leave Charleston by Route 17 South. After crossing the Ashley River Bridge, bear right onto Route 61. Travel about 10 miles.

Open February 15 to May 1 8 A.M. to 6 P.M. Adults $2.50, children under 12 admitted free.

This estate, formerly called "Magnolia-on-the-Ashley," has been the residence of the celebrated Drayton family since 1671.

The Draytons had been active in South Carolina public affairs since Revolutionary times. William Henry Drayton

(1742–1779), a brilliant orator, served as president of the Provincial Congress and a member of the Continental Congress. His son John (1767–1822) was a governor of the state (1800–1802, 1808–1810). During the War of 1812 Colonel William Drayton (1776–1846) commanded Fort Moultrie.

When, in the second decade of the nineteenth century, there was no direct male heir, the property passed to the son of the Draytons' eldest daughter, John Grimké-Drayton. He was an ordained minister, but because of ill health retired to this estate where he devoted his time to cultivating these beautiful gardens.

In 1843 Grimké-Drayton began importing *camellia japonica*, and later he planted the first *azalea indica* in the United States. This magnificent twenty-five-acre garden now has almost 700 varieties of camellias and many types of azaleas, as well as examples of *magnolia grandiflora*, Chinese yew, and French cypress.

DRAYTON HALL

The colonial brick mansion that once stood on these grounds was used by Lord Cornwallis as temporary headquarters. Soon after the Revolutionary War, Drayton Hall was accidentally destroyed by fire. A second structure, built of cypress, was razed by Union troops during the Civil War. The present house was completed in the late 1860s.

Middleton Place Gardens

Leave Charleston by Route 17 South. After crossing the Ashley River Bridge, bear right onto Route 61. Travel about 14 miles.

Open all year 8 A.M. to 5 P.M. Adults $2.50, high
school students, $1.50, youngsters (6–12) 75¢, children
(under 6) free.

These gardens were the property of the Middleton
family, renowned for their service to the state and nation.
Henry Middleton (1717–1784) served as one of the
presidents of the Continental Congress, and his son Arthur
(1742–1787) was a signer of the Declaration of Independence. Arthur's son Henry (1770–1846) became a governor
of South Carolina (1810–1812), and a United States Congressman (1815–1819).

In 1740 Henry Middleton sent to England for a landscape
gardener to design the formal gardens and ornamental
lakes for his estate. It took almost ten years to complete
the project. The forty acres—a series of terraces which
descend from the bluff of the Ashley River—are noted for
their stately oak trees and magnificent azaleas and camellias. The first camellias brought to America were planted
here in 1787.

MIDDLETON MANSION

The original brick mansion, built in 1741, was looted
and burned by Sherman's army as it marched from
Savannah to Columbia. Only the north wing remains, and
it has been restored. The plantation stableyards have
been renovated and are now used as workshops to display Colonial crafts such as candlemaking and weaving.

Georgetown

Revolutionary War History

The third oldest town in South Carolina, Georgetown was settled in 1734–1735. Surrounded by prosperous indigo and rice plantations, the town had become a thriving port by the middle of the eighteenth century.

When the nineteen-year-old Lafayette arrived from France on June 13, 1777, to join the Patriot cause, he and his companions disembarked from their ship *Victoire* at North Island across the bay from Georgetown.

VISITORS' CENTER Tourist information is available from the Chamber of Commerce, 1001 Front Street, phone 546–4921.

GUIDED TOURS During the summer tours are offered on Monday, Tuesday, Thursday, and Friday at 9:15 A.M., 11 A.M., and 2 P.M., leaving from the Chamber of Commerce Building, 1001 Front Street. Phone 546–4921 for information. Adults $1.00, children 50¢.

Soon after the British occupied Charleston in 1780, they established a small garrison at Georgetown. An attempt by the Patriots to regain control of the town in November 1780 ended in failure. In January 1781 forces under the command of Francis Marion and Henry ("Light-Horse Harry") Lee attacked the post, but because of a shortage of ammunition were forced to abandon the attempt. Four months later, Marion, learning that the garrison had been reduced to about eighty soldiers, gathered a large corps of militiamen and marched to Georgetown. On their arrival they were overjoyed to discover that during the night the British had fled to Charleston by ship. With the garrison under Marion's control, Georgetown and the countryside were free of British domination.

Colonial and Revolutionary War Sites

BELLE ISLAND GARDENS *Travel 4 miles south on Route 17, then about 2 miles east. Open November through August 8 A.M. to 6 P.M. Adults $1.00, children 50¢.* This plantation was owned by the father of Francis Marion (1732–1795) the "Swamp Fox" (so called for his skill in eluding British forces by slipping into the swamps). The lovely gardens were once noted for their varieties of azaleas and camellias. The area is presently under development, and the roads leading to the plantation house are gated.

BOLEN-BELLUME HOUSE *222 Broad Street. Not open to the public.* During the British occupation of Georgetown this two-story frame house served as the headquarters for the senior staff officers.

HOPSEWEE PLANTATION *12 miles south of Georgetown on Route 17/701. Open Tuesday through Friday 10 A.M. to 5 P.M. Adults $1.50, children 75¢.* A typical Low Country plantation house of the mid-eighteenth century, Hopsewee has on each floor four rooms opening onto a central hallway. The house is noted for its elaborate hand-carved molding and fine period furniture. This was the home of Thomas Lynch (1727–1776)

and Thomas Lynch, Jr. (1749–1779), both delegates
to the Continental Congress. The son's presence at the
Congress has been recorded for all ages through his
signature on the Declaration of Independence. Thomas,
Sr., had died before the document was signed.

KAMINSKI HOUSE   *622 Highmarket Street. Open Tues-*
day through Friday 10 A.M. to 4 P.M. Fee $2.00.   This
outstanding mansion was built in 1760 by Benjamin
Allston, a rector of Prince George Winyah Church. It
was willed to the city of Georgetown by his great-great-
granddaughter, Mrs. Harold Kaminski, and opened to
the public. The house is furnished with fine antiques,
including a pair of Acajou French Empire side chairs, a
rare Beluchistan rug, sixteen matched Duncan Phyfe
chairs, a silver coffeepot (*c.* 1790) made by Garrett
Schanck, and an unusual Hepplewhite letter cabinet.

MASONIC TEMPLE   *Prince and Screven Streets*   This
building, dating from 1740, served as the meeting hall
of the Georgetown Masonic Lodge. Washington was a
guest here in 1791 and addressed his fellow Masons.

PAWLEY-PARKER HOUSE   *1019 Front Street. Not*
open to the public.   Local historians believe that Washington stayed overnight in this house on his way to
Charleston in 1791. Arriving on Saturday, April 30, he
was greeted by a cannon salute, a company of infantry,
and cheering crowds. In the late afternoon he attended
a banquet given in his honor. The house (with the front
originally facing toward the Sampit River) was built
about 1760; the two bay windows facing Front Street
are later additions.

PRINCE GEORGE WINYAH CHURCH   *Broad and*
Highmarket Streets. Open daily 8 A.M. to 5 P.M.
Founded in 1721, this parish was named after the son of
King George II. The brick church was constructed be-
tween 1737 and 1750, and the belfry was added in 1824.
The English stained-glass window behind the altar was
originally a part of St. Mary's Chapel for Negroes at
Hagley Plantation on Waccamaw.

It is believed that the British used this church as a stable during the occupation of Georgetown. In the nearby cemetery are graves of Revolutionary and Confederate soldiers.

RICE MUSEUM   *Front and Screven Streets. Open on Saturday from 10 A.M. to 1 P.M. and on Sunday from 2 P.M. to 5 P.M. October through March. The schedule for the remainder of the year is Monday through Saturday 9 A.M. to 5 P.M. Adults $1.00, students free.*   Located in the Old Market Building (erected about 1835) is the Rice Museum, which is devoted to the history of the rice-growing industry in South Carolina. Dioramas, maps, photographs, and exhibits show the importance of the crop to the economic development of the region.

WINYAH INDIGO SOCIETY   *Prince and Cannon Streets. Open only to members.*   Organized in 1740, the Indigo Society was chartered by King George II as a "Convivial Club to meet to talk over the latest news from London."

The first president of the group was Thomas Lynch, Sr. Dues were paid in indigo. (Used in the manufacturing of blue dye, the indigo plant was one of South Carolina's main crops, playing an important role in the colony's economic growth.) In 1753 the Society established one of the first free schools in America.

The present meeting hall dates from 1857.

Important Colonial Houses

Other fine Colonial houses may still be seen in Georgetown. Although they are not open to the public, tourists to the city who are visiting the neighborhoods in which they are located may take the opportunity to view these dwellings.

Craft-Rodwell House (1749)   *212 Orange Street*
Ford House (1739)   *914 Highmarket Street*
Forster-Schneider House (1760)   *909 Prince Street*
Fraser House (1770)   *1028 Front Street*
Man-Doyle House (1775)   *528 Front Street*
McGrath House (1770)   *220 Queen Street*
Pacey House (1760)   *601 Highmarket Street*
Rumley-Miller House (1760)   *331 Screven Street*
Stewart-Congdon House (1750)   *513 Prince Street*
Tucker-Smith House (1760)   *15 Cannon Street*
Ward-Bull House (1750)   *614 Prince Street*
Withers-Porter House (1740)   *316 Screven Street*

Santee

Revolutionary War History

An air of complacency hung over the British camp at
Eutaw Springs (near Santee) on the morning of September
8, 1781. So certain was Colonel Alexander Stewart of the
security of his encampment that he sent a foraging party
of 100 unarmed men to bring back fresh food. Little did
he suspect that General Nathanael Greene was approaching with a Patriot force of 2,200 soldiers.

Stewart was soon alerted, however, by informers. Fearing an attack, he hurriedly dispatched a reconnoitering
patrol under Major John Coffin. They ran directly into the
vanguard of Greene's soldiers and in the ensuing skirmish
suffered heavy losses. When the retreating Redcoats returned to camp and sounded an alarm, Stewart commanded his men to prepare for battle. A single line of
troops was positioned so that the right flank was protected by the Eutaw Creek and the left by a dense thicket.

Near the steep bank of the Eutaw Creek nearly 300
men—six companies of grenadiers and light infantry—
under the command of Major John Marjoribanks were deployed at an angle to the main line.

The American forces now marshaled for the attack.
General Greene ordered the North Carolina militia to the
front, Andrew Pickens' South Carolina militia to the left
flank, and Francis Marion's South Carolina militia to the
right. "Light-Horse Harry" Lee's cavalry stood in readi-
ness at the outer right flank, and Colonel William Washington's cavalry was held in reserve at the rear of the

formation. Thus arrayed, the Patriots advanced on the enemy.

Fighting raged for nearly three hours. The steady thrust of the first line of militiamen sent the British scurrying in retreat. Only Marjoribanks' detachment remained in position. Colonel Washington and his men then charged into the murderous fire of Marjoribanks' troops. Almost half of Washington's men were killed or wounded, and he was captured.

The remaining Colonial forces pursued the British through the camp. Suddenly the action reversed itself. The hungry, exhausted Patriots fell on the spoils of a still-unachieved victory and began to loot the stores, eating the abandoned provisions and guzzling the liquor. Major Marjoribanks took advantage of this unexpected turn of events and swept down upon the plunderers, driving them from the field. Although the assault was successful, he sustained a mortal wound.

When the smoke had cleared over the battleground, the grim tally of casualties was taken: 522 Americans, 866 British (two-fifths of the force).

Colonial and Revolutionary War Sites

EUTAW SPRINGS BATTLEFIELD SITE   *From Santee, take Route 6 West for 11 miles to the intersection of Routes 6 and 45. Turn left onto Route 45 and travel 2½ miles to the battlefield site.*   Visitors to the battlefield may retrace the events of September 8, 1781, through several markers and monuments. The most noteworthy are:

THE BATTLE MONUMENT This granite shaft, dedicated to those who fought here, was erected in 1912 by the Eutaw Chapter of the Daughters of the American Revolution.

GRAVE OF MAJOR MARJORIBANKS AND MARKER After British officer John Marjoribanks was wounded, he was carried to Wantoot Plantation (now under nearby Lake Moultrie) where he died and was buried on October 22, 1781. His grave and marker were moved here in 1941 by the South Carolina Public Service Authority.

NORTHAMPTON MARKER This marker calls attention to the residence of General William Moultrie, Northampton Plantation, which was once located near here.

FORT WATSON SITE *From Santee, follow Route 15/ 301 North. Soon after crossing two bridges (over Lake Marion), turn left onto a narrow road, which leads into Santee State Park. Fort Watson is located on the north shore of Lake Marion.* From April 15 to April 23, 1781, British and Patriot troops fought here for possession of

Monuments and markers, Eutaw Springs Battlefield Site (ALPER)

this garrison. The conflict was stalemated because the Colonials lacked a cannon with which to batter down the walls of the fort. Colonel Hezekiah Maham offered an imaginative suggestion—the building of a tower so that the Patriot soldiers could fire down upon their enemy. During the night of April 22 a crude rectangular structure of rough logs was erected.

At dawn the surprised British discovered looming above the fort a fifty-foot tower manned by American riflemen. As they opened fire, other Patriots, under the commands of Francis Marion and Henry ("Light-Horse Harry") Lee, charged the fort. Unable to repel their adversary, the British surrendered.

At the present time the University of South Carolina is conducting excavations on the site.

Non-Revolutionary Site of Interest

WINGS AND WHEELS MUSEUM *Located ½ mile south of Santee on Routes 15/301. Open daily 9 A.M. to 9 P.M. Closed December 25. Adults $2.20, children $1.10.* A fascinating collection of antique airplanes, automobiles, and train engines is housed in this huge structure. On weekends in the summer months, visitors may ride in a reproduction of the nation's first passenger train (1830), *The Best Friend of Charleston.*

Camden

After the fall of Charleston in May 1780, the British established a series of posts across the northern section of the colony, with Camden as the principal garrison. To counter the growing British dominance in the Carolinas, Congress selected General Horatio Gates (1728–1806), the hero of Saratoga, to assume command of the Continental troops in the South. His appointment was a serious miscalculation.

Gates reached the camp of Baron de Kalb (Prussian officer who had come to America to fight for the Patriot cause) at Coxes Mill, North Carolina, on July 25, 1780, and immediately issued orders for a march to Camden. De Kalb proposed that they march southwest by way of Salisbury and Charlotte and then to Camden—a circuitous route, but one which would take them through fertile farmland cultivated by people sympathetic to the Revolution. Gates rejected this route for one fifty miles shorter, even though it ran through a region that was, for the most part, wilderness and it transversed Cross Creek County, an area hostile to the Patriot cause. Little food was available except peaches and green corn; soon intestinal disorders and dysentery were rampant. The march turned into a two-week nightmare as the exhausted, debilitated men trudged toward Camden. On August 13 they arrived at Clermont, South Carolina, several miles north of their objective.

On the night of August 15 Gates prepared to launch a surprise attack against the British. Before the march com-

General Charles Cornwallis
(NATIONAL PARK SERVICE, WASHINGTON, D.C.)

menced, he ordered one gill of molasses added to the troops' rations to bolster their energy. But this only added to their gastric distress.

That same evening General Cornwallis, unaware of Gates' plans, ordered a night march to surprise the Continentals. The two armies started moving along the same road toward one another. When the astonished forces encountered each other, they simultaneously opened fire. After the first burst of fire, both sides withdrew to await the morning light.

Dawn revealed a thinly-studded forest of pines flanked on both sides by swamps. The American line was formed for battle. To the right were stationed Delaware and Maryland Continentals, commanded by Baron de Kalb and General Mordecai Gist, but the center and left were manned by inexperienced militia.

They were no match for the overpowering army of scarlet and steel commanded by Cornwallis, Rawdon, and Tarleton. As the British phalanx advanced upon them, the terrified front and left lines threw up their muskets and ran frantically in retreat. Only the Maryland and Delaware veterans remained, locked in conflict with Rawdon's forces. While De Kalb rallied his men, he was seriously wounded and taken prisoner. A final charge by Tarleton's cavalry broke all American resistance.

The craven Gates ignominiously fled the battlefield and did not interrupt his retreat until he reached Charlotte, sixty miles to the north! Baron de Kalb was carried back to Camden where he died three days later.

The Battle of Camden was one of the worst defeats inflicted on the American army. While the British casualties numbered 324, almost 1,000 Patriot soldiers were killed or wounded.

VISITORS' CENTER   Touring information may be obtained from the Chamber of Commerce, 700 De Kalb Street, phone 432–2525.

PUBLIC TRANSPORTATION   Since Camden does not have an elaborate public transportation system, visitors to the city who do not wish to walk should use automobiles or taxis.

TAXI SERVICE   City Cab, phone 432–3211; Hill Top Cab, phone 432–8821; Red Top Cab, phone 432–2441.

Colonial and Revolutionary War Sites

BETHESDA PRESBYTERIAN CHURCH AND DE KALB MONUMENT   *De Kalb and Little Streets (Route 1). Open daily 9 A.M. to 4:30 P.M.*   Camden's first Presbyterian meeting hall was destroyed by the British during the Revolutionary War. This structure (the fourth Presbyterian church in the town) was built in 1820 by architect Robert Mills, the designer of the Washington Monument.

In front of this graceful Doric-columned church is a monument honoring Baron Johann de Kalb, the Prussian general who was mortally wounded (August 1780) while leading Patriot troops in the Battle of Camden. In the midst of the rout of the Patriot troops, the heroic De Kalb, unhorsed and continuing to fight on foot, directed the movements of the Maryland and Delaware troops. According to legend, he fell to the ground only after three musket balls and eight bayonet points had penetrated his body. British officers buried him in an obscure grave, but in 1825 his remains were reinterred in the Bethesda churchyard.

De Kalb's friend and comrade in arms, Lafayette, who was touring the United States in 1824–1825, laid the cornerstone of this monument on March 9, 1825. The monument is composed of twenty-four granite blocks, each representing a state of the Union at that time. The inscription reads: "Here lies the remains of Baron de Kalb —a German by birth, but in principle, a citizen of the world."

CAMDEN BATTLEFIELD SITE *Located 12 miles from downtown Camden—from the intersections of Routes 521 and 1—the battle monument is hidden in a cluster of pine trees off a quiet two-lane road (Country Road 58). To reach the area, travel 9.3 miles north on Route 521 until you see a cemetery on the left side of the highway and a sign pointing in the direction of De Kalb Baptist Church. (This cemetery is exactly 3 miles past the Shamokin Campground on Route 521.) Turn left on the road in front of the cemetery, proceed 1.2 miles to a stop sign, then turn left and travel 1.5 miles until you see the monument on the left side of the* road. (*Drive slowly on this road and use your odometer as a guide to the distances.*) The site of the Battle of Camden (August 16, 1780) is almost forgotten today, marked only by a solitary monument honoring the Prussian-born Baron Johann de Kalb (1721–1780), who sailed to America in 1777 to join the Patriot cause. De Kalb was wounded and captured here, and he died in Camden three days later.

HISTORIC CAMDEN *One mile south of the city on Route 521. Open June through Labor Day, Tuesday through Saturday 10 A.M. to 7 P.M., Sunday 1 P.M. to 7 P.M. From Labor Day through May 1 the schedule is Monday through Friday 10 A.M. to 4 P.M. Adults $1.00, children 50¢.* The oldest existing inland town in South Carolina, Camden was settled during the 1730s when

Bethesda Presbyterian Church and De Kalb Monument, Camden (ALPER)

several English families built crude log cabins along the Wateree River. The village was first known as Pine Tree Hill but changed its name to Camden in 1768 in honor of Charles Pratt, Earl of Camden, a member of the British Parliament who championed the rights of the colonies.

On the site of the original settlement—known today as "Historic Camden"—homes of the Colonial period have been restored and fortifications used during the British occupation have been reconstructed. The initial phase of development of this area was completed in 1970, and today visitors can see the following points of interest.

THE NORTHEAST REDOUBT The British erected this redoubt to block the intersection of Lyttleton and Bull Streets. A six-foot-deep ditch surrounded an earthen wall six feet high.

THE SOUTHEAST REDOUBT This small, isolated earthwork flanked the "Cornwallis House" (Kershaw Mansion) and protected the southeast approach of the town.

MAGAZINE SITE A powder magazine was constructed on this site by the town's residents in 1777. It was a rectangular brick building supported by four buttresses. It was demolished in 1794, but the foundations may still be seen.

KERSHAW MANSION Plans are under way to reconstruct the Kershaw Mansion, built in 1777 by Camden's leading citizen Joseph Kershaw, the wealthy proprietor of indigo works, a grist mill, tobacco warehouses, and a distillery. During the British occupation of Camden this house was commandeered and used as headquarters first by Cornwallis and later by Lord Rawdon. In 1865 the residence was destroyed by fire.

THE DRAKEFORD HOUSE This log cabin was originally located twelve miles north of Camden near Granny's Quarter Creek. Its first owner, Richard Drakeford, was a Virginian who settled in North Carolina about 1754. Both he and his brother fought in the Revolution. When

Battle of Camden Monument, Camden Battlefield Site (ALPER)

the house was removed to a site in Historic Camden, a mantel, some doors, and floorboards were replaced. Today, the Drakeford House is a small museum displaying Revolutionary War relics, pottery, armaments, and a model of the Kershaw Mansion.

THE CRAVEN HOUSE   This one-room house was built at 816 Mill Street shortly after the Revolutionary War. All that is known about its owner, John Craven, is that he was an accountant, unmarried, and, according to one legal document, "a lunatic." In 1806 a wealthy merchant and landowner named Zachariah Cantey purchased the property, and his family used the house as a recreation center, for card playing and for other forms of entertainment.

Moved to the present site in 1970, the structure was restored and furnished with representative period pieces.

A painting showing a group of soldiers assembled in front of the Kershaw Mansion is highly prized.

HOBKIRK'S HILL BATTLE SITE *A battle marker is located on Route 521—the 2000 block of Broad Street—about 1 mile north of the city.* A marker at the side of the highway is the only reminder of the battle that occurred along this ridge on April 25, 1781.

In the spring of 1781 Camden was still occupied by British forces. In late April General Nathanael Greene arrived in the vicinity with a force of nearly 1,400 Patriot soldiers and encamped along Hobkirk's Hill, a sandy ridge about one mile north of Camden. Alerted to Greene's presence, Lord Francis Rawdon marched his troops out and took the Americans by surprise. Disorder reigned in the camp but lines of battle were quickly formed, and at first the Patriots appeared to be winning. Suddenly, the Maryland regiment was thrown into confusion when they mistook an order to regroup for a command to withdraw. Taking advantage of this opportunity, Rawdon's soldiers pressed forward, routing the Americans.

Although Greene was forced to call a retreat, giving the day's victory to Rawdon, the presence of his and other Patriot forces in the area cut off Rawdon's supply lines. On May 9, after unsuccessfully trying to ferret out the ensconced adversary, the British evacuated Camden. As they withdrew, the town was set on fire.

According to local legend, the body of a soldier, whose head had been shot off by a cannonball during the battle, was carried off by his horse into the nearby swamps. Tradition has it that on certain nights when the fog is dense, the headless ghost, mounted on a skeleton steed, comes out of the swamp and rides around Hobkirk's Hill in a vain search for his head.

QUAKER CEMETERY *700 block of Meeting Street* In the mid-eighteenth century a small Quaker community that had settled here built a meeting house and established a cemetery. The Quakers have long since vanished from this area and their cemetery, much enlarged, now holds the graves of people of other faiths. Dates on the tombstones span a period from pre-Revolutionary times to the present century. Buried here are:

Agnes of Glasgow, who according to her tombstone, "departed this life February 12, 1780, age 20." Although nothing factual is known of Agnes' life, she is the subject of a romantic legend. The story relates that she was engaged to a lieutenant who was ordered to the colonies during the Revolutionary War. Finding the separation unbearable, she set out to be reunited with him. After a rough sea passage, she arrived in South Carolina and Loyalists directed the determined young lady to a hospital unit near Camden. She rushed to her stricken lover's side, arriving only to watch him die in her arms. With an agonized shriek, she threw herself across his body and

Colonial dwelling,
Historic Camden
(ALPER)

died of a broken heart. (Sticklers for historical detail point out that the British did not arrive in Camden until several months after her death.)

Dr. Isaac Alexander, who attended the wounded Baron de Kalb.

Dr. James Martin, a surgeon who fought in the Revolutionary War.

Richard Kirkland, a young Confederate soldier who gained fame by risking his life to take water to dying Union troops.

Generals J. B. Kershaw and John D. Kennedy, both heroes of the War between the States.

Dr. George Todd, brother-in-law of Abraham Lincoln, who was in charge of a hospital here during the Civil War.

Richard Hobson Hilton and John Cantey Villepigue, both recipients of the Congressional Medal of Honor during World War I.

Other Revolutionary War Sites and Important Colonial Houses

BLUE HOUSE SITE *300 block of Broad Street* The Blue House was the residence of Dr. Isaac Alexander, who attended the wounded Baron de Kalb. After his death, De Kalb was buried behind this house. In 1825 his body was reinterred in the Bethesda Presbyterian churchyard.

CARTER-LAFAYETTE HOUSE SITE *1100 block of Broad Street* The mansion that once stood on this site was in 1825 the home of John Carter, who placed it at the disposal of the visiting Marquis de Lafayette.

CENTRAL SQUARE *Intersection of Bull and Broad Streets* This area was the center of eighteenth-century Camden. George Washington addressed the local citizens here on May 26, 1791, during his tour of the South.

REVOLUTIONARY WAR JAIL SITE *600 block of Broad Street* During the Revolutionary War the small "gaol" here held many political and military prisoners. Among them was the young Andrew Jackson, who was captured by the British during a skirmish near Camden. A local legend relates his defiant refusal to clean the boots of a British officer who, in a vengeful mood, angrily struck Jackson with a saber.

WASHINGTON HOUSE *1413 Mill Street. Not open to the public.* This handsome house (originally located at the corner of King and Fair Streets) was the scene of a gala reception held in honor of President Washington during his brief visit to Camden in 1791.

Non-Revolutionary Sites of Interest

CONFEDERATE GENERALS' MEMORIAL (THE PANTHEON) *Rectory Square, Chestnut and Lyttleton Streets* This monument of six columns serves as a memorial honoring six Confederate generals from the Camden area. They are:

James Chestnut, a United States Senator from South Carolina, who resigned to become a delegate to the Secession Convention and later served on the staff of Jefferson Davis.

Joseph Brevard Kershaw, a prominent lawyer, saw action at Bull Run, Harper's Ferry, Fredericksburg, and Gettysburg.

John B. Villepigue, a graduate of West Point, died of malaria after only one year of service in the Confederate army.

James Cantey served under Stonewall Jackson until he was commissioned a general.

John D. Kennedy, although wounded several times, recovered to be promoted to his command at the age of twenty-four.

Zack C. Deas, who, with $28,000 worth of his own gold, purchased rifles for his men and led them to Shiloh.

CONFEDERATE MONUMENT *Monument Square, Laurens and Broad Streets* The monument here honors the Confederate dead. The inscription reads: "Brave sons who fell during the Confederate War; defending the rights and honor of the South."

Besides sacrificing their sons on distant battlefields, the residents of Camden suffered greatly as a result of a brutal attack in February 1865 by forces of Sherman's army.

KING HAIGLAR WEATHER VANE *On top of Clock Tower, 900 block of Broad Street* King Haiglar, a noble Catawba Indian chief, insisted on remaining friendly with the colonists during the Cherokee-Catawba wars (1758–1761). A grateful South Carolina Assembly provided the Catawbas with food and equipment. In 1763 King Haiglar was killed by members of a hostile tribe.

J. B. Mathieu designed and executed (between 1815 and 1825) this five-foot memorial weather vane, which has always been placed on the highest building in the city. Residents refer to the peace-loving King Haiglar as "the patron saint of Camden."

SPRINGDALE RACE COURSE *Knight Hall Road, about 1 mile outside of town on Route 21 North* Since 1930 the annual Carolina Cup, one of the nation's outstanding horse-racing events, has been held here. The Colonial Cup, an international steeplechase carrying a purse of $100,000, was first run at this track in 1970.

Recommended Side Trips

Winnsboro

To get to Winnsboro from Camden, travel west on Route 34 for about 30 miles.

After the American victory at King's Mountain (October 7, 1780), Lord Cornwallis led the remnant of his field forces in harried retreat. It had rained for days and the roads became so muddy that they were practically impassable. Provisions were low and the soldiers grew weak and ill. After fifteen days, they arrived, battered and weary, at Winnsboro.

While the British remained here from October 1780 to June 1781, reinforcements arrived and rebuilt the army's strength to almost 4,000. From here Cornwallis moved on to Charlotte, then toward Yorktown.

BRATTON HOUSE *Bratton and Zion Streets. Not open to the public.* Richard Winn, for whom Winnsboro was named, gave this property in 1777 to his daughter Christina, the bride of Colonel William Bratton of York County, who is thought to have fought in several Revolutionary War campaigns.

CORNWALLIS HOUSE *8 Zion Street. Not open to the public.* The original section of this house is presumed to have been used by Cornwallis as his headquarters during the occupation of Winnsboro.

FORTUNE SPRINGS GARDEN *Between High, Chalmers, and Park Streets. Presently under development.* John Buchanan, a captain in the Continental Army, gave this land to Pompey Fortune, his former slave who had served General Lafayette during the War of Independence. In 1825 Fortune rode to Columbia (about thirty miles away) to pay his respects to Lafayette, who had returned to the United States for a visit.

MOUNT ZION INSTITUTE *Walnut Street between Bratton and Hudson Streets. Not open to the public.* Mount Zion Institute was chartered February 13, 1777, by the General Assembly as a public school. The school was closed during the British occupation because the building was used to quarter soldiers. A marker recording the Institute's history was erected by the Thomas Woodward Chapter of the Daughters of the American Revolution.

Cornwallis House, Winnsboro (ALPER)

Ninety-Six

Ninety-Six is located near the town of Greenwood.

In mid-May 1781 Patriot General Nathanael Greene began marching 1,000 soldiers toward the village of Ninety-Six, a strategic enemy stronghold in the interior of South Carolina. When the troops arrived in the area on May 22, they immediately began digging entrenchments and erecting defenses in preparation for their siege.

Ninety-Six was heavily fortified: attached to the high walls which enclosed the village were a star-shaped redoubt (the Star Redoubt) on the east end and a stockaded fort (Fort Holmes) on the west end. Patriot artillery fire was first directed against the Star Redoubt, but it was bravely defended by the Loyalists within. Upon the suggestion of Henry ("Light-Horse Harry") Lee, Greene initiated efforts to launch an assault against Fort Holmes which, if successful, would also cut off the village's water supply.

But before this could be accomplished, the Patriot generals received a dispatch indicating that British reinforcements under Lord Rawdon were marching to relieve the besieged garrison at Ninety-Six. Realizing he must take immediate action, General Greene ordered an all-out attack. On the afternoon of June 18 Lee's detachment stormed Fort Holmes while troops under Lieutenant Colonel Campbell attacked the Star Redoubt. Although Lee's forces were able to fight their way into and take possession of the fort, Campbell's men were driven back during their attempt to penetrate the abatis surrounding the redoubt.

With nearly 130 Patriot casualties and with Rawdon's forces swiftly approaching, Greene ordered a general retreat on June 19.

General Nathanael Greene. *Mezzotint by Valentine Green (after Peale).* (METROPOLITAN MUSEUM OF ART, NEW YORK. BEQUEST OF CHARLES ALLEN MUNN)

NINETY-SIX BATTLEFIELD SITE *From Camden travel along Route 20 West. Near Columbia pick up Route 26 West and proceed for about 40 miles. In the vicinity of Clinton, take Route 72 South to Greenwood, then travel on Route 34 East for several miles to the site.* Visitors can see vestiges of the defenses and siege works as well as traces of some of the buildings of the village that once stood here. The Star Fort Historical Commission, which administers the site, is undertaking reconstruction of Fort Holmes. Ninety-Six recently was designated a National Historic Site.

Spartanburg Area

King's Mountain—Revolutionary War History

In late 1780, after Gates' disaster at Camden, South Carolina was virtually the undisputed possession of General Cornwallis' army. Major Patrick Ferguson, commanding a force comprised solely of Loyalists, was charged with patrolling the northern part of the colony to inspire local sympathizers to join the British forces. He was then instructed to meet Cornwallis at Charlotte, North Carolina.

As Ferguson was moving his army toward Charlotte, the frontiersmen from settlements west of the Blue Ridge Mountains (in present-day Tennessee, North Carolina, and South Carolina) were organizing forces to crush the Tory presence. Colonel Isaac Shelby and Colonel John Sevier, both respected Patriot leaders, issued an urgent call for volunteers to rally at Sycamore Shoals (near modern Elizabethton, Tennessee). More than 1,000 men responded. On the morning of September 26, 1780, they began their march over the mountains in pursuit of Ferguson's army. Moving southward through North Carolina, they were joined by a continuous stream of volunteers. Finally, the determined frontiersmen reached King's Mountain (just south of the present-day North Carolina border) where Ferguson's camp of 1,100 men was located on a tapering ridge 500 yards long and raised about 60 feet above the surrounding countryside.

In mid-afternoon on Saturday, October 7, 1780, the major Patriot leaders—Shelby, Sevier, Campbell, Williams, McDowell, Winston, and Chronicle—instructed their detachments to encircle the base of the ridge, then close in

Colonel John Sevier
(NATIONAL PARK
SERVICE, WASH-
INGTON, D.C.)

gradually from all sides. As the Patriots steadily ascended
—moving from boulder to boulder, tree to tree—the
Loyalists began to fire incessantly at them. A Loyalist
bayonet charge succeeded in repulsing two of the Patriot
units, but not for long. Finally, Campbell's and Shelby's
men captured the southwestern section of the ridge, and
Sevier's corps reached the summit. Within minutes Ferguson's forces were completely surrounded. Terrified, they
made a last desperate stand. At the height of the fray
Ferguson was mortally wounded.

An order to surrender was shouted by Captain Abraham
de Peyster, who had assumed command. But many Patriots,
wishing to avenge relatives and friends killed by the Tories,
continued to fire. When order was restored, the victorious
frontiersmen collected the prisoners' arms and counted the
dead.

While the Patriots lost only twenty-eight men, not one
of the Loyalists escaped death or capture. It is noteworthy
that, with the exception of Major Ferguson, the British
forces were composed of native Americans. Here in 1780
South Carolina saw brother fighting brother.

The Battle of King's Mountain was the turning point of the Southern campaign, the beginning of a series of Patriot victories that ended by driving the British from the Carolinas.

King's Mountain National Military Park

From Spartanburg take Interstate 85 North—about 17 miles past the town of Gaffney—to Route 216 South. Follow the signs to King's Mountain.

King's Mountain Battlefield site is now a military park (administered by the United States Department of the In-

The Battle of King's Mountain. *Painting by F. C. Yolin.* (NATIONAL PARK SERVICE, WASHINGTON, D.C.)

terior) which adjoins King's Mountain State Park, where swimming, camping, and picnicking are permitted.

VISITORS' CENTER   An information center and museum at the battlefield site houses a diorama of the battle, an electric map showing the deployment of troops, and a reproduction of a rare breech-loading rifle, invented by Ferguson. The building is open daily 8:30 A.M. to 6 P.M. from June to Labor Day; the remainder of the year it is open from 8:30 A.M. to 5 P.M. Closed December 25 and January 1. Free.

From here visitors may follow a foot trail that leads to the chief points of interest.

CENTENNIAL MONUMENT   Erected in 1880 in memory of the American Patriots who defeated Ferguson, this monument is placed on the highest peak of the battle ridge—where the men under Shelby, Campbell, and Sevier overpowered the Loyalists.

THE CHRONICLE MARKERS   When his troops wavered, Major William Chronicle urged them on, shouting, "Face to the hill!" They moved ahead even as he was struck and killed. Legend has it that he was buried wearing the ring presented to him by his fiancée, Margaret Alexander.

The marker to the left is the original stone erected in 1815 by Dr. William McLean, surgeon to the Patriot forces that participated in the battle. It marks the grave of the twenty-five-year-old Major Chronicle, a North Carolina officer, who is buried here alongside Captain John Mattocks, John Boyd, and William Rabb. In 1914 the King's Mountain Association of York, South Carolina, erected the second marker which stands to the right.

Ferguson's grave, King's Mountain National Military Park (NATIONAL PARK SERVICE, WASHINGTON, D.C.)

FERGUSON'S GRAVE   Born in Aberdeenshire, Scotland, Patrick Ferguson received his military training at an academy in London. He entered the British army in July 1759 and, after seeing service in Flanders and Germany, was sent to America in 1777. He fought at Brandywine and Charleston before he was assigned to organize and train the Loyalist militia in South Carolina.

His outstanding achievement to the science of weaponry was the development of the first breech-loading rifle to be used by troops in battle. Known as the Ferguson Rifle, it was effective for its rapid-firing capabilities which surpassed those of the front-loading muskets of the period. The rifle was first used in the Battle of Brandywine (September 11, 1777) by troops trained by Ferguson.

The large tablet marking Ferguson's grave was dedicated October 7, 1930, by President Hoover on the occasion of the Sesquicentennial Celebration of the Battle of King's Mountain. The headstone is seven feet high and two feet wide with a finely bordered oval circle bearing the inscription *"Dieu et mon droit"* (God and my right) and *"Honi soit qui mal y pense"* (Evil to him who evil thinks)—the respective mottoes of the British Royal Arms and the Order of the Garter.

Following the Scottish custom, visitors have placed stones on Ferguson's grave to prevent his spirit from wandering. Over the years the mound of rocks has grown steadily.

UNITED STATES OBELISK Congress authorized $30,000 for the erection of this monument, which was completed in 1909. The eighty-three-foot white marble obelisk was dedicated before dignitaries from the major Southern states.

United States Obelisk, King's Mountain National Military Park
(ALPER)

On the east side of the obelisk is a plaque listing the names of the Patriots who died in the Battle of King's Mountain. On the west side a plaque names the officers serving here.

Cowpens—Revolutionary War History

In late fall 1780, after General Gates' disastrous retreat from Camden, the Continental Congress appointed General Nathanael Greene commander of the Southern forces. On December 2 Greene arrived at Charlotte, North Carolina, where the bruised Americans had been preparing to encamp for the winter.

While bivouacked at Charlotte under Gates, the Americans had so pillaged the countryside for provisions that little more could be obtained, and local inhabitants were becoming increasingly hostile to the Patriot cause. Greene decided to remove his forces to South Carolina where they could repair their equipment and regain their strength. Against orthodox military strategy, he split his already meager forces and placed a unit of the men under Colonel Daniel Morgan with the intention of diverting the British from the American's southward movement. As Morgan marched toward the British, his ranks were swelled by groups of militia.

In early January 1781 General Cornwallis, fearing that Morgan would interfere with his plans to march northward toward Virginia, dispatched about 1,000 soldiers under Lieutenant Colonel Banastre Tarleton to drive Morgan's troops from the area. On January 17 the opposing forces met in South Carolina at Cowpens (so called because it was the spot where local farmers gathered their cattle before sending them to market).

Morgan devised a shrewd deployment of forces for the coming confrontation. Because the front line was composed of unseasoned militia, he directed them to fire only two rounds at the enemy and then to withdraw and regroup behind the second line. The second line—composed primarily of Maryland and Delaware Continentals—took positions on a low hill. They were to refrain from firing until after the first line had begun to drop back. Behind this formation Colonel William Washington's cavalry waited in reserve.

Tarleton's cavalry made the first advance, but the sharpshooting of the American militia caused them to cease their charge. After firing, the American first line withdrew as instructed.

Tarleton, mistaking this for a retreat, ordered his infantry and dragoons to advance. To their surprise the second American line held fast. Shooting low, they fired round after round, but the equally courageous Redcoats continued to attack. Sensing that they might be outflanked, a unit of Americans drew back to regroup. The British, seeing this as a sign of imminent victory, pushed forward. The Americans faced about and fired into their oncoming enemy. Simultaneously, Washington's cavalry circled around, striking the British from the rear. Seeing the disorder in the British ranks, the Americans then charged with their bayonets. At a call to surrender the Redcoats threw down their arms; some fled in panic while others begged for mercy.

Washington's horsemen followed the fleeing British cavalry, and at one point the two officers crossed swords. Tarleton managed to fire his pistol at his adversary and escape, but the bullet missed Washington, killing his horse instead.

Although the opposing forces were virtually equal in number, Morgan's leadership won the day. In preparing his battle formation he had carefully assessed the abilities of his men and had devised a strategy that minimized their inexperience. The Battle of Cowpens was a decisive victory for the Americans—110 British were killed and more than 800 were captured while only 12 Americans were lost.

Cowpens National Battlefield Site

From Spartanburg take Route 110 North for about 17 miles to the junction of Route 11. If you are near Interstate 85 North, take that highway to Route 110, then travel north on 110 (toward Chesnee) for about 6 miles. The Battle Monument is located at the junction of Routes 110 and 11.

BATTLE MONUMENT   In 1856 the Washington Light Infantry Brigade of Charleston made a pilgrimage to Cowpens to erect a commemorative stone on the spot where Colonel William Washington's troops had taken their stand.

They were cordially welcomed on their arrival in Spartanburg (then a town of about 2,000 inhabitants) on Saturday, April 19, and spent the weekend as guests of the townspeople. Early Monday morning the men of the Washington Light Infantry, bearing the standard carried by Colonel William Washington's regiment seventy-five years before, journeyed to the Cowpens Battlefield site.

The day was spent in erecting a monument—an octagonal marble slab base on which a fluted iron shaft topped by a bronze eagle was set. The following day (April 22) at noon a gala dedication was held with speeches, military drills, lively music, and picnicking. This original monument was destroyed by vandals.

In 1931 the Sesquicentennial of the Battle of Cowpens led to plans for a second monument. By this time,
the section of Spartanburg County in which the battlefield lay had been taken for the formation (in 1898)
of Cherokee County, with its courthouse at Gaffney.
The Daughters of the American Revolution of Gaffney
raised $1,000 and bought an acre of the battlefield area
for the purpose of erecting a second monument a few
hundred yards from the Washington Light Infantry
shaft. The next year the impressive monument was dedicated with appropriate pomp and ceremony.

Proposals for the Bicentennial include enlarging the
battlefield site, building a Visitors' Center, and possibly
rerouting Highways 11 and 110.

Downtown Spartanburg

MORGAN STATUE *Morgan Square, 100 block of West
Main Street*   Under the joint auspices of the Washington Light Infantry and a committee of citizens of
Spartanburg, the Centennial of the Battle of Cowpens
was celebrated by the erection in Spartanburg's public
square of a stately column surmounted by a statue of
General Daniel Morgan (1736–1802).

In the spring of 1881 large blocks of stone were
brought to Spartanburg to form the base and shaft of the
monument. After the foundation was in place, the bronze
statue (sculpted by J. Q. A. Ward) arrived and was
hoisted to the top of the Doric column. The statue represents Morgan in frontier garb; a powder horn is slung
over his left shoulder and in his right hand he holds a

*Battle Monument,
Cowpens National
Battlefield Site*
(ALPER)

sword. (It is believed that the likeness is based on a
sketch by artist John Trumbull.)

On May 11, 1881, a cannon salute inaugurated the
dedication festivities. Bands blared martial music, flags
fluttered gaily in the breeze, and brigades of soldiers
marched to the square. Next, eight young ladies—escorted by officers of the Washington Light Infantry—
prepared to unveil the statue. In response to a signal,

they pulled cords attached to the bunting covering the monument, and the striking statue was seen outlined against the blue sky. Afterward, the assembled crowd listened to speeches by distinguished politicians, including Governor Hagood. Senator Hampton conveyed a message from President Garfield.

SPARTANBURG REGIONAL MUSEUM *501 Otis Boulevard. Open Tuesday through Saturday 10 A.M. to noon and 3 P.M. to 5 P.M., Sunday 3 P.M. to 5 P.M. Closed December 25, January 1, Easter and Thanksgiving. The museum is also closed on Sunday during summer. Free.* The museum houses thirty displays on regional history as well as a map collection and exhibits of Indian artifacts.

*Morgan statue,
Spartanburg
(ALPER)*

Recommended Side Trip

Walnut Grove Plantation

From Spartanburg take Interstate 85 South to Route 26, then travel south on 26 until the intersection of 26 and 221. Take the nearest exit. Immediately after leaving the exit ramp, make a left turn, go under the bridge, then after a short distance turn right (at the Walnut Grove Plantation sign) onto Stillhouse Road. Proceed 1 mile, then turn right onto Otts Shoals Road and continue until you see the Plantation, which is located on the right-hand side of the road.

Walnut Grove Plantation is open Tuesday through Saturday 11 A.M. to 5 P.M. from March to November. During the remainder of the year it is open only on Sunday from 2 P.M. to 5 P.M., and by appointment (576–6546). Closed holidays. Adults $2.00, children $1.00.

Walnut Grove Plantation was the home of Charles and Mary Moore, who had first settled in Pennsylvania, and then migrated to South Carolina in the early 1760s. After traveling down the Great Wagon Road through Virginia and North Carolina, they finally arrived here, in a land that was a wilderness. They hewed down the great walnut and oak trees and in 1765 built this sturdy Georgian-style structure.

This house is furnished with many fine period pieces, which have been chosen with great care. In front of the **Living Room** fireplace, with its Queen Anne–style mantel,

stands a fine eighteenth-century gaming table set up for
a game of draughts (similar to checkers). Behind the handsome Chippendale sofa is a chest on which may be seen
a 1675 Bible box brought by the Moores to South Carolina.
The prints of plants and birds gracing the walls were
executed by Alexander Wilson, an artist who traveled
throughout the Carolinas in the early 1800s. A family
memento on display is the diploma of one of Thomas
Moore's sons, Dr. Andrew Moore, who graduated from
Dickenson College in 1795, studied with Dr. Benjamin
Rush in Philadelphia, and returned to South Carolina to
practice medicine.

The **Dining Room,** a post-Revolutionary addition, contains a fine drop-leaf dining table, a Hepplewhite sideboard, a sugar chest, and serving pieces of pewter and
delft.

Among the important furnishings in the **Master Bedroom**
are a four-poster bed (made in Charleston), a tape loom
(used for making narrow tapes or ties), and a trunk (made
of European "deal" wood, similar to pine). The portrait
above the mantel is of Kate Moore Barry, who served as
a spy and courier during the War of Independence. She is
said to have gathered valuable information for Colonel
Daniel Morgan as he was preparing to confront the British
at Cowpens. An excellent horsewoman, she rode through
the countryside warning the local Patriots of the British
presence.

The large upstairs room was used as a **Bedroom-Dormi-
tory** by the Moore children. Today it is filled with games,
dolls, and beds such as the youngsters might have used.
The partition that separates the small rooms to the side is a
later addition. The older children, who needed more pri-
vacy, slept here. **Kate's Bedroom** is furnished with a blue-
painted Queen Anne bed and a matching blanket chest.

In this upstairs room a friend of the Moores, Captain
Steadman, an officer in the Colonial forces, recuperated
from a serious illness. Two fellow soldiers were visiting

Walnut Grove Plantation (ALPER)

when word arrived that "Bloody Bill" Cunningham—a Tory notorious for his terrorism of the local community—was on his way to wreak vengeance on Steadman for the execution of one of his friends. As Cunningham and a gang approached the Moore house, their raucous shouts unintentionally served as a warning. Steadman's two visitors fled through the back door in an attempt to seek aid but were cut down before they could make their escape. "Bloody Bill" bounded up the stairs and bayoneted the bedridden Captain Steadman.

The house, which is steeped in history, may still contain one of its Revolutionary inhabitants. On several occasions a ghost is reported to have been sighted. Some observers claim that this spectral creature is a woman (perhaps Kate Moore Barry?), while others believe it is Captain Steadman in his nightshirt.

The outbuildings on the grounds of Walnut Grove Plantation include:

A **Kitchen** where the food was prepared and other chores

performed, such as making candles, preparing dyes, and spinning flax.

A **Blacksmith Forge** where horseshoes, locks, nails, and-irons, skewers, and trivets were made.

The **Well House** with a dry cellar in which dairy products kept in covered crocks and jugs were stored.

The **Meat House** where meats were smoked and salted.

The **Academy,** a one-room schoolhouse, the first in Up-Country South Carolina. Charles Moore was the first schoolmaster here.

Several hundred yards from the house and outbuildings is the **Cemetery** where members of the Moore family, including Kate Barry, are buried. The graves of Captain Steadman and his two companions are also located here.

North Carolina

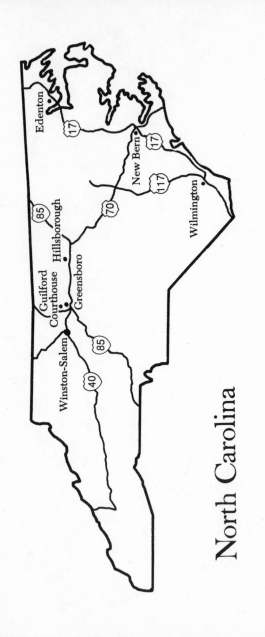

North Carolina

Greensboro Area

Guilford Courthouse—Revolutionary War History

In February 1781 Cornwallis had sent Greene's Patriot forces retreating to safety in Virginia. While the British seemed momentarily to have gained the advantage, their provisions were low and the soldiers were weary from their effort to overtake the Americans.

In Virginia the Patriots' numbers were increased by the local militia, and Greene decided to return to North Carolina to cut off Cornwallis' supply lines and, by his presence in the colony, to discourage Carolina Loyalists from joining the British.

Throughout the beginning of March Greene managed to harass the British while avoiding a direct conflict. By mid-March he had assembled about 4,400 men. Although unsure of their effectiveness in battle, he decided that he would have to confront Cornwallis before the militiamen became discouraged and drifted back to their homes.

On March 15, 1781, Greene waited near Guilford Courthouse for the arrival of Cornwallis. As the Redcoats approached from the west, Greene deployed his troops into three lines, then opened cannon fire. The British quickly brought a gun forward and returned the fire while they drew into battle formation.

The British soon attacked the American first line. (Composed mostly of newly recruited North Carolina militiamen, they—like Morgan's first line at Cowpens—were expected to fire two rounds and fall back.) As the Redcoats stubbornly pushed forward until they reached the position of the first line, they suffered heavy casualties.

Then they proceeded toward the American second line (composed primarily of Virginia militiamen). These inexperienced Patriots, no match for the well-trained British, were driven back. The British advanced 400 yards to the American third line. At the sight of the onrushing scarlet-coated soldiers, one of the unseasoned regiments of the third line turned in retreat. But the First Maryland Regulars stood firm; they discharged a volley and sprang forward in a bayonet charge. At that moment the cavalry of Colonel William Washington swooped down from a nearby hill to join in the fray. The soldiers were engaging in fierce hand-to-hand fighting when Cornwallis, in a desperate maneuver to save the remnant of his battalion of Guards, ordered his cannon to fire "grapeshot" into the melee, even though it would endanger his own men.

The tactic was effective. The British troops regrouped and charged again. Greene, realizing he would have to sacrifice too many of his men to counter another assault, ordered a general retreat. Only after the other regiments had withdrawn did Greene's unit quit the field.

Although the day's victory went to Cornwallis, it was purchased at a high price. More than a fourth of his army had fallen and the endurance of the British soldiers had been sorely tried.

With his nearest source of food 200 miles away at Wilmington, no foraging party could be safely dispatched into the surrounding countryside nor could the safety of provisions sent from Wilmington be guaranteed. Cornwallis' forces had been so demoralized that he would have to avoid another major battle, for should he sustain substantial losses his army would be prey to the hostile militia.

Subsequently he decided that if Britain was to hold the South, the only hope lay in his pushing north to Virginia and consolidating his forces with those of General Phillips.

First Maryland Regiment Charging British Guards at the Battle of Guilford Courthouse (NATIONAL PARK SERVICE, WASHINGTON, D.C.)

Guilford Courthouse National Military Park

Take Route 220 North (running through downtown Greensboro), which becomes Battleground Avenue. Follow Battleground Avenue for about 8 miles to New Garden Road, turn right and proceed until you see the Visitors' Center on the left side of the road. (*Note:* In Greensboro you can take any road paralleling Route 220—such as Eugene Street or Westover Street—to get to Battleground Avenue.)

Open daily 8:30 A.M. to 6 P.M. June to Labor Day; the remainder of the year the park is open from 8:30 A.M. to 5 P.M. Closed December 25. Free.

The development of the Guilford Courthouse Battleground site was the inspiration of Judge David Schenck of

Greensboro, who in October 1886 purchased thirty acres of the land here. During the next thirty years additional land was acquired and numerous monuments were erected. In 1917 federal legislation created the Guilford Courthouse National Military Park, and since 1933 it has been administered by the National Park Service of the Department of the Interior.

VISITORS' CENTER This building houses a small museum with dioramas and Revolutionary War relics. A ten-minute slide show describes the battle.

To see the major points of interest, visitors to the area may either walk along the footpaths or drive their automobiles down the two-lane roads.

Driving Tour

Start at Turner Monument about ½ mile before the Visitors' Center:

> Turner Monument
>
> Signers Monument
>
> Greene Monument
>
> Maryland Monument
>
> Delaware Monument
>
> Third Line Monument
>
> Stewart Monument
>
> Francisco Monument
>
> Winston Monument
>
> Winston-Franklin Graves

End at the traffic circle near the graves of Winston and Franklin.

DELAWARE MONUMENT In July 1888 the founder of the Guilford Courthouse Battle Ground Company, Judge David Schenck, was searching the battlefield for mementos when he noticed bones protruding from the ground near a small gully. He excavated the area, finding the remains of three men and buttons identifying them as Continental soldiers of Captain Robert Kirkwood's Delaware command. At the intersection of Bruce Road and New Garden Road the bones were reinterred and a marker was erected on the spot. Soon afterward a shaft of marble was added. The dedication took place in 1892.

FRANCISCO MONUMENT On the hill opposite the Third Line Monument stands a cenotaph to Peter Francisco (1760–1836), the seven-foot-tall soldier who was a member of Colonel William Washington's cavalry, which charged the British Guards in the vale below.

Francisco spent his childhood in Virginia. Shortly after the outbreak of the Revolutionary War, he joined the Colonial army and fought in many battles. He is said to have removed an 1,100-pound cannon during the Battle of Camden. According to legend, Francisco, wielding an oversized sword, ferociously slew eleven men in the Battle of Guilford Courthouse before he was critically wounded. He lay close to death on the battlefield for hours before he was discovered by a local farmer who nursed him back to health.

The octagonal shaft—with alternating rough and dressed sections—was erected about 1909 by Peter Francisco Pescud, a descendant of the hero. The monument also serves to commemorate the contribution of the Marquis de Bretigny (a Frenchman who came to America to fight for the Patriot cause) at the Battle of Guilford Courthouse. Leading a company of North Carolina cavalrymen, he participated in the charge of Colonel William Washington.

GREENE MONUMENT Directly opposite the Visitors' Center—on the ground where the Virginia militia of the American second line took their stand—is the impres-

Francisco Monument, Guilford Courthouse National Military Park (ALPER)

sive statue of Nathanael Greene. Born in Warwick, Rhode Island, Nathanael Greene (1742–1786) became active in Colonial politics and served (1770–1772, 1775) in the Rhode Island Assembly. At the beginning of the American Revolution he commanded a detachment of militia at the siege of Boston and was in charge of the city after the British evacuation (1776). He fought with Washington (1776–1777) at Trenton, Brandywine, Germantown, and Valley Forge. After Gates was defeated at Camden, Greene was given command of the Southern forces.

On the monument base (white granite on a concrete foundation with a granite exedra) stands a ten-foot-high pedestal topped with a bronze equestrian statue (fifteen feet, nine inches high).

At center front is a bronze statue of an allegorical

figure who is crowned with a laurel wreath and is holding two palm branches in her right hand. In her left hand she holds a shield bearing the emblem of an eagle and thirteen stars.

In 1911, after two decades of determined but unsuccessful efforts by the concerned citizens of North Carolina, Congress passed a bill appropriating $30,000 for a monument to honor Greene. A Commission of Fine Arts was established to supervise a competition for the design of an appropriate statue.

In January 1912 the commission selected a model by Augustus Lukeman. But Paul Schenck, Congressman Charles Steadman, and Senator Lee Overman—a special committee overseeing the project—preferred a model submitted by Francis H. Packer, whose work was finally selected. The preliminary full-size model was approved in 1914 and in the following year was sent to the foundry

Greene Monument, Guilford Courthouse National Military Park (ALPER)

for casting. Construction of the monument was started in April 1915 and was finished only a few days before the dedication ceremonies on July 3.

Another competition was held for the words to be inscribed on the bronze tablet that was to be placed on the front pedestal. The inscription submitted by Dr. C. Alphonso Smith of the University of Virginia was chosen, but the second sentence with a comment disparaging to the British was so strongly opposed by the commission and by the Secretary of War that it was deleted.

The festive dedication ceremonies were held on July 3, 1915. Before a crowd of thousands, North Carolina dignitaries welcomed the honored speakers: Judge Conrad of the Delaware Supreme Court, Lieutenant Governor Bethea of South Carolina, and Ogden Person, president of the Georgia Senate.

MARYLAND MONUMENT   In 1891 the Maryland Historical Society passed a resolution to erect a monument to the memory of the Maryland regiments who fought at Guilford Courthouse. Through voluntary contributions about $350 was raised, and a granite monument—four feet square and six feet high—was unveiled on October 15, 1892. For the dedication ceremonies the positions of the Patriot and the British regiments during the Battle of Guilford Courthouse were marked by flags. Professor Edward Daves, who had conceived the idea of the monument, delivered the main address.

NO NORTH–NO SOUTH STONE   This small monument has an unusual history. In 1903 the Southern Railway Company had planned to erect a monument to Patriot Calvin Graves but was forced to abandon the project. By this time, however, the stone had been cut and polished. Realizing the face of the stone was too narrow for a full inscription, the members of the Guilford Courthouse Battle Ground Company decided on the following wording:

No North
Washington

No South
Greene

The monument, unveiled July 4, 1904, signifies the common cause that joined North and South during the War of Independence: Washington, a Virginian, commanded Northern troops, and Greene, a Rhode Islander, led the Southern forces.

SIGNERS MONUMENT This monument honors three North Carolina signers of the Declaration of Independence: Joseph Hewes (1730–1779), John Penn (1741–1788), and William Hooper (1742–1790).

It is interesting to note that none of the three was born in North Carolina. Hewes, a native of New Jersey, settled in Edenton, where he became a successful merchant. He served as a member of North Carolina's Committee of Correspondence and was a delegate to the Continental Congress.

Penn, born in Virginia, moved to Williamsboro, North Carolina, at the age of thirty-three. He was elected to the Continental Congress in 1775.

Boston-born William Hooper settled in the Wilmington area in 1765. He headed the North Carolina delegation to the Continental Congress and later served in the state legislature.

The remains of Hooper and Penn were reinterred here in 1894; Hewes' grave is located in Philadelphia. The bronze figure of Hooper, which was sculpted by A. Pelzer, was dedicated on July 3, 1897.

STEWART MONUMENT Standing near the road in front of the Third Line Monument is the Stewart Monument, which was erected in 1895 on the spot where Colonel Stewart's sword was discovered during excavations.

According to legend, Colonel James Stewart (leader of the Second Battalion of the British Guards) had dueled in January 1781 with Captain John Smith (of Maryland) at the Battle of Cowpens. When the duel prove ! inconclusive, the two antagonists vowed to fight to the death if they should ever meet again. Two months later, they encountered each other on the Guilford Courthouse battlefield. A fierce hand-to-hand combat ensued and Colonel Stewart was killed.

THIRD LINE MONUMENT The tall white column marks the midpoint of the third line, where almost 1,500 American troops resisted the British assault. Little is known about this monument, which was erected in 1910.

TURNER MONUMENT This bronze statue depicts Mrs. Kerrenhappuck Turner. After her son had been wounded at the Battle of Guilford Courthouse, she came on horseback from her Maryland home to nurse him back to

Winston Monument, Guilford Courthouse National Military Park (ALPER)

*Turner Monument,
Guilford Court-
house National
Military Park*
(ALPER)

health. This valiant lady and loving mother is said to
have lived to the age of 115. Several of her descendants
became prominent citizens of the South.

The monument was commissioned by Major James
Turner Morehead of New York City and was designed
by W. H. Mullins of Salem, Ohio. When it was unveiled
on July 4, 1902, only the base was in place. The statue
was not completed until two months later.

The small triangular marker several yards to the left
of the Turner Monument is a memorial to a grandson of
Mrs. Turner, James Morehead (1750–1815), who also
fought at Guilford Courthouse. The monument, cut in
the shape of a small tent, was placed here in September
1900.

WINSTON MONUMENT   The base of this monument
was erected on June 6, 1893, as a memorial to the North

Carolina troops who fought here under Major Joseph
Winston. The next year a statue was commissioned and
was mounted during the spring of 1895.

At the age of twenty-three, Virginia-born Joseph
Winston moved to North Carolina and settled in Surry
County. He served throughout most of the Revolutionary
War in the North Carolina Militia. At Guilford Court-
house his troops were almost in constant contact with the
Redcoats until Greene ordered the retreat. After the war,
Winston served in the state legislature and in the United
States Congress. The city of Winston-Salem is named in
part for him.

The statue, representing Winston leading a charge of
his Surry County Riflemen against Tarleton's Dragoons,
was dedicated on July 4, 1895.

WINSTON-FRANKLIN GRAVES   Buried here are Major
Joseph Winston (1746–1815) and Captain Jesse Franklin (1760–1823), a member of the Surry County Riflemen and later a U.S. Senator and a governor of North
Carolina. Their remains were reinterred here in 1906.
Nothing is known about Winston's stone; Franklin's stone
was removed from the original grave at Fisher's Peak,
North Carolina. On July 13, 1966, the Joseph Winston
Chapter of the Daughters of the American Revolution
of Winston-Salem donated a commemorative plaque to
mark the gravesite.

Alamance—Revolutionary War History

During the decade preceding the formal severing of ties
with England, rebellion was stirring in the colonies.
Frontiersmen from the western part of North Carolina

for several years had openly opposed the taxes and dishonest officials of the Colonial government. These defiant backwoodsmen became known as "Regulators" because they created disturbances to convince the royal governor that regulation of local officials was necessary.

When in December 1770 the Assembly passed the Johnston Riot Act—designed to expedite the arrest and conviction of disturbers of the public peace—the Regulators denounced the repressive act by threatening death to all court clerks and lawyers. They also vowed to assassinate Edmund Fanning, a high government official whose actions had made him a target of their anger. (He had served as a representative to several Colonial assemblies, was register of deeds of Orange County, and was a judge of the Superior Court).

As the unstable conditions continued to prevail, Royal Governor William Tryon prepared a show of force. In early spring he led the eastern militia, totaling over 1,000 men, toward Hillsborough and ordered General Hugh Waddell to enlist the support of the western militia and meet him there. Waddell, however, could raise only 200 men. On May 9 Tryon's army reached Hillsborough without incident, but on the same day Waddell's march was halted by 2,000 Regulators who blocked his movement at the Yadkin River. Tryon began moving his army westward and on Monday, May 13, encamped on the west bank of Alamance Creek. Remaining there three days, the royal governor tried to negotiate with the Regulators, but no compromise could be reached.

On the morning of May 16 Tryon's militia marched to within a half-mile of the Regulators' camp, and he dispatched a final message ordering the rebels to disperse. When it was rejected, the militia launched a two-hour attack sending the Regulators fleeing in panic. Eighteen prisoners were taken, along with supplies, ammunition, and seventy horses. Nine Regulators and nine militiamen lay dead on the Alamance battlefield and many more were wounded.

This show of force by the British added fuel to the spreading fire of Colonial unrest.

Alamance Battleground State Historic Site

Take Interstate 85 North to Route 62 South (Alamance Exit). At the end of the exit ramp turn right and travel 6 miles.

Open Tuesday through Saturday 9 A.M. to 5 P.M., Sunday 1 P.M. to 5 P.M. Closed Thanksgiving and Christmas Day. Free.

VISITORS' CENTER   An informative audio-visual show presents details of the Battle of Alamance.

ALLEN HOUSE   This small log cabin was moved here from its original location fifteen miles away. It was built by John Allen, who migrated from Ireland to settle in Pennsylvania. Upon receiving a land grant in North Carolina from Lord Granville, he traveled to this locale in the late 1750s. Allen's sister Amy married Herman Husband, a leader and pamphleteer of the Regulator movement. Generations of Allens lived in this house until 1929.

Included among the furnishings, which date from

Allen House, Alamance Battleground State Historic Site (ALPER)

about 1765 to 1825, are a fine tall-case clock, a handsome Chippendale desk, and a walnut blanket chest.

The one-room house also has a loft where the ten Allen children slept. The little porch-room in the rear was used as a general store. The family papers and account books record the sale of items such as herbs, spices, corn, medicines, yarns, cloth, and tools.

BATTLE MONUMENT This small granite monument, unveiled on May 29, 1880, was given as a memorial to the battleground by Alamance County. The inscription reads: "Here was fought the Battle of Alamance, May 16, 1771, between the British and the Regulators."

HUNTER MONUMENT The statue which crowns this monument honors James Hunter, often called the "General of the Regulators." Hunter, a red-headed Scotsman, presented a Regulator petition citing grievances to Royal Governor Tryon at Brunswick Town in June 1768, but Tryon refused to take action. Three years later, during the battle here, Hunter led his valiant men, although in the spirit of brotherhood he proclaimed, "We are all free men and every man must command himself." Following the defeat at Alamance, he escaped to Maryland and went into hiding. While in exile Tryon placed a sentence of death on him for his part in the rebellion. After the Revolutionary War, Hunter returned to North Carolina and represented the Guilford Courthouse area in the state legislature.

The stone monument base was originally erected on the Guilford Courthouse battleground site in 1901 through donations raised by the Hunter family. Its design is attributed to William C. Noland of Richmond, Virginia. The following year the statue of Hunter (which cost $2,850) was added.

In 1962 the entire monument was transferred to the Alamance battlefield site.

Hunter Monument, Alamance Battle-ground State Historic Site (ALPER)

PUGH'S ROCK   According to tradition, James Pugh, one of the Regulators, hid behind this rock during the battle and fired at his enemy. During the height of the fray he courageously captured one of Tryon's cannons. Pugh was captured and, along with five other Regulators, was hanged at Hillsborough.

Winston-Salem
(Old Salem)

Revolutionary War History

The Moravian Brethren are followers of Jan Hus (1369–1415), the Bohemian religious reformer who was condemned as a heretic by the Council of Constance and burned at the stake. In the 1740s the Moravians established settlements in Pennsylvania, and in 1753 a group of them traveled to North Carolina, where they built a small community named Bethabara (meaning "House of Passage"). Because the town (near present-day Winston-Salem) was primarily engaged in agricultural activity, the Brethren decided in 1766 to build a commercial center on a nearby site. The town, which they named Salem, was carefully planned, street by street; after six years of construction, the first section of houses and shops was completed.

In early 1781 the Revolutionary War reached Salem, bringing with it chaos, fear, and disease. First to arrive were units of General Nathanael Greene's army, which were supplied with provisions. Later, a field hospital was established here briefly and the seriously wounded were left behind to be cared for by one of Salem's physicians, Jacob Bonn.

On February 9 about 5,000 Redcoats swarmed the area in pursuit of General Greene's forces. Foraging parties seized livestock and supplies and ripped apart fences and outbuildings to provide wood for campfires. When Corn-

wallis issued an order for the delivery of twenty horses,
many residents hid their horses in the nearby forest.

On February 22 Colonel William Preston and his Patriot
soldiers stopped over in Salem on their way to Guilford.
He ordered none of his men quartered in the houses but

VISITORS' CENTER   Information and books about the
community of Old Salem are available here.

Old Salem, Inc., was organized in 1950 to restore the
Moravian settlement founded here in 1766. Buildings
erected in the late eighteenth century have been restored or reconstructed, many on the original sites.
Visitors should park their automobiles in the lot in front
of the Visitors' Center. The major points of interest may
be viewed leisurely by walking down Main Street.

Walking Tour

Start at the Winkler Bakery on South Main
Street, just north of Academy Street:

Winkler Bakery

Miksch Tobacco Shop

Wachovia Museum

Single Brothers' House

Vogler House

Salem Tavern

Museum of Early Southern Decorative Arts

End on Main Street near Race Street.

---

asked whether they might be sheltered from the rain in
sheds and stables. That evening many of the officers were
entertained by a program of organ music, and several of

the men spent the night repairing weapons at the black-smith's forge.

In November 1781, and again in January 1782, the peripatetic North Carolina Assembly met in Salem, but both times it failed to transact business because a quorum was not present.

After the signing in 1783 of the Treaty of Paris—which officially ended the war with England's formal recognition of the independence of the American colonies—the North Carolina Assembly issued a proclamation recommending a statewide observance of the Fourth of July "as a day of Solemn Thanksgiving." The Moravians of this community planned a celebration, the first such observance by legislative fiat in America.

On the morning of July 4, 1783, the residents of Salem gathered in the Congregation House to pray, sing hymns, and listen to a sermon delivered by Brother Ludwig Benzien. At 2 P.M. everyone assembled for a "Lovefeast," a

Townspeople singing hymns at a Fourth of July celebration,
Old Salem (ALPER)

Fourth of July candlelight and torch procession, Old Salem
(ALPER)

simple meal consisting of buns and wine. At dusk a candlelight procession, led by a brass choir, marched singing
through the streets.

On the last day of May 1791 President George Washington visited Salem. He spent the day touring the shops,
the school, and the waterworks. In the evening he attended
a church service after which he retired for the night to the
Salem Tavern.

From Greensboro take Interstate 40 West toward Winston-Salem. Pick up Route 52 for a short distance (about
⅕ mile), then turn right onto Stadium Drive. Follow the
green signs to Old Salem by traveling along Stadium Drive
and Salem Avenue, and then by turning right onto Old
Salem Road. The Visitors' Center is located on the corner
of Old Salem Road and Academy Street.

Open Monday through Saturday 9:30 A.M. to 4:30 P.M.,
Sunday 1:30 P.M. to 4:30 P.M. (Hours may be extended
during the summer months.) Closed December 25. A ticket
to the six major Exhibition Buildings is $2.50 for adults and

60¢ for students. A combination ticket to the Exhibition
Buildings and to the Museum of Early Southern Decorative
Arts is $3.50 for adults, $1.25 for students. Single-admission
tickets to some buildings may also be purchased.

Old Salem Sites

MIKSCH TOBACCO SHOP *On South Main Street, just
off Academy Street* When Johann Matthew Miksch
built this small house in 1771, he went into business as
a bookbinder. Not achieving great success in this en-
deavor, he opened a tobacco shop, where he sold cut
tobacco, chewing tobacco, and snuff. Later, he also sold
such items as herbs, spices, seed, soap, and small tools.

The oldest piece of furniture in this house is the
eighteenth-century chest brought here from the Moravian community in Bethlehem, Pennsylvania. Highly
prized also is the desk made by John Krauss, a Salem
resident. The "perpetual" calendar-clock downstairs
stopped in 1785.

Bedrooms are located on the second floor.

**MUSEUM OF EARLY SOUTHERN DECORATIVE
ARTS** *926 South Main Street. Open Monday through
Saturday 11 A.M. to 6 P.M., Sunday 1:30 P.M. to 4:30
P.M. Closed December 25. Adults $1.50, students $1.00.
Guided tours are offered.* Opened in 1965, this museum
houses a splendid collection of decorative arts and furni-
ture (1660–1820) from various regions of the South.
Among the fifteen period rooms, visitors should not miss
the elegant Chippendale pieces in the **Edenton Parlor**,
the sophisticated decor of the **White Hall Dining Room**,

Salem Tavern,
Old Salem (ALPER)

and the finely carved woodwork in the **Edgecombe Room.**

SALEM TAVERN *800 South Main Street* The first Salem Tavern, completed in August 1771, was built on the Town Square. The two-storied half-timbered building, which measured forty-three feet by thirty-one feet, also had several outbuildings: a kitchen, smokehouse, cow shed, stable, and woodshed.

The first occupants of the tavern were Brother Jacob Meyer, his family, and servants. At first Meyer was paid a salary of £ 30 a year; later he was permitted to retain a third of his profits as well. His activities were strictly regulated by the laws of the colony and by the Aufscher Collegium. One stricture was that the innkeeper must not allow a guest to become intemperate and run himself into debt. (No one's account could total more than forty shillings.)

After the devastating fire of January 1784, which

destroyed this section of town, another tavern was constructed at a new location. Jacob Meyer and his wife Dorothea moved into their second establishment on December 20, 1784, and remained there until 1787, when they retired from the business.

The new tavern keeper was Jacob Blum, who had previously managed the tavern in the nearby community of Bethabara. A justice of the peace, he performed civil wedding ceremonies and collected taxes in Salem.

In the **Gentlemen's Room** of the Salem Tavern—with its Chippendale furniture and fine tablecloths—food was served at any hour. In the **Public Room** across the hall, however, meals were served only at specified hours three times a day.

Food for as many as forty guests was prepared in the large **Kitchen.** The meat and vegetables were cooked in the heavy iron pots hung in the twin fireplaces and were served on pewter platters.

No furniture in the tavern is original except possibly the stretcher table in the **Keeper's Parlor.** The bedrooms are sparsely furnished, and George Washington is said to have spent two nights (in 1791) in the **Blue Room** on the second floor.

SINGLE BROTHERS' HOUSE   600 *South Main Street*
This large building housed the unmarried men and older boys of the Moravian community. It was their home and place of business.

The congregation of Salem was divided into groups or "choirs" according to age, sex, and marital status. Single people lived in one of the Choir Residences—the Single Brothers' House or the Single Sisters' House. Married couples lived in their individual homes with their children who, upon reaching the age of fourteen, went to live in the Choir Residences.

After a general education in the Boys' School, the young men came to live here and learned a craft by serving an apprenticeship until they were twenty-one years old.

This structure was built in 1769; in May scores of workmen gathered for a house-raising bee, and in two days the timbers and rafters were in place. In December sixteen men and four boys moved in. Seventeen years later the kitchen was enlarged and additional space for shops was provided.

Visitors can still see in the **Dining Room** the original oak plank floor and the old stove that was used to provide heat. The room is furnished simply, with plain tables and benches. The tables are set with pewter utensils imported from England.

The **Kitchen** is very large and well equipped. The housework was done by the men and one brother served as a fulltime head cook, assisted by young boys. Among the kitchen equipment here is a sifter with a bottom made of horsehair, a lard press, rolling pins, cake pans, and a coffee roaster. The fireplace with its elevated hearth has not been altered. The brick floor is slanted and an opening appears in the left wall so that dishwater thrown on the floor could be drained out of the building.

The southern rooms were used as **Shops.** The tinsmith made household articles such as pots, pans, cookie cutters, candle molds, and even butter churns. The gunsmith crafted fine rifles for hunting, which were sold only to members of the community; in addition, he spent much of his time making door locks, nails, and traps. The joiner's shop—now equipped with two lathes from the shop of Johann Simon Leicht and a workbench from the shop of Henry Leinbach—produced custom-made furniture of walnut, cherry, or maple.

On the second floor is the room of the **Vorsteher** or supervisor of the house. The folding bed was raised during the day to create space. The chest of drawers was made locally, and the washstand may be either the

original one used here or one from the Single Sisters'
House.

Brothers attended services in the **Chapel** on the top
floor at least once a day (usually in the evening), when
the scriptures were read and hymns were sung. The
organ, which is still in use today, was originally used
across the square in the large sanctuary that accom-
modated the entire congregation. (The benches and
brass chandeliers here were also taken from that structure.) The organ was built in Pennsylvania by Daniel
Tannenburg, famous maker of musical instruments, and
was brought to Salem in 1797.

VOGLER HOUSE   *Facing Salem Square*   This house
was built in 1819 by thirty-six-year-old John Vogler for
his new bride Christina.

Vogler, who lived to be almost ninety-eight, tried his
hand at many occupations. As a young man he served

*Children dressed in
Colonial costumes
playing games,
Old Salem*
(ALPER)

an apprenticeship to a gunsmith but later decided to become a silversmith. He opened a shop on the ground floor of this house, where he not only sold his silver work but also sold and repaired clocks.

The French Empire clock here was presented to his daughter when she married in 1838. The profile-making machine standing in a corner was invented by Vogler, who had seen the art practiced in Philadelphia. Cutting silhouettes soon became a lucrative "hobby" for him.

This house was the first in the village to use wallpaper; the paper in the **Family Room** is a reproduction of an eighteenth-century pattern. Articles in the room which belonged to the Vogler family include the ivory chess set, the secretary, and the rocking chair. The paintings above the mantel are of John and Christina Vogler.

Visitors can view some of the original tools Vogler used as well as the old forge that melted the metal for his fine silver objects.

WACHOVIA MUSEUM (BOYS' SCHOOL) *Corner of South Main and East Academy Streets* This building, constructed in 1794, was used as a boys' school until 1895. The first floor served as the living quarters of the schoolmaster; the classrooms and chapel were located on the second floor; and the students slept in the dormitory on third floor.

One of the most impressive displays in the museum is the collection of early local pottery by Gottfried Aust and Rudolf Christ. Other important exhibitions include musical instruments (such as harps, dulcimers, tubas, and cornets) and paintings (such as Thomas Sully's *Self Portrait*, Gustavus Grunewald's *Portrait of a Boy*, and Moravian artist John Valentine Haidt's *Queen of Sheba Visiting Solomon*).

The Annex houses stage coaches, a costume and doll collection, and many Indian artifacts.

WINKLER BAKERY *525 South Main Street* John Cristian Winkler was born near Blumenstein, Switzer-

Winkler Bakery, Old Salem (ALPER)

land, in 1766, and as a young man was apprenticed to
a blacksmith. In 1791 he journeyed to Neuweid (now in
West Germany) to be received into the Moravian Congregation. Later, he traveled to Ebersdorf where he
learned the baker's trade and was placed in charge of
the Brothers' House bakery.

Winkler sailed to America in 1799, was ordained a
deacon in Bethlehem (Pennsylvania) in 1802, and finally
settled in Salem in 1807, where he purchased this small
building for a bakery.

His business flourished. Records indicate he baked
almost 200 loaves of bread (in various sizes) in a
week. At that time a five-and-one-half-pound wheat loaf
sold for one shilling. In addition, rye bread, cakes, and
other baked goods were offered for sale.

Hillsborough

Hillsborough (also spelled Hillsboro) was the scene of the Regulator uprising of 1768. It began when a government official seized a Regulator's horse and saddle for nonpayment of taxes. An outraged band of Regulators rode into town, bound the sheriff, harassed several citizens, and fired shots over the house of Edmund Fanning, one of the royal governor's representatives in the area. Fanning summoned the local militia to search for the leaders of the rioters, and two well-known Regulators, Herman Husband and William Butler, were captured and imprisoned. Enraged by this act, 700 Regulators marched into Hillsborough and forced Fanning to free the prisoners on bail.

When Husband and Butler were tried at the September term of court, almost 3,000 Regulators encamped on the hills that surrounded the town. Husband was acquitted but Butler was found guilty.

In September 1770, when the court was hearing a case against several other Regulators, a mob of sympathizers, wielding sticks and cudgels, filled the courtroom. A riot soon erupted. John Williams, an attorney, was severely whipped; William Hooper (later a signer of the Declaration of Independence) was assaulted; and the hated Edmund Fanning was dragged through the streets. Before evening the mob looted homes and shops and ransacked Fanning's residence.

On June 19, 1771, six Regulators who had fought in the Battle of Alamance (May 16, 1771) were hanged in Hillsborough.

Other significant events occurred at Hillsborough. As hostilities with the British intensified and after Royal Governor Martin had fled the colony, a Provincial Congress met here in August 1775, with Samuel Johnston as moderator, and voted to arm two regiments and organize the county militia. The town served as a supply post for Patriot troops and in 1780 as a rendezvous point for General Horatio Gates' demoralized army after their defeat at Camden.

Cornwallis occupied Hillsborough for five days in 1781 and raised the royal standard in front of the old courthouse. He tried to induce the young men of the area to join his forces by offering ten days' rations, but few accepted.

In September 1781 Hector McNeill and David Fanning, two daring Tories, marched with 300 men from British-held Wilmington to Hillsborough and captured Governor Thomas Burke (a native of Hillsborough), several members of his Council, and a number of Continental officers. The prisoners were taken back to Wilmington.

Hillsborough was the site of five General Assemblies (1778, 1780, 1782, 1783, and 1784). The state convention which met here in the summer of 1788 refused to ratify the Federal Constitution. (Every state except North Carolina and Rhode Island had already accepted it.) A second state convention meeting at Fayetteville in November 1789 finally voted to ratify the Constitution.

Hillsborough Sites

THOMAS BURKE GRAVE   *Drive 2 miles northeast of Hillsborough on Highway 57, then .8 mile. Turn right* *onto dirt side road and drive ⅛ mile.* The tall granite stone here marks the grave of Thomas Burke (1747–1783), member of the Continental Congress (1777–1781) and governor of North Carolina (1781–1782). On September 12, 1781, at his estate Tyaquin, Burke was captured in a surprise attack by the Tories and taken prisoner to Wilmington.

COLONIAL INN *153 West King Street* Since Colonial days a tavern has stood on this site. The L-shaped section, the east wing, was built in 1768. Cornwallis, who pitched camp in Hillsborough in February 1781, probably visited this tavern. According to tradition, he ordered his soldiers to pave the muddy street here with flat flagstones similar to those now in front of the Inn.
The building is now used as a hotel.

FANNING HOUSE SITE *Churton Street (Route 70A)* A marker indicates the site of Edmund Fanning's house. It is believed that the fine mansion which once stood here was built from money extorted in official fees.

HOOPER HOUSE *118 West Tryon Street. Usually not open to the public.* This home was purchased in 1781 by William Hooper, a signer of the Declaration of Independence, and it was owned by the Hooper family for seventy-two years. When the structure was renovated in the nineteenth century, Hooper's law office, an outbuilding on the northeast corner of the lot, was demolished.

ORANGE COUNTY HISTORICAL MUSEUM *Old Courthouse (second floor), East King and Churton Streets. Open daily except Monday 1:30 P.M. to 4:30 P.M. Donations accepted.* This small museum is devoted to eighteenth-century local history. Especially interesting are pieces by early Hillsborough silversmiths, a reproduction of a Colonial kitchen, and a set of standard weights and measures (made in England and purchased by Orange County in 1760).

PRESBYTERIAN CHURCH CEMETERY *Northwest corner of Churton and West Tryon Streets (behind the Presbyterian Church)* William Hooper (1742–1790), one of the North Carolina signers of the Declaration of Independence, was buried here before his remains were removed to the Guilford Courthouse battleground site in early 1920s. But this original grave is still marked by a large stone slab.

The first pastor of the Presbyterian Church, Reverend John Knox Witherspoon (1791–1853)—a grandson of John Witherspoon, a New Jersey signer of the Declaration of Independence—is buried in the Nash family plot near the west wall of the cemetery.

REGULATOR MARKER *About .1 mile on the lane leading from East King Street to the rear of St. Matthew's Episcopal Church* A bronze marker and a concrete slab indicate the place where six Regulators were hanged on June 19, 1771, after the Battle of Alamance. They were James Pugh, Benjamin Merrill, and Robert Matear, and three others whose names have been lost to posterity. The prisoners were escorted to the place of execution by a guard of militiamen.

When they reached the execution site, the condemned men were allowed to speak. Pugh delivered an impassioned defense of the Regulators' cause, and Merrill pleaded for his family's safety. Then they mounted the gibbet, where they were blindfolded and nooses were placed around their necks. As a wail arose from the assembled crowd, they were hanged.

SITE OF TRYON'S MILITARY CAMP *Area below West Margaret Lane (between Wake and Occoneechee Streets)* In May 1771, before proceeding to Alamance to crush Regulator resistance, Governor William Tryon set up a temporary camp in the meadow along the south bank of the Eno River.

Wilmington Area

Revolutionary War History

When the Stamp Act was passed by the British Parliament in 1765, the people of eastern North Carolina vowed to defy it and large crowds met in Wilmington in open opposition. During the evening of October 31, 1765—the night before the Stamp Act was to take effect—a mob of rowdy demonstrators burned an effigy of "Liberty" to dramatize England's abuse of their rights. Two and a half weeks later, an angry crowd harassed Stamp Master William Houston into resigning his office. These acts of civil disobedience and other spontaneous outbreaks throughout the colonies forced Parliament to repeal the act in the following year. But still injustices against the colonies continued to multiply.

In June 1775 the Patriots of the Wilmington area assembled at the courthouse to proclaim their unity in supporting the acts of the Provincial Council; they passionately declared themselves ready to defend North Carolina even if it meant the sacrifice of their "lives and fortunes to secure her freedom and safety."

In early February 1781 Cornwallis decided to establish Wilmington as a supply base and as a center for military operations. He dispatched Major H. Craig with a battalion of 400 men and a small naval force under Captain Barclay to capture the city. Their timing was propitious, for the bulk of the Patriot troops was engaged elsewhere, making the capture of Wilmington an easy victory. On April 7 Cornwallis set up his headquarters in the home of George Burgwin, a leading businessman.

The British troops, making forays into the surrounding countryside, plundered farms and homes and captured Patriot leaders.

One evening several Patriots were meeting at the Rouse House, a tavern several miles outside of Wilmington, to play whist and socialize, but the innocent gathering was interpreted as a clandestine political meeting. A squadron of Major Craig's dragoons marched to the inn and slaughtered every man, except one who had concealed himself in a large chimney. The infamous deed has gone down in local history as "The Massacre of the Rouse House."

Cornwallis and the army left Wilmington on April 25, 1781, and marched toward Virginia. A few units under Major Craig, supported by the British warships in the harbor, remained in the town until mid-November 1781— about one month after Cornwallis' surrender at Yorktown.

VISITORS' CENTER   Tourist information and maps of historic Wilmington may be obtained from the Chamber of Commerce, 514 Market Street, phone 762–2611.

PUBLIC TRANSPORTATION   Bus service is provided by the Wilmington City Bus Line Company, phone 762–4226.

TAXI SERVICE   Yellow Cab, phone 762–3322; Coastal Cab, phone 762–4464.

Colonial and Revolutionary War Sites

CORNWALLIS HOUSE (BURGWIN-WRIGHT HOUSE)
224 Market Street. Open Monday through Friday 9 A.M.

Cornwallis (Burgwin-Wright) House, Wilmington (ALPER)

to 4 P.M. During the spring the house is also open on weekends—Saturday 9 A.M. to 4 P.M. and Sunday 2 P.M. to 6 P.M. Closed holidays. Adults $1.00, children 25¢

This handsome house was built in 1770–1771 by John Burgwin, formerly treasurer of the colony under Royal Governor Arthur Dobbs. Prior to the signing of the Declaration of Independence, Burgwin was traveling in England and injured his leg, which caused him to extend his stay. When conditions in the colonies worsened, he decided to remain in England until order had been restored.

After Burgwin's departure, the residence was occupied by Judge Joshua Wright and his family, although he did not purchase the property until April 1799.

On April 7, 1781, when Lord Cornwallis arrived in Wilmington after the Battle of Guilford Courthouse, he selected this eight-room, two-story house for his headquarters. The basement was probably used as a prison during the British occupation.

According to legend, one of the Wright daughters was attracted to a young British staff officer, and the couple frequently met under the crab apple tree in the front yard to sip tea and exchange tender glances. To record their affection, the officer engraved their initials on a windowpane.

The house has been restored and furnished with eighteenth-century antiques. Among the notable pieces here are a wing chair from the home of Betty Washington Lewis, a chair from Tryon Palace, a convex mirror owned by Colonel William Washington, a tea table made in Edenton in the 1790s, a Lowestoft punch bowl used by Royal Governor Arthur Dobbs, a 1790 chest of drawers by Philadelphia cabinetmaker Henry Connelly, and a pair of black-and-gold torchères made in England in 1780.

HARNETT MONUMENT *Fourth and Market Streets* This granite shaft was erected by the Colonial Dames of America to honor Cornelius Harnett (1723–1781), a Revolutionary War Patriot who has been called the "Samuel Adams of North Carolina." Harnett served in the Colonial Assembly (1771–1775), accepted the presidency of the Provincial Council of Safety (1776), was a member of the Congress that adopted North Carolina's first constitution (1776), was selected as a delegate to the Continental Congress (1777), and signed the Articles of Confederation (1780).

In the winter of 1781 he was taken prisoner while visiting the home of a friend, Colonel Spicer. Harnett's captors forced him to walk beside the mounted officers as they rode the thirty miles back to Wilmington. When at last he fell exhausted to the ground, they tossed his limp body across a horse and galloped to the town, where he was thrown in prison and died of illness in April. He was buried in the churchyard of St. James.

ST. JAMES EPISCOPAL CHURCH *Third and Market Streets. Open for Sunday services.* St. James Parish, established by an act of the Colonial legislature, was organized in 1729, and the first rector was Reverend John La Pierre. Since construction of the church building was not begun until 1751, members of the parish met for worship in the courthouse.

The first St. James (which had no belfry) was seized by Cornwallis' troops in 1781 and converted into a stable. The present church was erected in 1839.

The painting of Christ entitled *Ecce Homo* (Behold the Man) that hangs here is attributed to the Spanish artist Pacheo (1571–1654). It was taken from a pirate ship that attacked Brunswick Town (fourteen miles away) in 1748, and the North Carolina General Assembly presented it to the parish three years later.

In the churchyard are buried Cornelius Harnett, a Revolutionary War Patriot; Philadelphia-born Thomas Godfrey, author of *The Prince of Parthia* (1767), the first American play performed by a professional company; and Major George W. Glover, the first husband of Mary Baker Eddy, founder of Christian Science.

STAMP ACT DEFIANCE MONUMENT *Front and Market Streets* This stone marker tells of the armed resistance in 1765 to the Stamp Act imposed by Parliament. On this spot, the location of the courthouse, a mob forced the stamp master appointed by the Crown to resign his office on November 16, 1765. In June 1775 citizens of New Hanover County assembled here to express their support of the Provincial Congress.

Important Colonial Houses

CAPTAIN COOK HOUSE *321 South Fourth Street. Not open to the public.* This dwelling was built in 1784 by

Captain William Cook, an English-born sea captain who made his residence in Wilmington.

SITE OF THE HOOPER HOUSE   *Third Street between Market and Princess Streets*   William Hooper, a signer of the Declaration of Independence, lived in Wilmington from 1764 until the close of the Revolutionary War, when he moved to Hillsborough.

SITE OF THE QUINCE-WASHINGTON HOUSE   *Southeast corner of Dock and Front Streets*   On Sunday, April 24, 1791, President George Washington visited Wilmington after his tour of New Bern. He was escorted by the Light-Horse Guards (Wilmington's military company), and he entered the town to the thunder of artillery and the cheering of crowds. He occupied rooms at the residence of Mrs. John Quince. The following evening bonfires illuminated the town as a ball was held in the Assembly Hall to honor the distinguished guest. Washington departed on Tuesday, April 26.

St. James Episcopal Church, Wilmington (ALPER)

Non-Revolutionary Sites of Interest

CONFEDERATE MONUMENT *Intersection of Dock and Third Streets* Designed by Francis Packer of Baltimore, this stirring statue of a Confederate soldier was erected with funds provided by Gabriel James Boney, who served in the War between the States and wished to honor his comrades.

DUDLEY MANSION *Front and Nun Streets. Not open to the public.* This was the residence (constructed *c.* 1830) of the first governor elected by the people of North Carolina, Edward Bishop Dudley (1837). It is now used as the Elks Club.

NATIONAL CEMETERY *Twentieth and Market Streets* More than 2,000 Union soldiers, many of whom participated in the 1864 assault on Fort Fisher (about twenty-five miles south of Wilmington), are buried here.

U.S.S. *NORTH CAROLINA* BATTLESHIP MEMORIAL *Just south on US 17/74/76 on the Cape Fear River. Open daily 8 A.M. to sunset. Adults $1.00, children 25¢. During the summer a sound and light show is presented at 9 P.M. Adults $1.50, children 75¢.* Dedicated to the North Carolinians who sacrificed their lives in World War II, this ship is now open to visitors. A museum provides a visual history of the many Pacific campaigns in which the *North Carolina* participated, earning twelve battle stars.

SITE OF ANNA WHISTLER HOUSE *Orange and Fourth Streets, marker at Orange and Third Streets* The home of the mother of the artist James Abbott McNeill Whistler (1834–1903) was once located here.

She served as a model for his painting *Arrangement in Black and Gray* (1872), commonly known as *Whistler's Mother.*

Brunswick Town—Revolutionary War History

A thriving port town stood on this site two centuries ago.

In 1725 Maurice Moore was granted 1,500 acres of land on the west side of the Cape Fear River. He set aside 320 acres for a community, Brunswick Town. Cornelius Harnett, Sr., of Edenton bought the first two lots in June 1726, and after he built his home, he began operating a ferry across the river. Other houses and shops sprang up, and a small town soon flourished here.

In 1731 Brunswick Town became the official port of entry of the Cape Fear River: all ships entering and leaving were required to get clearance to pass here.

After the Stamp Act went into effect in 1765, about 450 armed residents of the area marched on Governor Tryon's residence (then located at Brunswick Town). Another angry mob later forced William Pennington, comptroller of customs, to swear under oath that he would not issue stamped paper.

The next year a British man-of-war seized three merchant ships—the *Dobbs*, the *Patience*, and the *Ruby*—because the papers granting them permission to sail were not properly stamped. The outraged residents of Brunswick Town retaliated by refusing to sell the British much-needed provisions, and a group of several hundred armed men from the lower Cape Fear region finally coerced the British naval officer, Captain Jacob Lobb, into permitting the American ships free access.

In the spring of 1776 (following the Loyalist defeat at Moore's Creek Bridge), British troops began arriving off Cape Fear. On May 12 Sir Henry Clinton's ships shelled Brunswick Town and a force of more than 900 men came ashore. Although no major engagement was fought, the soldiers pillaged property and sent residents fleeing. The British finally burned the town, leaving it a deserted ruin.

Brunswick Town State Historic Site

Follow Routes 17 South and 74 West (17/74) through Wilmington. (This can be done by taking 16th Street to Wooster Street.) Outside the city, cross a large bridge over the Cape Fear River, then pick up Route 133 South. After traveling several miles along this highway, watch closely for the route signs, as 133 South veers sharply to the left, becoming a two-lane road. Proceed about 12 miles until you come to a fork in the road. Take the road bearing toward the left; it leads to Orton Plantation (½ mile) and to Brunswick Town (3 miles).

Open Tuesday through Saturday 9 A.M. to 5 P.M., Sunday 1 P.M. to 5 P.M. Closed Thanksgiving and December 24–26. Free.

VISITORS' CENTER Audio-visual displays vividly describe the history of Brunswick Town. A map of the historic area is available at the reception desk.

Visitors should follow the foot trail to view the major points of interest.

The foundations of several Colonial Brunswick Town buildings have been excavated and are maintained by the state of North Carolina as archaeological exhibits. At the present time reconstruction of the dwellings is not planned.

SITE OF COURTHOUSE   With the creation of Brunswick County in 1764, a courthouse was built which was used until 1769, when it was destroyed by a hurricane. A partition wall at the east end once divided the official chambers and the public courtroom. The foundation is twenty-five feet square.

SITE OF HEPBURN-REONALDS HOUSE   Two wealthy merchants, George Reonalds and Charles Hepburn, bought this lot in 1734 for ten shillings and built a residence and a shop. Even with the expenses of construction, they realized a handsome profit when they sold the property eight years later for £580.

SITE OF JOBSON-LEACH HOUSE   This was one of the earliest houses in Brunswick Town. James Leach sold it to the Jobsons of Pennsylvania in 1728. The deed indicates that three years later James Espry, who owned the adjacent lot, purchased it.

SITE OF WILLIAM LORD HOUSE   The structure once located here may have been a tavern or inn, as records show that William Lord was a "Tavern Keeper." In his will, dated July 5, 1748, he left his property to a wife and six children.

SITE OF MAURICE MOORE HOUSE   Judge Maurice Moore, son of the founder of Brunswick Town, built in 1759 an impressive house facing Front Street (the road that ran parallel to the river). A porch extended across the entire front of the large structure, and formal gardens graced the grounds.

SITE OF NATHANIEL MOORE HOUSE   Built in the late 1720s, the structure that once stood here had three dormer windows, two brick chimneys on each side of

Foundation of a Colonial building, Brunswick Town (ALPER)

the house, and a porch raised above the ground. Even after 1733, when Nathaniel Moore sold this river-view property, it continued to be known as "Nat Moore's Front."

SITE OF ROGER MOORE HOUSE Colonel Maurice Moore, founder of the town, sold this lot to his brother Roger. Since Roger was residing at nearby Orton Plantation, the house on this site was occupied by tenants.

SITE OF NEWMAN-TAYLOR HOUSE The two-story brick structure that once stood on this site was built in 1766 by Captain Stephen Newman. Since this house was not burned by the British, it is assumed he was a Loyalist sympathizer. In the late 1770s the dwelling was purchased for £600 by N. Taylor, who added two rooms (one at the back, the other at the front). The house was torn down about 1800.

SITE OF PUBLIC HOUSE The Public House was probably a six-room stone structure with a peaked roof, several dormer windows, and three chimneys. A low wall enclosed the grounds of the property. Archaeological evidence indicates that a tailor shop was located in one of the rooms here.

SITE OF RUSSELLBOROUGH   Royal Governor Arthur Dobbs, wishing to improve his health, established a residence in Brunswick Town in 1758; he purchased the large house of Captain John Russell of His Majesty's Sloop *Scorpion*. It is evident that the air of Brunswick Town had a salubrious effect on Dobb's health, for four years later the seventy-three-year-old gentleman fell in love and married Justina Davis, a fifteen-year-old resident of the area.

After Dobbs' death in 1765, Royal Governor William Tryon purchased the property. (Construction of the Governor's Palace in New Bern did not begin until 1767.) He changed the name to "Castle Tryon," built a three-room kitchen outbuilding, planted formal gardens, and constructed a tunnel leading from the cellar to the river. Rice was grown in fields along the riverbank northward from the house.

When Governor and Mrs. Tryon moved in 1770 into their luxurious residence in New Bern, William Dry of Brunswick Town became owner of this estate. Although located some distance from the center of the town, Dry's elegant house and furnishings did not escape destruction at the hands of the British in 1776.

WALLS OF ST. PHILIP'S CHURCH   St. Philip's Church was begun in 1754 and construction of the building took fourteen years. Because of the great expense involved, in 1760 the Reverend John McDowell was forced to raise more money to continue work on the structure. With the aid of Richard Quince (a prominent local merchant) and Royal Governor Arthur Dobbs (who wished to make St. Philip's the King's Chapel of North Carolina), sufficient funds were collected. But shortly afterward construction was further delayed by natural causes—lightning struck the roof, which collapsed.

By the time the church was dedicated on May 24, 1768, both McDowell and Dobbs had died and had been buried here. The original communion plate, surplice, and Bible were gifts of King George III.

Many distinguished colonists worshipped at St. Philip's, including Governor William Tryon, Judge Maurice Moore, Robert Howe, and John Wilkens.

When the British burned Brunswick Town in 1776, this fine church was left in ruins.

Orton Plantation—Revolutionary War History

Orton Plantation is located 2½ miles from Brunswick Town. The gardens are open daily 8 A.M. to 5 P.M. The

Remains of St. Philip's Church, Brunswick Town (ALPER)

mansion, Orton Hall, is closed to the public. Adults $2.00, children 75¢.

Orton Hall was built in 1725 by "King" Roger Moore, brother of Colonel Maurice Moore, founder of Brunswick Town. Named for the ancestral home of the Moores in England, Orton Plantation was a leading producer of rice.

A relative of the Moores, Richard Quince, was the next owner and held possession of the estate for thirty years. The property then passed to Benjamin Smith, who had served as an aide-de-camp to General George Washington and later became a governor of North Carolina. In the early 1840s Dr. Frederick Hill purchased the estate and enlarged the house with a second story and an attic. He further enhanced the mansion by adding a Greek Revival facade with four imposing columns. During the Civil War, Orton Hall was used as a hospital for Northern troops.

In the early twentieth century the estate was purchased by the Sprunt family, who added the side wings to Orton Hall and planted the beautiful gardens.

Currie (Moore's Creek)— Revolutionary War History

The Battle of Moore's Creek Bridge was fought on February 27, 1776, between a contingent of Loyalists led by Colonel Donald McDonald and a unit of Patriots organized by Colonel James Moore.

In early 1776, as rebellion was beginning to spread throughout the colonies, Royal Governor Josiah Martin issued a call for subjects loyal to the king to unite and take up arms against the insurrectionists. Donald Mc-

Donald raised a force of almost 1,500 Loyalists, most of them Scots.

The Patriots had, at the same time, organized themselves into fighting units, and for about two weeks the two opposing forces managed to avoid each other as they rallied sympathizers to their respective standards. Colonel Moore sent word to Colonel Richard Caswell (commanding about 800 Patriots) and to Colonel Alexander Lillington (commanding about 400 men) to join forces with him at the Moore's Creek Bridge.

Through a series of military maneuvers and subterfuges, the Patriots triumphed over their foe. On the night of February 26 Caswell and his men marched to the bridge, abandoning their encampment and leaving the fires smoldering to indicate a hasty retreat. Before sunrise they removed much of the bridge's log floor and coated the remaining logs with tallow and soap.

At dawn (before Colonel Moore had arrived) the Loyalist forces started to rush across the bridge. Colonel Donald McLeod (who had assumed command from McDonald, who had fallen ill) instructed his followers to maintain their balance by thrusting their swords into the slippery logs. Within a moment the first wave of men was riddled by the volley of musket fire that swept across the bridge. Almost every man—including McLeoad—fell dead. Panic gripped the other Loyalists, who dashed to cover in the nearby swamp as Caswell's and Lillington's men pursued them.

Although the entire battle lasted only three minutes, at least thirty Loyalists were killed and hundreds were taken prisoner. Yet only one Patriot, Private John Grady, fell mortally wounded.

Man in Colonial costume takes aim with his musket, Moore's Creek National Military Park (NATIONAL PARK SERVICE, WASHINGTON, D.C.)

Moore's Creek National Military Park

From Wilmington travel 17 miles north on Route 421, then about 3 miles west on Route 210. The park is located near the town of Currie.

Open daily 8 A.M. to 5 P.M. Sections of the park where picnicking is permitted are open until dusk. Closed December 25. Free.

BRIDGE MONUMENT   Although the original bridge no longer exists to mark the spot where the Patriots under

Colonels Richard Caswell and Arthur Lillington defeated the Loyalists, a monument—which was erected near the creek in 1931 by the United States War Department—now pays silent tribute to those brave men.

GRADY MONUMENT John Grady, a farmer from Duplin County, was the only Patriot killed during the battle. As he poked his head above the earthwork to take surer aim at the enemy, he was shot. No one knows for certain where he is buried; local historians speculate that he may have lingered several days before he died, and thus may have been buried in Wilmington.

On February 27, 1857 (the eighty-first anniversary of the Battle of Moore's Creek Bridge) a cornerstone was laid in the presence of the Wilmington Light Infantry, the Wellington Rifle Guards, and a large crowd that had come to participate in the ceremonies.

The Grady monument was erected sometime between 1860 and 1876. The date is obscure as no record of the dedication ceremonies has been discovered.

LOYALIST MONUMENT Erected by the Moore's Creek Monument Association in 1909, this monument honors the Loyalists who fought and died here.

JAMES F. MOORE MONUMENT James Fulton Moore (1852–1912), the first president of the Moore's Creek Battleground Association, helped to develop this park as a memorial to the Patriots who fought here. In appreciation for his fourteen years of selfless service the Association erected this eight-foot obelisk soon after his death in July 1912.

ORIGINAL LINE EARTHWORKS The low earthworks here were hastily erected by the Patriots in preparation for meeting the Loyalist assault.

MARY SLOCUMB MONUMENT A fascinating legend has grown around Mrs. Mary Slocumb who, having dreamed that her husband lay wounded on the Moore's Creek battlefield, rode alone at night for sixty-five miles to tend his injuries. When Mary arrived here, she was

Mary Slocumb Monument, Moore's Creek National Military Park
(ALPER)

relieved to find her husband Ezekiel unharmed. She immediately proceeded to give aid to the other soldiers.

In 1907 the Moore's Creek Monumental Association, with $2,000 appropriated by Congress, erected this statue to Mary Slocumb. It also serves to honor all the devoted and self-sacrificing women of the Cape Fear Region.

SLOCUMB GRAVES In front of the statue are the graves of Mary (nicknamed "Polly") Slocumb and Ezekiel. Their remains were removed from the cemetery at Mount Olive (about 100 miles to the north) and reinterred here in 1929.

New Bern

Serving as the Colonial capital of North Carolina, New Bern was the location of the royal governor's official residence. The North Carolina Assembly appropriated £ 15,000 (about $75,000) for the building of the impressive structure, and construction was begun in 1767 under the supervision of John Hawks, an English architect. Skilled artisans were brought from England and Pennsylvania, and within three years the luxurious mansion was completed. The first residents were Royal Governor William Tryon, his wife Margaret, and their nine-year-old daughter. In 1771, when Tryon was appointed governor of New York, he and his family moved to that colony.

His successor, Josiah Martin, lived in the New Bern Governor's Palace until 1775. After the Patriots of the area received news of the Battles of Lexington and Concord in April 1775, they held Martin prisoner for a short time; soon afterward he was forced to flee.

On January 16, 1777, Richard Caswell was inaugurated in the palace as governor under the first constitution of the independent state of North Carolina. Three months later the first state General Assembly was convened, and it continued to meet regularly until 1794, when the state capital was moved to Raleigh.

Although serving for a time as the seat of government of North Carolina, New Bern saw little military involvement in the Revolutionary War except for a brief occupation in August 1781 by a raiding party from British-held Wilmington.

During George Washington's visit to New Bern in April 1791 he was entertained at a banquet and a ball at the Governor's Palace. On the afternoon of Thursday, the 21st, an address of welcome was followed by fifteen toasts, each announced by the thunder of cannon. A member of the President's party then read an official reply to the greetings. That evening Washington, clad in black velvet and wearing a powdered wig, attended a ball held in the Council Chamber. The wife of Richard Dobbs Spaight (a signer of the Constitution and later a governor of North Carolina) danced the first minuet with the distinguished guest. Washington's visit was perhaps New Bern's last moment of political glory.

Colonial and Revolutionary War Sites

TRYON PALACE COMPLEX *George Street between Eden and Metcalf Streets. Open Tuesday through Saturday 9:30 A.M. to 4 P.M., Sunday 1:30 P.M. to 4 P.M. Closed Thanksgiving, December 24–26, and January 1. Adults $2.00, children $1.00. A combination ticket for Tryon Palace, Stanly House, and Stevenson House costs $4.00 for adults, $1.50 for children. It may be purchased at the gift shop across the street from the Palace entrance gates.* Most of the Tryon Palace was destroyed by fire on the night of February 27, 1798. Only the west wing was still standing in 1952 when restoration was begun. It took $4 million and years of dedicated work to restore the buildings and grounds to their original beauty.

THE PALACE Re-creation of the interior was aided by the discovery of Governor Tryon's inventory of furnishings.

The **Library**—to the left of the main entrance—contains 400 editions, including volumes of philosophy, history, and military science. Among the interesting items in the room are an eighteenth-century barometer, rare Stuart-period brass candlesticks, a chess table, an Edward Aldridge silver inkstand, and an Eglomise painting of Queen Anne.

The **Council Chamber** served a dual purpose: for Council meetings, when the governor and his advisors met to discuss official business, and for state parties and balls. The most distinguished visitor entertained here was George Washington.

Today the room is furnished with a desk and master armchair, a large mahogany table with twelve Gothic Chippendale chairs, and two Irish cut-glass chandeliers. An unusual musical clock (made by Charles Clay of London in 1736) not only records the time, the day of the month, and the phases of the moon, but also chimes and plays operatic airs!

The Sienna marble mantel is almost an exact duplicate of the one described in Tryon's inventory. Flanking the fireplace are a pair of full-length portraits of King George III and his consort Queen Charlotte in their coronation robes. The portraits, painted in England during the 1760s, are attributed to the School of Sir Joshua Reynolds.

The handsome Chippendale table in the **Dining Room** is set for a dessert course—with a Worcester porcelain dessert service and unusual enamel and metal knives and forks. The portrait of Queen Anne (attributed to the School of Sir Godfrey Kneller) honors the patron of Baron Christopher de Graffenreid, who founded New Bern in the first decade of the eighteenth century. (He had come from Bern, Switzerland, and named the settlement in honor of his former home.)

In the **Music Room** the women congregated to gossip, sip tea, and hear music. Exhibited here are a spinet

Council Chamber, Tryon Palace, New Bern (COURTESY, TRYON PALACE COMMISSION, NEW BERN)

(Hitchcock, London, *c.* 1720), a flute (Camusac, London, *c.* 1760), and other representative instruments of the period. The dress worn by Eunice Kelley at the gala ball given for George Washington is displayed on a mannequin in one corner of the room. (The dress was in the possession of a local family and was presented to the Tryon Palace Restoration Commission.)

Other distinguished furnishings in the music room are worth noting. The Turkish carpet dates from the sixteenth century; the seven George II chairs—originally made for the Earl of Shaftesbury—are covered in rare Soho tapestry; the elaborately carved mahogany card table with folding top was made by William Vile, a highly respected cabinetmaker to the royal household of King George III; and the painting *Landscape with Huntsmen* is by Claude Lorrain.

Although food was cooked in the east wing, it was brought to the **"Housekeeper's" Room** and placed in warming cupboards before being served. Trays, china, glassware, and dinnerware which once were stored here are now on display. One may also see syllabub glasses (for "syllabub," a dessert of sweetened cream flavored with wine and beaten to a froth) and a silver papboot (for "pap," bread boiled or softened in milk or water that was fed to infants and invalids). The small chest or "tea caddy" contains three canisters—one might have held a green tea, the other a black tea, and the third a blend.

The second floor was used for the family quarters. The **Ochre Bedroom** and the **Mauve Bedroom** are furnished with majestic four-poster beds with floral bedspreads, delft washbasins, mirrors, and dressing tables. The **Governor's Bedroom** features an English carved canopy bed (with paw feet and spiral-twist fluting), a Queen Anne bonnet-top highboy, and a portrait of Charles Tryon, father of Royal Governor William Tryon. The **Daughter's Room**—occupied by Tryon's daughter when the family resided here—has dolls, a wooden birdcage, a delicate tea set, and miniature furniture (which originally may have been samples of traveling cabinetmakers).

Visitors may also wish to see the **East Wing**, which houses the kitchen, the secretary's office, and a servants' dining room. Not to be missed are the **Kitchen Garden** (with herbs, vegetables, and fruit trees) and the magnificent **Latham Memorial Garden** (completed in 1959 at a cost of over $1 million).

STANLY HOUSE   *307 George Street. Open Tuesday through Saturday 9:30 A.M. to 4 P.M., Sunday 1:30 P.M. to 4 P.M. Adults $2.00, children $1.00. (Admittance also with combination ticket.)*   This house was designed by John Hawks (the architect of Tryon Palace) for his friend John Wright Stanly and was completed in the early 1780s. The center door of the two-story structure is framed with Doric columns supporting a denticulated pediment, and the windows on the first floor have decorative carved moldings. The structure is topped with a hipped roof with a balustrade.

As a young man, Stanly was engaged in the export business in Kingston, Jamaica, and in Philadelphia. In 1772 he was emigrating to Charleston, South Carolina, when a violent storm at sea forced him ashore at Beaufort, North Carolina. There John Sitgreaves, a traveling companion, invited him to settle in New Bern. According to tradition, soon after his arrival in the community he met Ann Cogdell at a palace ball given by Royal Governor Josiah Martin, fell in love, and married her within the next year.

Stanly built a flourishing business; he owned ships engaged in the West Indies trade as well as a local molasses distillery.

As the hostilities between the colonies and Britain intensified, he engaged about fifteen privateers (privately owned armed ships) to keep the ports of

Music Room, Tryon Palace, New Bern (COURTESY, TRYON PALACE COMMISSION, NEW BERN)

Ocracoke and Cape Lookout open, thereby permitting supplies to move through New Bern. After the war erupted, his ships carried munitions to the Patriots from their French allies and even attacked and captured British ships, confiscating foodstuffs and other items useful to the Patriot cause.

John Wright Stanly also advanced more than $80,000 to General Nathanael Greene to support his military campaigns. The loan was never repaid. After the Revolution Washington appointed him First Judge of the Maritime Court of North Carolina in gratitude for his wartime services.

Stanly's life was snuffed out prematurely during the yellow fever epidemic of 1789. He died at the age of forty-seven on June 1, 1789; his wife died a month later.

Although no one occupied this house for several decades after the demise of the Stanlys, it was the scene of a joyous occasion in 1791. When President George Washington stayed here on April 20–21, the residence was cleaned and new furniture was brought in for his sojourn.

The house, which passed through the hands of many owners, was moved to its present location in 1966 and was restored to its original splendor.

Records show that the Stanlys were visited by many distinguished guests. The **Dining Room**—with its Waterford chandelier, fine furniture, Chinese export porcelain, and a portrait of the Washington family (after Edward Savage)—was the center for entertainment. In the evening guests might have played cards in the **Parlor** at the fine gaming table. It stands near a Philadelphia lowboy (by William Savery) and a wing chair covered in its original needlepoint.

The hourglass, telescope, and two globes (London, c. 1770) are appropriate fittings for the **Library** of a ship-owner. Near the secretary-bookcase, made by cabinet-maker Thomas Burling of New York, hang engravings of Nathanael Greene and George Washington.

Among the appointments in the **Master Bedroom** are a gentleman's wig stand and two japanned dressing boxes. On the desk is a copy of a letter written by Mrs. Stanly to her husband scolding him for not writing more frequently and asking him to purchase a pair of shoes for one of the children.

The house, standing on the grounds near Tryon Palace, is an extraordinarily fine restoration.

STEVENSON HOUSE *611 Pollock Street. Open Tuesday through Saturday 9:30 A.M. to 4 P.M., Sunday 1:30 P.M. to 4 P.M. Adults $1.00, children 50¢. (Admittance also with combination ticket.)* A fine example of early-nineteenth-century architecture, this dwelling was built by a sea captain whose ships sailed between New Bern and the West Indies. During the War between the States it was used as a hospital. In 1957 the structure was purchased by the Tryon Palace Commission for restoration.

Today it is furnished with Federal and Empire antiques. Among the outstanding pieces are a pair of Crown Derby urns signed by William Duesbury, a Hepplewhite inlaid mahogany secretary-bookcase, a Sheraton dining table and sideboard from Philadelphia, an Empire gilt chandelier, a mahogany sleigh bed, and rare porcelains.

CHRIST EPISCOPAL CHURCH *Pollock and Middle Streets* The first brick church to stand on this site was completed in 1750. Two years later, King George II presented the parish with a Bible and a silver communion service, which are still in use today. When Royal Governor Josiah Martin fled from New Bern in May 1775, he tried to confiscate the silver but failed. (During the Civil War the communion service was secretly carried to a parish in Fayetteville, where it was hidden.)

The first Christ Episcopal Church was set ablaze by a band of incensed colonists who objected to the royal arms of England being displayed conspicuously above the door. The structure was rebuilt soon after the Revolutionary War. The first rector here, the Reverend James Reed, is buried in the churchyard.

CLERMONT CEMETERY *Moore's Lane* This land was part of the plantation owned by Colonel William Wilson and his wife, Mary Vail. In 1756 their daughter, Elizabeth, married Richard Spaight, a member of the Council of Royal Governor Arthur Dobbs (1757–1766). Their son, Richard Dobbs Spaight (1758–1800), became the first native-born governor of North Carolina (1792–1795). He is buried in this cemetery near his parents.

CYPRESS TREE *520 East Front Street (on the grounds of the Morrison house, a private residence)* According to tradition, this cypress tree was witness to many important moments of history. Here, under the spreading branches, the first boat built in North Carolina was ribbed, sheathed, and caulked. Here John Wright Stanly pledged his unwavering support to General Nathanael Greene. Here George Washington paused for a few moments to relax during his tour of New Bern. (None of these assertions, of course, can be substantiated.)

LADY BLESSINGTON CANNON *Pollock and Middle Streets* This cannon was captured during the War of Independence from the *Lady Blessington*, a British warship, by one of John Wright Stanly's privateers.

Important Colonial Houses

HAWKS-LASITTER HOUSE *306 Hancock Street. Not open to the public.* Built in the mid-1700s, this house was sold in April 1807 to Francis Hawks, son of John Hawks, architect of Tryon Palace.

HOWARD HOUSE *520 New Street. Not open to the public.* This handsome Georgian house (built in the early 1770s) was the home of Martin Howard, first master of the local Masonic Lodge.

GASTON OFFICE *Craven Street between Broad and Pollock Streets. Not open to the public.* This is a reconstruction of the office of Judge William Gaston, a justice of the North Carolina Supreme Court. His father, Alexander, was killed on August 20, 1781, by a Loyalist as he and his family were fleeing to safety. (British soldiers had arrived in New Bern on August 19.) According to tradition, the Gastons escaped through a tunnel running from their house to a small outbuilding. Alexander Gaston was cut down as he and his family were about to board a boat at the waterfront.

MASONIC MEETING HALL *516 Hancock Street. Not open to the public.* This structure served as the meeting place for the local Masonic Lodge. (Chartered in 1772, it is the second oldest lodge in the state.) The first master was Martin Howard, chief magistrate of the Royal Colony of North Carolina from 1767 to 1773. President Washington visited his Masonic brothers here during his visit to New Bern.

Edenton

Ten months after the Boston Tea Party fifty-one women of the Albemarle region gathered at Edenton to protest the British tea tax and the royal government's harsh policies. The defiant ladies drew up a resolution boycotting East India tea, which prompted one local resident to boast that Edenton possessed "more female artillery" than any other town in America. Among the signers of that resolution at the so-called Edenton Tea Party on October 25, 1774, were Anne Johnston, Abigail Charlton, Penelope Barker, Elizabeth Creacy, Jean Blair, and Sarah Littlejohn.

During the Revolutionary War a supply depot was located at Edenton. Although British troops never attacked the town, in May of 1779 the enemy fleet entered Hampton Roads and took Portsmouth, Virginia. As the vessels sailed toward Suffolk, Virginia, residents of Edenton—fearing that troops would disembark and march southward—loaded their furnishings and belongings onto carts and fled. But the Redcoats never reached the town.

In late May 1781 a British galley, the *General Arnold*, slipped into Edenton Harbor at night and made off with the schooner *Small Hopes*, owned by William Littlejohn. The men of Edenton armed several small boats and bravely pursued the galley, which they captured. But they arrived too late to save the American vessel; *Small Hopes* had gone up in smoke.

Several prominent Revolutionary leaders lived in Edenton. Joseph Hewes (1730–1779) served in the North Carolina Assembly (1766–1775), the First Provincial Congress (1775), and the Continental Congress (1774), and was a signer of the Declaration of Independence (1776). He gained the dubious distinction of being the only signer to die in Philadelphia (1779). (Fate seemed to balance things in 1798 when James Wilson, a Pennsylvania signer, died in Edenton while a guest at the James Iredell house.)

VISITORS' CENTER An information center is located in the Barker House at the end of South Broad Street, phone 482–3663. A slide show describes the history of the Albemarle region, and books and pamphlets are offered for sale. Visitors may purchase tickets here for admittance to the major historic houses.

GUIDED TOUR Groups form at the Visitors' Center for guided tours of the Cupola House, Chowan County Courthouse, James Iredell House, and St. Paul's Church. Tuesday through Saturday 10 A.M. to 4:30 P.M., Sunday 2 P.M. to 5 P.M. Adults $2.00, children 50¢

The life of Edenton resident Dr. Hugh Williamson (1735–1819)—merchant, writer, and physician—was rich and eventful. While traveling in Europe in 1775, he sent a document to Lord Mansfield, *The Plea of the Colonies*, defending the disloyalty and unrest in the colonies. Returning by ship to North Carolina in December 1776, he was captured by the British but managed to escape. Later, he was appointed surgeon-general of the North Carolina troops and was ordered to New Bern to vaccinate the soldiers against smallpox. (Immunity to smallpox through inoculation was known in the early eighteenth century—decades before Edward Jenner's experiments in the 1790s.) At the Battle of Camden Williamson treated many of the wounded. After the war, he served as a delegate to Congress (1782–1785, 1787–1788) and was a signer of the Constitution in 1787. In 1789 he attended the Fayetteville Convention and voted for the ratification of the Constitution.

Edenton is rightfully proud of its sons who served the cause of liberty.

Colonial and Revolutionary War Sites

BARKER HOUSE   *Facing Edenton Bay, at the tip of South Broad Street*   This two-story structure was built in 1782 for Thomas Barker, a successful lawyer who took an active role in Colonial politics. Before the Revolutionary War he served as the London agent for the North Carolina colony. His wife, Penelope, presided over the Edenton Tea Party.

In the early nineteenth century the building was purchased by Augustus Moore, a prominent judge. Members of his family occupied the house until 1952, when it was purchased and moved to the present site. Now the headquarters of Historic Edenton, Inc., it serves as a Visitors' Center.

CHOWAN COUNTY COURTHOUSE   *East King Street. Open Monday through Friday 9 A.M. to 5 P.M., Saturday 10 A.M. to 4:30 P.M., Sunday 2 P.M. to 5 P.M. Free.* Built in 1767, this structure is the oldest courthouse still in use in North Carolina. The courthouse design is quite sophisticated and is attributed to John Hawks, the architect of Tryon Palace in New Bern. The District Court meets here every Tuesday and the Superior Court convenes several times a year.

For two centuries the same offices have been used by the register of deeds and the clerks of court. The Masons once used the second-floor east room for meetings of Unanimity Lodge.

The courtroom also served as a public meeting hall. When court was in session, the judge presided from the tall chair in the center of the front of the room. On the second floor the large paneled room—which occupies three central bays and the depth of the building—was used as a ballroom for important occasions. President James Monroe danced here during his visit in 1819.

CHOWAN COUNTY JAIL *Off Courthouse Green. Not open to the public.* One of the oldest jails in the United States, this white brick building surrounded by high walls was built in 1787. Plans for an Edenton "gaol" were drawn up as early as 1773 by John Hawks (architect of Tryon Palace), but the design was modified by Charles Sheeter, who supervised the construction of this structure. Today it is used for offices.

COURTHOUSE GREEN

REVOLUTIONARY WAR CANNON   The cannon facing the waterfront were salvaged from a shipment of armaments carried on a French vessel that sank in Albemarle Sound in 1778. They had been purchased by Benjamin Franklin, Arthur Lee, and Silas Deane, who were the American Commissioners to France.

TEAPOT MEMORIAL   This small bronze teapot on a five-foot pole marks the site of the home of Mrs. Elizabeth King, where fifty-one Edenton women met in 1774 to protest the high taxes on tea.

CUPOLA HOUSE *408 South Broad Street. Open Tuesday through Saturday 10 A.M. to 4:30 P.M., Sunday 2 P.M. to 5 P.M. Adults $1.00, children 25¢.* Named for the small octagonal structure surmounting the roof, the Cupola House was built for a sea captain, Richard Sanderson, about 1725. The building is characterized by prominent gables and a second-floor overhang. The interior woodwork was probably added in the late 1750s by Francis Corbin, an agent for Lord Granville, one of the Lords Proprietors. Corbin had the finial on the front of the house added; it bears the initials "F.C." and the date 1758. His heirs sold the house in 1777 to Dr. Samuel Dickinson, who lived here with his eleven children. His descendants resided here for 141 years.

Since the original woodwork was purchased and removed by the Brooklyn Museum, the woodwork on the first floor is a reproduction. Especially fine are the moldings around the windows, the rosettes and designs above the built-in cupboards, the carving of the doors, and the elaborate mantels.

The fireplace in the **Main Room** has a fireback with an oak tree depicted on it. It is dated 1660 with the initials "C.R." for "Charles Rex." According to legend, King Charles II (1630–1685) saved his life during a battle by hiding in the branches of an oak tree. The

Teapot Memorial, Courthouse Green, Edenton (ALPER)

Chowan County Courthouse, Edenton (ALPER)

fireback has a dual purpose: to protect the back of the fireplace and to throw off heat.

The room is furnished with eighteenth-century pieces. The china on the Queen Anne tea table once belonged to the Dickinson family. The imposing figure in the portrait is Penelope Barker, who presided at the Edenton Tea Party.

In the **Hall** hangs a portrait of Thomas Hodgson (by Wolleston), Penelope Barker's nephew and stepson. (Thomas was the son of Penelope's sister. After her death, the widowed Penelope married the father of Thomas, thereby becoming his stepmother and aunt at the same time.) The calendar clock is the only piece of furniture that has remained in this house since the eighteenth century. It was purchased in England for Dr. Dickinson by Charles Pettygrove.

The comfortable **Sitting Room** has a wing chair (1740) covered in crewel and a fine Chippendale secretary. The little "toddy" table, made in Edenton in the early 1700s, is one of the few North Carolina pieces in this dwelling. Several of the pictures are painted on the reverse side of the glass, a popular technique of the eighteenth century.

Articles discovered in the house during the restoration are on display in Dr. Dickinson's **Study**: four antique maps, a three-footed child's bench, a trunk, a foot-warmer, and a newspaper dated 1797. One item of unusual interest is the three-sided crib, which could be either pulled up to the mother's bed at night or placed against a wall during the day to ensure the infant's safety.

The upstairs **Dressing Room** contains a dress worn by the wife of James Iredell (Associate Justice of the Supreme Court, appointed by George Washington). The pencil post bed in the **Master Bedroom** has an unusual bedspread of pieced appliqué on a white background. On the Queen Anne commode chair near the elm high-boy a doll with china feet is perched. This doll was typical of those sent by English merchants to model the latest London fashions, which could be purchased and shipped to the colonies.

Two delightful items in the upstairs rooms are a decorated patchbox used for keeping the fake beauty marks that women wore and a 1794 valentine with a poem ending, "And if these fair lines you do refuse/ Pray burn the paper and me excuse."

From the **Servants' Quarters** on the third floor—where objects such as a pewter bedpan, an old sewing machine, and a wine press are stored—one can climb a circular barrel staircase into the cupola. There one is rewarded with a panoramic view of Edenton.

IREDELL HOUSE *107 East Church Street. Can be visited on tour or individually; Tuesday through Saturday 10 A.M. to 4:30 P.M., Sunday 2 P.M. to 5 P.M. Adults $1.00, children 25¢.* When seventeen-year-old James Iredell came to America from England in 1751, he was

Cupola House, Edenton (ALPER)

ready to assume his duties as deputy collector for the port of Roanoke. He studied law and eleven years later became attorney general of North Carolina. Following the Revolutionary War, he was appointed Associate Justice of the United States Supreme Court by George Washington.

In 1778, five years after his marriage to Hannah Johnston (sister of the future governor Samuel Johnston), Iredell purchased this property from local silversmith Joseph Whedbee. The structure was significantly enlarged in 1799 by a two-story addition and porches.

The house passed through the hands of several owners (in the 1850s it was used as a rectory for St. Paul's) until the Edenton Chapter of the Daughters of the American Revolution purchased it in 1949.

Although the house is fully restored, it is still being furnished. Many of the pieces are fine antiques of the early nineteenth century.

ST. PAUL'S EPISCOPAL CHURCH *South Broad and West Church Streets. Open daily* 8 A.M. *to* 5 P.M. Organized under the Vestry Act of 1701, St. Paul's parish holds one of the oldest charters in North Carolina. The church building, which was completed in 1760, fell into disrepair and was restored between 1806 and 1809. Four decades later, the present chancel woodwork was added.

While the church was being refurbished in 1949, fire destroyed the roof and steeple, but since the furnishings had already been removed, they were not damaged.

Among the cherished possessions of St. Paul's Church are a book of vestry minutes (1701), a silver chalice and paten (1725), an alms basin (*c.* 1812), and a pair of silver-plated vases (1852).

Several Revolutionary War leaders were members of this parish: Joseph Hewes (a signer of the Declaration of Independence), James Iredell (a lawyer who became Associate Justice of the first United States Supreme Court), and Samuel Johnston (clerk of the Superior Court, later a governor of North Carolina and Senator from the state).

A large group of colonists convened here in 1774 to elect delegates to the Provincial Congress. On June 19, 1776—two weeks before the adoption of the Declaration of Independence—parishioners signed "The Test," a document protesting unfair English taxation policies and supporting the actions of the Continental Congress.

In the churchyard are buried three Colonial governors, all members of St. Paul's: Thomas Pollock, Henderson Walker, and Charles Eden, for whom Edenton was named. (Until 1725, the year of Eden's death, the village had been called Queen Anne's Town.)

Important Colonial Houses

CHARLTON HOUSE *West Eden Street near South Granville Street. Not open to the public.* Jasper Charlton, owner of this home, was active in Revolutionary politics. His wife Abigail is said to have been the first signer of the "Tea Party" Resolutions.

LEIGH-BENNETT HOUSE *West Queen Street between South Broad and South Granville Streets. Not open to the public.* William Bennett, a member of the North Carolina Committee of Safety, bought this dwelling in the early 1770s. His wife Lydia was a signer of the "Tea Party" Resolutions.

MILLEN HOUSE *East Water Street between South Oakun and Court Streets. Not open to the public.* Quentin Millen, a successful merchant, built this house in the early 1770s. A fiery Tory, he was forced to leave the country during the Revolution, although his family remained in Edenton.

PAXTON-McCULLOCH HOUSE *West King Street between South Broad and South Granville Streets. Not open to the public.* This house was owned by Henry Eustace McCulloch, a cousin of James Iredell. Loyal to England, McCulloch returned home when hostilities in the colonies began to intensify. His property was confiscated during the War of Independence.

PEMBROKE HALL *West King Street between South Broad and South Granville Streets. Not open to the public.* In the mid-eighteenth century this property was bought by Thomas Childs, one of Lord Granville's agents. During the Revolution the house was occupied by Mrs. Mary Littledale, one of the organizers of the Edenton Tea Party and a signer of the Resolutions.

WESSINGTON-EVERARD HOUSE *West King Street near the corner of South Granville Street. Not open to the public.* This house was originally the residence (1730) of Sir Richard Everard, royal governor of North Carolina. During the Revolutionary War it was occupied by George Russell, a sea captain, who is remembered for his generous gift of the master's chair to the local Masonic Lodge.

Virginia

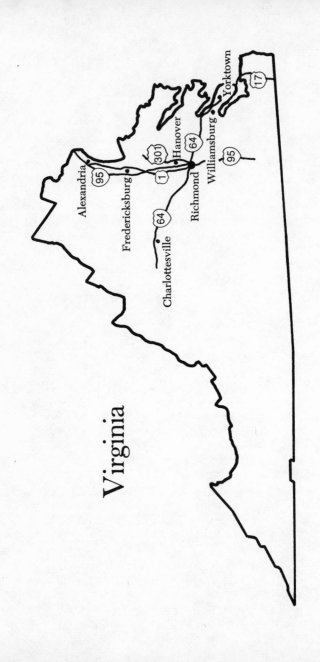

Williamsburg

Revolutionary War History

After the Indian Massacre of 1622 at Jamestown (Virginia's capital), a palisade was built across the narrow peninsula between the James and York Rivers. Many colonists then moved to the safety of the higher ground and established a settlement along the palisade called Middle Plantation.

Here in 1676 Nathaniel Bacon (1647–1676) and discontented frontiersmen met to plan a revolt against Royal Governor William Berkeley. High taxes, patronage of a favored clique, and vacillation in establishing adequate frontier defenses led to the uprising. Berkeley was forced to flee, but soon regained power after Bacon contracted malaria and died, leaving the insurrectionists without a strong leader. The chief rebels were captured, declared traitors, and hanged.

In 1693 Middle Plantation was chosen as the site of the College of William and Mary (the second oldest college in the country, preceded only by Harvard). Five years later, after the Jamestown State House was destroyed by fire, the legislators voted to move the seat of government to Middle Plantation, which they renamed Williamsburg in honor of King William III. The new capital—gradually developing into a town of about 200 houses and 1,500 residents—became the political, social, and cultural center of Virginia.

Delegates elected to the House of Burgesses met in Williamsburg twice a year, in April and October. During these "Publick Times" the population of the town swelled to between 6,000 to 8,000.

Leatherworker demonstrating his craft, Colonial Williamsburg (ALPER)

The colony's first printing press was brought here in 1736 by William Parks, who published Virginia's first newspaper. Before the Revolution, Patrick Henry made fiery speeches against the British in the Capitol; Thomas Jefferson, Peyton Randolph, and their compatriots formed a Committee of Correspondence; and the House of Burgesses adopted the Virginia Resolution for American Independence, which called upon the Continental Congress to sever all ties with England.

But the glory that was Williamsburg came to an end in 1780 when the seat of government was transferred to Richmond. Many of Williamsburg's handsome buildings then fell into disrepair; others burned to the ground.

In 1926 John D. Rockefeller, Jr., and Dr. W. A. R. Goodwin, rector of Bruton Parish Church, initiated plans for the restoration of Colonial Williamsburg. After years

VISITORS' CENTER The Information Center—which is located at the junction of the Colonial Parkway and Route 132—is open 8:30 A.M. to 10 P.M. daily. Phone 229–1000.

Since some sections of the Historic Area are barred to automobile traffic, visitors should park their cars in the parking lots and use the free shuttle buses, which make a complete circuit of the area every few minutes. These buses originate from the downstairs platform of the Information Center.

Before touring the buildings, visitors may wish to see a thirty-five minute film, *Williamsburg: The Story of a Patriot*, which is shown continuously in the two theaters here (until 10 P.M. in July and August, until 6:05 P.M. the remainder of the year).

Sightseeing information and admission tickets to the exhibition buildings are available at the Information Center. A one-day combination ticket may be purchased permitting admission to the Capitol, Magazine, Public Gaol, James Geddy House, Peyton Randolph House, George Wythe House, Raleigh Tavern, and Wetherburn's Tavern. The cost is $5.00 for adults, $3.00 for children. A three-day admission ticket to the major exhibition buildings and the craft shops costs $7.00 for adults, $4.00 for children. A tour of the Governor's Palace is an additional $2.00. The exhibition buildings are open 9 A.M. to 5 P.M. daily.

At the many craft shops in the town visitors may observe craftsmen in eighteenth-century costume practicing their trades in the fashion of their Colonial predecessors.

GUIDED TOURS **Lanthorn Tour,** a candlelight tour of Colonial craft shops, $2.00. **Tricorn Hat Tour,** a two and one-half-hour guided tour for youngsters; 10 A.M. and 2 P.M. during July and August, $2.50. **Garden Tour,** a one-hour tour of Williamsburg's finest gardens; 10:30 A.M. and 2:30 P.M. from April through August, $2.00.

For all the above tours, make arrangements at the reception desk in the Information Center.

WALKING TOURS Most of Williamsburg's major points of interest can be seen in two walking tours. (During the summer entrance lines may be long, so visitors should plan their time accordingly. A minimum of two days is suggested.)

Tour A	Tour B
Area bounded by Lafayette Street on the north, Francis Street on the south, Queen Street on the east, and Nassau Street on the west.	Area bounded by Nicholson Street on the north, Francis Street on the south, Waller Street on the east, and Botetourt Street on the west.
Start at north end of the Palace Green:	Start on Duke of Gloucester Street, just east of Botetourt Street:
Governor's Palace	Wetherburn's Tavern
Brush-Everard House	Raleigh Tavern
Peyton-Randolph House	Capitol
Courthouse	Public Gaol
Magazine	
James Geddy House	
Bruton Parish Church	
George Wythe House	
(Craft shops in the area include those of the bootmaker, weaver, cooper, and basketmaker)	(Craft shops in the area include those of the jeweler, wigmaker, and gunsmith; also the bakery and the apothecary)
End on west side of the Palace Green.	End on Nicholson Street, just north of the Capitol.

of painstaking historical and archaeological research, the rebuilding and renovations began. Today, the Historic Area covers about 170 acres extending one mile in length. Eighty-five eighteenth-century houses, taverns, shops, and public buildings have been restored, and fifty important structures have been rebuilt on their original sites.

Williamsburg Sites

BRUSH-EVERARD HOUSE   *East side of Palace Green*
Built in 1717, this small structure served as the residence and workshop of John Brush, an armorer and gunsmith who also served as the first keeper of the Williamsburg Magazine. At that time the dwelling consisted of one room on each side of a central hall and a loft.

About mid-century the property was acquired by Thomas Everard, who held several important civic positions, including clerk of the General Court and mayor of Williamsburg. He enlarged the house by adding two wings to the rear, thus creating the U-shaped structure. The interior was enhanced by an elaborate staircase and fine woodwork.

Today, the rooms are furnished with antiques of the period. Of special interest is the **Child's Room** (on the second floor) with its miniature furniture and accessories. The **Library** is stocked with about 300 books, reproducing as nearly as possible Everard's fine collection (which was purchased after his death by Thomas Jefferson).

BRUTON PARISH CHURCH   *Duke of Gloucester Street near the west side of the Palace Green*   Organized in 1674, Bruton Parish was named for an English parish in Somerset, the native home of several prominent residents of the Virginia colony. The present brick church, completed in 1715, was designed by Royal Governor Alexander Spotswood. The altar was placed at the east end, and a special area was set aside for the use of the governor and his council. Because of the rapidly growing congregation, the church was enlarged in 1744. The first organ was installed in 1755, and the bell (presented to the parish by James Tarpley, a local merchant) was mounted in the steeple in 1761.

After reports arrived in Williamsburg in 1774 that Parliament had closed the port of Boston, the burgesses proclaimed June 1 a day of fasting and prayer with services at Bruton Parish. Years later, the church bell rang out the news of the adoption of the Declaration of Independence (1776) and the signing of the Treaty of Paris formally ending the Revolutionary War (1783).

Among the important political leaders who worshipped here were George Washington, Thomas Jefferson, George Mason, Patrick Henry, James Madison, and James Monroe.

CAPITOL   *East end of Duke of Gloucester Street*   Construction of the Capitol began in 1701 under the supervision of master builder Henry Cary. The building was laid out in the shape of an H—two wings with a connecting section. One wing housed the Hall of Burgesses and committee rooms, and the other contained the General Courtroom and Council Chamber. When fire destroyed the structure in 1747, Royal Governor William Gooch ordered it rebuilt. The second Capitol, which was completed in 1753, fell into disrepair after the government moved to Richmond in 1780. In the early nineteenth century it burned to the ground.

The first Capitol has been reconstructed on the site, and it is one of America's most cherished historical shrines.

In this building representatives convened from the

Bruton Parish Church, Colonial Williamsburg (ALPER)

entire Virginia colony (which at one time stretched almost to the Ohio River). Burgesses, who were elected for one-year terms, traveled to Williamsburg twice a year—in April and October, the "Publick Times"—when the House of Burgesses sat to consider legislation. A bill was read in the House of Burgesses, then assigned to one of six standing committees. After the language was refined, amendments added, and revisions completed, the bill was read twice more in the House to be adopted or dismissed. Once passed, major bills were sent to England for the king's signature.

The day-to-day affairs of government were superseded by a crisis of immense proportions when the British Parliament passed the Stamp Act in 1765. Young Patrick Henry delivered an impassioned oration here protesting the policies of the mother country. Several conservative burgesses interrupted with cries of "Treason" to which Henry retorted, "If this be Treason, make the most of it."

In 1776, when relations between England and the colonies had passed the point of compromise, the burgesses selected Edmund Pendleton to draft the document which became known as the "Virginia Resolution for American Independence." It was introduced to the Continental Congress in Philadelphia by the Virginia delegation. When they returned home, the burgesses asked George Mason to form a committee to draft a constitution for Virginia, thus signifying the official ending of the role of England in their internal affairs. In June 1776 Patrick Henry was elected to serve as the first American governor of the newly established commonwealth.

Sessions of the General Court (the highest in the territory) were held concurrently with the sitting of the House of Burgesses. The royal governor and twelve counselors (who were appointed for life by the Crown) presided in the paneled courtroom, where they heard criminal cases involving loss of life or limb and civil cases amounting to more than £10. After a trial, the jurors (who had been brought to Williamsburg at public expense) retired to a third-floor chamber, without benefit of food or drink, to consider their verdicts. Not until the last day of court were all sentences passed.

COURTHOUSE *Facing Market Square* Constructed in 1770 to replace an earlier courthouse (at Francis and England Streets), this building housed the county and the municipal courts. The structure is typical of Colonial Virginia courthouses: it is built on a T-shaped design and has arched windows and a cupola. In 1911 columns were added to the overhanging pediment, but they were removed in 1932 when the building was restored to its original eighteenth-century appearance.

The square on which the courthouse stands was the site of town fairs (in April and December) and served as a farmer's market. Here, too, local militiamen mustered. In July 1776 the Declaration of Independence was read in the square, and the joyous event was celebrated with fireworks and the salute of guns.

The interior of the building is now being renovated; it will be furnished in the style of a local eighteenth-century courthouse.

JAMES GEDDY HOUSE *Duke of Gloucester Street near east side of Palace Green* Gunsmith James Geddy, a Scottish immigrant, settled in a small house on this site in the late 1730s. In 1750, six years after his death, Geddy's widow built the present two-story house and the one-and-a-half-story extension. A son, James, purchased the property in 1760 and established his residence and shop here. Becoming one of Williamsburg's most successful metalworkers, James Geddy II not only crafted utensils of pewter and brass but also fashioned fine jewelry of silver and gold. A respected member of the community, he was elected to the city's Common Council.

The house is a rare example of eighteenth-century Williamsburg architecture because of its L-shaped plan, low-pitched roof without dormers, and front porch crowned with a balcony. The furniture—mostly Colonial American—reflects the economic and social status of a prosperous eighteenth-century craftsman.

GOVERNOR'S PALACE   *Facing the Palace Green*   In 1706 the House of Burgesses granted £3,000 for the construction of an official governor's mansion. Henry Cary, architect and master builder, was appointed overseer of the project. Because of innumerable crises—lack of sufficient funds, incompetence of the workmen, and delivery of damaged materials—the Governor's Palace was not completed until 1720.

The most elegant building in Williamsburg, the palace was the home of seven royal governors: Alexander Spotswood, 1720–1722; Hugh Drysdale, 1722–1726; William Gooch, 1727–1749; Robert Dinwiddie, 1751–1758; Francis Fauquier, 1758–1768; Norborne Berkeley, Baron de Botetourt, 1768–1770; John Murray, Earl of Dunmore, 1771–1775.

The last royal governor of Virginia, who in his zealous execution of British edicts had incurred the wrath of the

Garden view of the Governor's Palace, Colonial Williamsburg
(ALPER)

colonists, found it expedient to secretly flee the palace one night in June 1775 and to take refuge on a British man-of-war anchored in Chesapeake Bay.

The first two governors of the independent common-wealth of Virginia also occupied this mansion: Patrick Henry, 1776–1779, and Thomas Jefferson, 1779–1780.

In 1780 the capital was moved from Williamsburg to Richmond because of the presence of the British fleet off the Virginia coast. The Governor's Palace was then converted into a hospital for wounded Colonial soldiers, and it was destroyed in 1781 through the carelessness of patients.

The east wing was originally used to house the offices of the governor, the lieutenant governor, and a staff of secretaries (who may have lived in the quarters on the second floor).

The main building, with its cupola rising above the balustraded roof, is furnished with magnificent antiques. The **Little Dining Room,** used by the governor and his family, contains a mahogany Chippendale table and Queen Anne chairs with the original needlework seats. The tea set on the mantel is Whieldon agateware. Domi-nating the **Great Bedchamber** is an impressive four-poster oak bed (six feet long by five feet wide) that was made in England in the seventeenth century. The chest on chest, made by a Boston cabinetmaker, is a rare ex-ample of this type. In the **Governor's Study** is found the only original piece of furniture from the palace—the tall-case clock that once was the property of Royal Gov-ernor Dunmore.

Through the **Ballroom** doorway—now flanked by Allan Ramsey's coronation portraits of George III and Queen Charlotte—passed Virginia's most distinguished residents to enjoy an evening of music and dancing. The most elaborate celebration was held on the king's birth-day, when fireworks blazed through the night sky above the palace Green and guests filled the dance floor beneath the ballroom chandeliers.

The **Supper Room,** used for receptions or for refreshments during balls, shows a strong Chinese influence: pagodalike pediments above the doorway, hand-painted wallpaper with Oriental nature motifs, and Chinese-style Chippendale furniture.

In the formal gardens behind the palace a plot of ground is marked by a simple plaque to commemorate the burial place of 156 Revolutionary War soldiers, some of whom were probably veterans of the Yorktown campaign. A holly maze, similar to the one at Hampton Court, England, provides a pleasurable game for visitors who wish to try to make their way through its labyrinthine pathways.

MAGAZINE   *Duke of Gloucester Street, one block East of Palace Green*   The octagonal brick magazine was built in 1715 on the orders of Royal Governor Alexander Spotswood as a central military warehouse for arms and ammunition used in defense against Indian attacks, slave uprisings, and pirate raids.

Six decades later, on the eve of the Revolutionary War, Lord Dunmore, royal governor of Virginia, directed that munitions be removed from the magazine and transferred to a British ship. Irate colonists marched on Williamsburg demanding either return of the supplies or full payment. Restitution was made, and the mob dispersed.

The magazine, which is the original structure, now houses an outstanding collection of eighteenth-century pistols and muskets.

PEYTON RANDOLPH HOUSE   *North England and Nicholson Streets*   This was the residence of one of Williamsburg's most distinguished citizens, Peyton Randolph (1721–1775), who served as a Speaker of the House of Burgesses for a decade preceding the Revolutionary War, was chosen chairman of the Virginia Committee of Correspondence, and was elected president of the First Continental Congress.

Magazine, Colonial Williamsburg (ALPER)

In 1715 Randolph's father built the western section— a two-story house with a central chimney—and in 1724 he acquired the story-and-a-half dwelling standing on the neighboring lot. Several years later, these two structures, were linked by a two-story middle section.

Before the outbreak of the Revolution, Patriots frequently held meetings at this house. On one occasion Randolph read aloud Thomas Jefferson's document known as *A Summary View of the Rights of British America.*

While attending the Second Continental Congress, Peyton Randolph died and his body was sent back from Philadelphia to be buried at the College of William and Mary in Williamsburg. His home continued to be occupied by his widow, the former Elizabeth Harrison (sister of Benjamin Harrison, a signer of the Declaration of Independence). In October 1824 Lafayette was a guest here while visiting the town.

The interior contains some of the finest paneled rooms in Williamsburg. Among the noteworthy furnishings are an octagonal George II walnut dining table, a silver punch bowl by Richard Gurney and Thomas Cook (London, c. 1740), an imposing English carved mahogany bookcase (c. 1765), an Ushak carpet with an arabesque design (late 1600s), a portrait by eighteenth-century artist Matthew Pratt, and an unusual single-legged corner table with a shell and C-scroll carved on the knee.

PUBLIC GAOL　*Nicholson Street, just north of the Capitol*　The public gaol (jail), completed in 1704, was designed by Henry Cary, the master builder who supervised the construction of the Capitol and the Governor's Palace. In 1722 quarters for the keeper, a lifetime political appointee, were added to this small brick structure.

Three types of prisoners were incarcerated here: debtors, persons accused of minor offenses, and those convicted of major crimes.

Debtors, held here for twenty days, were expected to pay their debts after release. For minor offenses—such as disturbing the peace and wife-beating—men served sentences of several weeks with some time in the pillories and stocks. Persons convicted of major crimes, such as treason, arson, and murder, were shackled in leg irons and held in separate cells until they were hanged.

During the War of Independence this jail was crowded with spies, Loyalists, and British soldiers.

RALEIGH TAVERN　*Duke of Gloucester Street, east of Botetourt Street*　This tavern was named for Sir Walter Raleigh (1552–1618), the English courtier, navigator, and poet of the Court of Elizabeth I.

The **Ballroom** and **Apollo Room** were the settings for significant historical events. In 1769 Royal Governor Botetourt, outraged at the colonists' protest against the British Revenue Act, dissolved the Virginia legislature, but the resolute burgesses reconvened at the Raleigh Tavern where they planned a boycott of British goods. Four years later, several Patriots—including Thomas Jefferson and Patrick Henry—met here to organize the

Virginia Committee of Correspondence. When the British closed the port of Boston in 1774, Virginia leaders congregated at the Raleigh Tavern to determine a course of action.

Many joyous occasions were celebrated here. Peyton Randolph, the first president of the Continental Congress, was honored at a banquet after returning from Philadelphia in 1774. When, in 1783, the Treaty of Paris was signed ending the Revolutionary War, local citizens paraded through the streets, then attended an elaborate reception at the Raleigh. During his visit to Williamsburg in 1824 Lafayette was feted in the Apollo Room by the gentlemen of the community.

This building, which was erected about 1740, was destroyed by fire in 1859. It was not reconstructed until 1930. The tavern boasts an outstanding collection of eighteenth-century furniture of English and American origin.

WETHERBURN'S TAVERN *Duke of Gloucester Street, east of Botetourt Street* Henry Wetherburn, one of the

Public Gaol, Colonial Williamsburg (ALPER)

most successful innkeepers in eighteenth-century Williamsburg, gained his wealth and influence through two marriages. In 1738 he married the widow of a tavern proprietor and landowner. A week after her death in 1751, he married the widow of another prosperous innkeeper, thereby acquiring a controlling interest in a second business.

The Wetherburn Tavern has been in continuous use for more than 200 years. The eastern section, the earliest part of the structure, was built about 1740 and the western extension was added ten years later. The detailed inventory made at the time of Wetherburn's death in 1760 served as a guide in furnishing the restored tavern.

During "Publick Times," when the burgesses converged on Williamsburg, Wetherburn's Tavern was bustling with activity.

In the **Great Room**—with its fine Chippendale-style tables and chairs set around a marble fireplace—gentlemen would dine, drink, and discuss politics. On the center table sits a delft punch bowl decorated with scenes of the Seven Years' War. When William Randolph and Peter Jefferson (the father of Thomas) were involved in a land transaction in the 1740s, they sealed their agreement over glasses served from this bowl.

The **Middle Room,** or Club Room, was reserved for gambling. The gaming tables here (made in England) have three surfaces—the regular table top, one for backgammon, and another for cards. The corner cabinet displays valuable pieces of ceramic and crystal.

The small room on the first floor is known as **Mr. Page's Room** because Colonel John Page rented this chamber by the year to be sure of accommodations whenever he visited Williamsburg on business.

Fourteen beds were placed in the **Bedrooms** on the second floor. It was often necessary for two or three

George Wythe House, Colonial Williamsburg (ALPER)

persons to share a bed; sometimes beds were even used in shifts!

In 1751 the tavern was the setting for a banquet honoring newly appointed Governor Dinwiddie. George Washington, who served in the House of Burgesses from 1759 to 1774, frequently dined here.

GEORGE WYTHE HOUSE *West side of Palace Green*
In 1754 George Wythe (1726–1806) settled in Williamsburg and soon married Elizabeth Taliaferro, whose father, Colonel Richard Taliaferro, designed this dignified Georgian mansion for the young couple.

Wythe became one of the most influential men in the colony. A burgess during the years preceding the Revolution, he fought for the rights and independence of the colonies. He later served as mayor of Williamsburg and Chancery Court judge. It was appropriate that he should be the first delegate from Virginia to sign the Declaration of Independence and that he should be a member of the Federal Convention of 1787, which framed the United States Constitution. From 1779 to 1790 he was professor of law at the College of William and Mary, where he taught John Marshall (who became a Chief Justice of the United States Supreme Court) and Henry Clay (who became Secretary of State). The young Thomas Jefferson spent several winters in Williamsburg studying law with Wythe, whom he called "my faithful and beloved mentor."

Wythe's house was used by George Washington as his headquarters prior to the Battle of Yorktown, and the Comte de Rochambeau was a guest here after the British surrender.

In 1806, at the age of eighty, Wythe's life ended as a result of a bizarre incident. He was poisoned by his grand-nephew George Sweeney, who, finding himself hopelessly in debt, expected to inherit a substantial fortune as his uncle's principal beneficiary. But Wythe survived several days—long enough to change his will. Because the only witness to the crime was a slave whose testimony was deemed inadmissible by the court, Sweeney was never convicted.

Recommended Side Trip

Carter's Grove Plantation

Carter's Grove Plantation is located 6 miles southeast of Williamsburg on Route 60. It is open daily 9 A.M. to

5 P.M. March 1 through November 30. Adults $2.00, children 6 through 12, $1.00.

The magnificent Georgian mansion of this estate was built in the 1750s by Carter Burwell, a member of the House of Burgesses. He was the grandson of Robert "King" Carter, one of Virginia's wealthiest and most powerful men.

Both George Washington and Thomas Jefferson visited here frequently. According to legend, both men proposed to their sweethearts and were rebuffed in the room now known as the "Refusal Room." Another legend attached to the house tells that the ruthless British officer, Colonel Banastre Tarleton, charged his horse up the stairway hacking the balustrade with his saber.

In 1927–1928 the roof of the mansion was raised to provide additional space, dormers were introduced, and units connecting the main structure with its dependencies were built. The furnishings are primarily antiques of the eighteenth and nineteenth centuries.

Yorktown

By mid-summer 1781 American morale had reached a low point. Despite military advances, the colonists had begun to weary of the war, and the securing of financial aid and the recruiting of fighting men were becoming increasingly difficult. Although George Washington had only about 3,500 Continentals at his command, he knew that an offensive action would have to be taken if the will to win was to be maintained.

In early August Washington received a communication that the Comte de Grasse, commanding the French fleet, was preparing to sail from the West Indies toward Virginia. Washington determined that the time was appropriate for decisive action.

The British troops under Cornwallis were at that time garrisoned in Yorktown. Washington sent orders south to Lafayette to prevent Cornwallis from withdrawing into North Carolina. Then, on August 20, after having joined with the French forces under General de Rochambeau near New York City, Washington began to march the Allied troops toward Virginia, where they planned to rendezvous with the French fleet. As they moved southward, their ranks were swelled by local militiamen who were persuaded to join in this campaign.

When the British became cognizant of the Allied strategy, a combined fleet under Admirals Hood and Graves was dispatched from New York with orders to keep De Grasse from entering the Chesapeake Bay. On September 5, 1781, the two fleets met outside Hampton Roads,

Virginia. The superior strength of the French fleet won the engagement, and Admiral de Grasse was not only able to sail up the bay but he was also able to disembark 3,000 troops to join Lafayette. On September 14 the combined American and French armies had arrived at Williamsburg, twelve miles from Yorktown.

When, on September 28, the Allied armies approached Yorktown, their strength totaled 16,650 men. Of these 8,850 were Americans, commanded by Washington, and 7,800 were French, under Rochambeau. Their foe, Cornwallis, was in command of about 6,000 soldiers.

To defend Yorktown the British general ordered a series of redoubts, earthworks, and batteries constructed around the town. Redoubts 9 and 10, on the eastern end of the British line, and the Fusiliers' Redoubt, on the extreme northwest, were the most heavily manned. The Allied army took positions extending in a six-mile curve from the York River above the town to Wormley Creek in the south.

On the morning of September 30 the Allies were surprised to discover that Cornwallis had evacuated all his outer defense posts except Redoubts 9 and 10 and the Fusiliers' Redoubt. The action was mistakenly construed as a retreat, but Cornwallis had received a dispatch from General Henry Clinton stating that a large fleet and 5,000 men would soon be sailing to relieve the beleaguered army. (Clinton was unable to fulfill his promise immediately, though, and the fleet set sail the same day the British surrendered.)

The Americans and French, taking advantage of the British withdrawal, seized the abandoned outposts and began constructing additional redoubts, batteries, and trenches.

By the end of the first week in October a line of fortifications nearly 2,000 yards long had been erected parallel to the British main defense line. French soldiers took up

Storming Redoubt 10 at Yorktown. *Painting by Louis Eugene Lami.* (NATIONAL PARK SERVICE, WASHINGTON, D.C.)

positions on the left half of the siege line, and the Americans took positions on the right.

Throughout October 9 and 10 Allied guns fired on the town, badly damaging British artillery and setting three enemy ships anchored in the York River ablaze. The Allies then moved their positions forward toward the British camp and constructed a second siege line. Now that they were within reach of Redoubts 9 and 10, the American and French troops prepared to attack.

On the night of October 14 the French forces (under Colonel Guillaume de Deux Ponts) stormed Redoubt 9. In less than thirty minutes they crashed through the abatis, dashed upon the redoubt, and mounted the parapet. The simultaneous attack launched by the Americans against Redoubt 10 (under Lieutenant Colonel Alexander Hamilton) lasted only ten minutes. Their bayonet charge pushed across the ditch and into the fortification, creating havoc among the enemy.

On the morning of the 16th Cornwallis sent forth a detachment of 350 men in retaliation for the attack. Lieutenant Colonel Abercrombie led an assault on the batteries of the American second line, spiked four guns, and routed the soldiers. But the British initiative was soon repulsed.

Realizing the hopelessness of his situation, Cornwallis decided that the only way to avoid the annihilation of his army would be to cross the York River to Gloucester Point and retreat northward toward Clinton's army. The plan was for the boats to transport the soldiers to the opposite shore and then return to Yorktown; the action was to continue until the entire force had been evacuated. Under the cover of darkness the first British regiments embarked, but a sudden storm scattered the boats, driving many of them down the river and causing the maneuver to be discontinued.

The Allies again began to bombard the town on the morning of the 17th. A red-coated drummer boy soon appeared on the parapet and beat a "parley." The Americans, understanding the message, ceased fire. A British officer

Cornwallis Sues for Cessation of Hostilities Under a Flag of Truce. *Fresco by Constantino Brumidi.* (OFFICE OF THE ARCHITECT OF THE CAPITOL, WASHINGTON, D.C.)

under the protection of a white flag was brought blind-folded to Washington's camp, where he asked for a short armistice and the appointment of commissioners to discuss terms of surrender.

The next day the commissioners met at the Moore House and drew up the Articles of Capitulation.

At 2 P.M. on October 19, 1781, the British marched out from Yorktown. In a large field selected for the occasion the defeated army marched between two lines of Allied troops. Cornwallis, on the excuse of illness, sent Brigadier General Charles O'Hara to tender his sword in surrender. Washington refused to accept the sword from a subordinate officer and directed O'Hara to present it instead to his second-in-command, Major General Benjamin Lincoln.

A total of 7,247 soldiers and 840 seamen surrendered; 244 pieces of artillery and thousands of small arms were captured. Casualties from the siege were light: Americans, 20 killed and 56 wounded; French, 52 killed and 134 wounded; British, 156 killed and 326 wounded.

The surrender virtually ended the war in America, although minor skirmishes did continue. News of Cornwallis' defeat caused shock and consternation in London. A strong vote in Parliament to authorize the king to propose a peace conference left him with no recourse but to end the war. With the signing of the Treaty of Paris on September 3, 1783, Great Britain formally acknowledged the independence of the American colonies.

Yorktown Battlefield Site

From Williamsburg take the Colonial Parkway to Yorktown. (*Note:* There are no gas stations or stores along this highway.) From Norfolk travel north on Route 17. Open 8 A.M. to 6:30 P.M. during the summer, 8:30 A.M. to 5 P.M. the remainder of the year. Free.

The Yorktown Battlefield Site was established by an Act of Congress in 1936. The area is administered by the National Park Service of the Department of the Interior.

VISITORS' CENTER A slide show and film are shown here as part of an orientation program for visitors. Dioramas and exhibitions are also very informative. Phone 887–2241.

Most of the points of interest can be seen by driving your automobile along the narrow roads. The sites are identified by markers.

Driving Tour

Start at Visitors' Center:

Redoubt 9

Redoubt 10

Allied First Siege Line

Supply Depot Site

Moore House

Surrender Field

Allied Encampment

Washington's Headquarter's Site

French Battery

End at Route 238 or return to the Visitors' Center.

ALLIED ENCAMPMENT The road moving south from Surrender Field (past the intersection of Route 17) leads through the area of the American and French encampments. Markers indicate the headquarters of Rochambeau and Washington.

ALLIED FIRST SIEGE LINE   Allied engineers studied the layout of the British lines before planning their own defenses. The first siege line stretched from the York River southeast of Yorktown to Yorktown Creek. During the night of October 6 almost 1,500 men began constructing redoubts and digging a series of trenches. By the next evening the Allied troops and artillery pieces were in position.

FRENCH BATTERY   Sections of the gun platforms and magazines of the French Battery have been reconstructed. Eighteenth-century artillery pieces—including several cannon used during the siege of Yorktown—have been mounted here.

MOORE HOUSE   *Open 9 A.M. to 5 P.M. from mid-April to mid-October. Fee 50¢.*   On October 17, 1781, Cornwallis sent George Washington a note proposing a cease-fire and a meeting of commissioners to draw up the terms of his surrender. The following day the British officers Lieutenant Colonel Thomas Dundas and Major Alexander Ross met the Allied representatives. Lieutenant Colonel John Laurens and Second Colonel Viscount de Noailles at the house of Augustine and Lucy Moore.

Negotiations continued late into the evening because of arguments over Article III, which denied the defeated army the right to march out in salute to the victor with flags unfurled and with drums resounding. Laurens vehemently insisted that the rites of an honorable surrender should not be granted because General Clinton had denied the Americans similar privileges when he captured Charleston in 1780. The British were forced to retract their demand.

The Articles of Capitulation were first sent to Yorktown, where they were signed by General Charles Cornwallis and Captain Thomas Symonds, the senior British naval officer. The document was then delivered to the

Moore House, Yorktown Battlefield Site (ALPER)

Allies and signed by Washington, Rochambeau, and Admiral de Barras.

Visitors to the Moore House—the gambrel-roofed, wood frame structure built about 1725—may view the **Surrender Room.** Since none of the original furniture has survived, the Yorktown Restoration Committee has furnished the room with a round mahogany drop-leaf Queen Anne table and Queen Anne cambriole-legged side chairs.

REDOUBTS 9 AND 10 On the night of October 14, 1781, these two redoubts were seized by the Allies. Soon afterward, they began digging trenches to connect the redoubts with the second siege line. A battery was also erected. Several days later, after the Articles of Capitulation had been accepted and signed by the British commanders, the Allied leaders met in Redoubt 10 to affix their signatures to the document.

SUPPLY DEPOT SITE A sign and large painting now mark the location of the small American arsenal established here during the Battle of Yorktown.

SURRENDER FIELD On October 19, 1781, the surrender ceremonies were held in this large field. At noon the French and American troops formed two parallel lines facing each other and extending more than one mile. Two hours later the British army marched out of the garrison at Yorktown to the tune "The World Turned Upside Down."

General Cornwallis, claiming illness, was represented by Brigadier General Charles O'Hara. He first tried to surrender to Rochambeau, who turned away. When O'Hara next began to present Cornwallis' sword to General Washington, Washington, already insulted, refused to accept the token of surrender from a subordinate officer and directed him to present it instead to Major General Benjamin Lincoln. Once the ritual had been accomplished, the sword was returned to O'Hara. The Redcoats then marched between the columns of Allied troops—the Americans to the east and the French to the west—to an open field where they laid down their arms. Under militia guard, the British soldiers were taken away to prison camps in Virginia and Maryland.

WASHINGTON'S HEADQUARTERS SITE The site of George Washington's headquarters is now marked by a painting of the tent used by the Commander-in-Chief. (The original tent is on display in the Visitors' Center.) American officers refreshed themselves from the nearby spring.

Yorktown—"Town of York"

The community of Yorktown, which was established in 1691, is located near the battlefield. Fine examples of Colonial architecture may still be seen.

ARCHER COTTAGE *Water Street near the corner of Read Street. Not open to the public.* A modest structure was built here in the 1730s by local merchant Abraham Archer. One of his grandsons, who inherited the property, became a naval officer and later a county magistrate. After the devastating fire of 1818 (which leveled the entire section of the town along the waterfront), the present story-and-a-half cottage was rebuilt on the original stone foundations.

CUSTOM HOUSE *Corner of Main and Read Streets. Open during the summer 9 A.M. to 5 P.M.* In 1721 a small frame dwelling and a two-story brick storehouse were built on this lot. From here Richard Ambler conducted his business—registering the goods of ships which anchored in the York River, collecting marine taxes levied by the Crown, and issuing sailing papers to itinerant seamen.

During the Revolutionary War the buildings were seized by the Virginia militia for use as barracks.

Redoubt silhouetted against the evening sky, Yorktown Battlefield Site (NATIONAL PARK SERVICE, WASHINGTON, D.C.)

Surrender of Lord Cornwallis at Yorktown. *Painting by John Trumbull.* (OFFICE OF THE ARCHITECT OF THE CAPITOL, WASHINGTON, D.C.)

DIGGES HOUSE *Main and Read Streets. Not open to the public.* An early owner of this house was Dudley Digges, who served in the House of Burgesses for twenty-five years before the Revolution. Along with Patrick Henry and Thomas Jefferson, he was a member of the Virginia Committee of Correspondence. After the war, he was selected as a member of the Virginia Council.

During the Yorktown campaign of 1781 British soldiers were quartered here and several American cannonballs penetrated the outer walls.

GRACE CHURCH *Church Street near Water Street. Open daily 9 A.M. to 5 P.M.* This Episcopal church was built of native marl in 1697. During the siege of Yorktown the British ripped out the pews and converted the building into a powder magazine. Thomas Nelson, Jr., a native of Yorktown and a signer of the Declaration of Independence, was buried in the churchyard.

NELSON HOUSE *Nelson and Main Streets. Under restoration; usually open 9 A.M. to 5 P.M.* This impressive brick Georgian house was built in the 1740s by "Scotch Tom" Nelson and was later the home of his grandson Thomas Nelson, Jr. (1738–1789), a burgess from York County, a delegate to the Continental Congress, a signer of the Declaration of Independence, and a commander of Virginia militia units during the Revolutionary War. Nelson is remembered for the generous use of his own money to pay public debts, which left him impoverished.

It is believed that this dwelling served as Cornwallis' headquarters during the last days of the siege. Several cannonballs that penetrated the eastern wall give graphic evidence of the severity of the Allied bombardment of Yorktown. During Lafayette's 1824 tour he was given a reception here by local dignitaries.

SWAN TAVERN *Main Street between Ballard and Church Streets. Open during the summer 9 A.M. to 5 P.M. daily, open during the winter Sunday 1 P.M. to 5 P.M.* The Swan Tavern opened for business in March 1722 with Robert Wills serving as innkeeper. Colonial travelers and townspeople gathered here for drink, food, and entertainment. On hearing news of the Boston Massacre in 1770, a band of angry men left the tavern and began harassing British soldiers.

In December 1863 the building was destroyed by fire and was not reconstructed until the late 1930s. Today exhibition rooms occupy the first floor of the building, once one of Virginia's most famous "Publick Houses."

VICTORY MONUMENT *Main Street off Comte de Grasse Street* Visitors to Yorktown may wish to end their tour at the Victory Monument. In 1881 the United States Congress appropriated $100,000 for the erection of a monument commemorating the 100th anniversary of the Allied victory. The joint design of three artists— R. M. Hunt, J. A. Ward, and H. Van Brunt—was selected, and a cornerstone was laid on October 18, 1881, in the presence of President Chester A. Arthur and thousands of spectators.

Years later, after the ninety-five-foot shaft was completed, an allegorical figure, "Liberty Goddess," sculpted by Oskar J. W. Hansen, was placed on top of the monument. The statue lost its head when struck by lightning in 1942; a new figure was erected in 1956.

Recommended Side Trip

Jamestown

Jamestown was the first permanent English settlement in North America. On May 13, 1607 (twenty-three years after the first attempted settlement at Roanoke Island and thirteen years before the Pilgrims landed at Plymouth), three ships carrying 104 passengers arrived at this site on the James River. The settlers were unprepared for what awaited them in the wilderness: starvation, disease, and hostile Indians. During the severe winter of 1609–1610 (the "Starving Time") 90 percent of the settlers died. The survivors were preparing to return to England when Lord De la Warr arrived (in June 1610) with men and supplies. From that moment Jamestown began to grow and prosper.

Tobacco, which was first cultivated here in 1612 by John Rolfe, became an important export. After Rolfe married Pocahontas in 1614, relations with the Indians were greatly improved. In 1619 the first Africans were brought to the colony on a Dutch warship.

The British concept of representative government was transplanted to Jamestown. When the first legislature of the colony convened here in 1619, Jamestown became the seat of government of Virginia.

In 1676 many persons openly opposed the policies of the royal governor, and Nathaniel Bacon organized an armed revolt. The rebels attacked and burned Jamestown, which they considered the stronghold of oppression. Although the town was partially rebuilt, it began to decline after the government moved to Williamsburg in 1699.

On July 6, 1781, near Green Spring Plantation on the Williamsburg-Jamestown road, troops under the command of General Anthony Wayne made a valiant stand against Cornwallis' army. Lafayette sent a detachment to aid Wayne, but the Patriots were outnumbered and were forced to withdraw. Almost 140 Patriots (out of 900 engaged in the battle) were casualties.

In 1934 excavations were conducted in the Jamestown area and plans were undertaken for a restoration. The site is jointly administered by the Association for the Preservation of Virginia Antiquities and the Colonial National Historic Park Service.

VISITORS' CENTER Displays, dioramas, paintings, and an audio-visual program provide background information.

GUIDED TOURS During the summer free tours originate from the Visitors' Center. Check the schedule at the information desk.

HISTORIC JAMESTOWN COLONIAL PARK *From Williamsburg travel south on the Colonial Parkway or*

*take Route 31 South. From Yorktown travel north on the
Colonial Parkway. Open daily 9 A.M. to 5 P.M. Closed
December 25 and January 1. Adults $1.00, students (12–
17) 50¢, youngsters (7–11) 25¢, children (under 7) free.*

HOUSE OF BURGESSES MONUMENT   On July 30, 1619,
the first representative assembly in the New World met
in a little cedar frame church here to discuss matters of
importance to the colony. The monument lists the names
of those first burgesses.

HUNT MEMORIAL   Erected to the memory of Reverend
Robert Hunt, the first minister of Jamestown, the monument features a plaque depicting in relief one of the
settlement's early communion services.

MEMORIAL CROSS   During the terrible winter of 1609–
1610 more than 400 colonists died from hunger and
disease. This impressive stone cross marks the area
where they were laid to rest.

NEW TOWNE AREA   Still standing here are the foundations of several seventeenth-century dwellings. Near
the river once stood the first State House, which served
the colony from 1641 to 1656.

OLD CHURCH TOWER   This brick tower is all that remains of the church built here in 1639. After 1750 the
building fell into ruin. Behind the tower is Memorial
Church, erected in 1907 by the National Society of the
Colonial Dames of America.

POCAHONTAS STATUE   This statue by sculptor William Ordway Partridge represents Pocahontas (c. 1595–
1617), daughter of the Indian chief Powhatan. She is
remembered for saving the life of Captain John Smith,
who had been captured by the Indians and sentenced to
death. In 1613 Pocahontas was seized by a party of
settlers so that an exchange might be arranged for
English prisoners held by her father. While in Jamestown she was converted to Christianity and baptized
Rebecca. John Rolfe fell in love with the Indian princess,

Cannon and dwelling inside James Fort, Jamestown Festival Park (ALPER)

and after marriage took her (in 1616) to England, where she fell ill and died.

JOHN SMITH STATUE   Designed by William Couper, the statue overlooking the James River honors one of the significant figures of Jamestown's early history. Captain John Smith (*c.* 1579–1631). A member of the governing council of the settlement, he established trade with the Indians and his resourceful leadership helped see the colony through periods of intense suffering.

TERCENTENARY MONUMENT   Rising 103 feet above its base, this granite shaft was erected in 1907 to commemorate the 300th anniversary of the settlement of Jamestown.

JAMESTOWN FESTIVAL PARK *Adjacent to Historic Jamestown Colonial Park. Open daily 9 A.M. to 5 P.M.*

*Full-scale replica
of a Colonial ship,
Jamestown Festival
Park* (ALPER)

Closed December 25 and January 1. Adults $1.00, students (12–17) 50¢, youngsters (7–11) 25¢, children (under 7) free. This site was constructed in 1957 for the celebration of the 350th anniversary of the settling of Jamestown. The park is maintained by the Commonwealth of Virginia.

VISITORS' CENTER Tickets and guidebooks may be purchased here.

THE GALLERY OF STATES   In this curved arcade the flags of the fifty states are displayed.

JAMES FORT   James Fort is a full-scale reconstruction of the triangular palisade built by the settlers in 1607 for protection against the Indians and animals.

Within the walls are the guardhouse, storehouse, church, and more than a dozen small log cabins.

NEW WORLD PAVILION   Displays which illustrate the achievements of Virginians and trace the development of the commonwealth are housed in this structure.

OLD WORLD PAVILION   The British government has provided exhibitions here showing the culture that seventeenth-century Englishmen sought to transplant to the colonies.

POWHATAN'S LODGE   This small structure is a reconstruction of a typical ceremonial hut used by the Indians who lived in this region.

THREE COLONIAL SHIPS   Full-scale replicas of the three vessels that carried the first settlers to Jamestown are located at the dock facing James Fort—the *Susan Constant* (76 feet, 100 tons), the *Godspeed* (50 feet, 40 tons), and the *Discovery* (38 feet, 20 tons).

Richmond

In 1737 William Byrd II (1674–1744), a wealthy land-owner and member of the House of Burgesses, laid plans for a settlement on the James River. Incorporated as a town in 1742, Richmond had about 2,000 inhabitants by the time of the Revolutionary War. In March 1775, after Royal Governor Dunmore dissolved the House of Burgesses in Williamsburg because of their advocacy of a boycott on British goods, the legislators came to Richmond to meet at St. John's Church. The approximately 120 members included George Washington, Thomas Jefferson, Patrick Henry, Benjamin Harrison, George Wythe, and George Mason. The following July, after the battles of Lexington and Concord, a group of Patriots held meetings in Richmond, where they appointed a Committee of Safety and prepared a plan for bolstering the strength of the colony's militia units.

In 1780 the capital of Virginia was moved from Williamsburg to Richmond, which then became a bustling town and important port. British soldiers, under Major John G. Simcoe, soon began a series of devastating raids on the area which lasted nearly a year. In January 1781 the forces of the turncoat Benedict Arnold for three days burned and plundered Richmond. The Patriot militia was unable to repel these attacks and Washington, at the urging of Governor Thomas Jefferson, finally sent reinforcements. On April 29 Lafayette arrived leading regiments of the New England and New Jersey Light Infantry. They pushed back the British assault and remained in

Richmond for a month before marching northward to meet other units of the Continental Army.

On June 16 Cornwallis' troops, moving from the Carolinas toward Yorktown, passed through Richmond.

In June 1788, five years after the formal end of the Revolutionary War, the Virginia Convention held to ratify the Federal Constitution convened in this city. Despite the persuasive arguments of Patrick Henry to reject the document, the delegates voted to unite with the other states under a federated government.

VISITORS' CENTER Information and brochures may be obtained from the Richmond Tourist Center, 1700 Robin Hood Road, open daily 9 A.M. to 6 P.M., phone 358–5511. Also contact the Chamber of Commerce, 616 East Franklin Street, phone 649–0373.

PUBLIC TRANSPORTATION The Greater Richmond Transit Company provides local bus service. For information and schedules, phone 358–8421.

TAXI SERVICE Yellow Cab, phone 355–4321; Veterans Cab, phone 329–1414; Southside Cab, phone 232–4000.

WALKING AND DRIVING TOURS Most of Richmond's important sites can be seen in two downtown walking tours and a drive (traveling west) along Monument Avenue. (NR signifies an important *Non-Revolutionary site*; P indicates a historic Colonial house which is now a *private residence*.)

Walking Tour A	**Walking Tour B**
Area bounded by Leigh Street on the north, Main	Area bounded by Broad Street on the north, Main

Street on the south, 13th Street on the east, and 5th Street on the west.

Start at the Capitol:

Capitol

Capitol Square

St. Paul's Church (NR)

Lee House (NR)

John Marshall House

Valentine Museum (NR)

Museum of the Confederacy (NR)

End near 12th and Clay Streets.

Street on the south, 25th Street on the east, and 18th Street on the west.

Start at Broad near 24th Street:

St. John's Church

Craig House (P)

Philip Morris Co. (NR)

Poe Museum (NR)

End at Main Street near 19th Street.

Driving
Tour C

Start at Capitol Square, drive west on Grace Street until you come to Lombardy Street. Turn left and proceed to Monument Avenue, where you turn right. When you reach Westmoreland Avenue—several blocks past Boulevard—turn left and travel until you come to Cary Street Road. Stop at the appropriate sites along this route.

Hopkins-Call House (P)

Monument Avenue (NR)

Virginia Historical Society

Wilton

End on Wilton Road, off Cary Street Road.

Colonial and Revolutionary War Sites

THE CAPITOL *Capitol Square, between 9th and 12th Streets. Open Monday through Friday 8:15 A.M. to 5 P.M., Saturday 9 A.M. to 5 P.M., Sunday 1:30 P.M. to 5:30 P.M. Closed December 25. Free.* Built in the late 1780s, the central structure of the Capitol is an adaptation by Thomas Jefferson of the Maison Carrée in Nîmes, France. The Virginia Assembly convened in the old hall of the House of Delegates from 1788 until 1906. A major structural change of the building was made in 1906 when wings for the two houses of the legislature (the Senate and the House of Delegates) were added.

In the Rotunda stands the famous marble statue of George Washington by Jean Antoine Houdon (1741–1828). In 1784 the Virginia Assembly voted appropriations for a statue of General Washington. Thomas Jefferson, then in France, commissioned the renowned sculptor Houdon for the project. In October 1785 he arrived at Mount Vernon where he made a model of his distinguished subject, then fifty-three years old and four years away from the presidency.

In the niches around the Capitol Rotunda are marble busts of Lafayette and several Virginia-born Presidents.

A significant event in the history of the Capitol occurred in 1807 when Aaron Burr (1756–1836), Vice President under Thomas Jefferson from 1800 to 1804, was tried and acquitted of treason during a six-month trial here.

CAPITOL SQUARE At the northwest corner of Capitol Square stands Richmond's celebrated sculpture of Virginia's Revolutionary leaders. At the center of the sixty-foot-high monument is an equestrian statue of George Washington flanked by figures of Jefferson, Henry, Marshall, Lewis, and Nelson. The sculptor was Thomas Crawford. The cornerstone was laid February 22, 1850, in the presence of President Zachary Taylor and other distinguished guests.

JOHN MARSHALL HOUSE *818 East Marshall Street, at 9th Street. Open Monday through Saturday 10 A.M. to 4:30 P.M., Sunday 2 P.M. to 5 P.M. Closed January 1, Easter, Thanksgiving, and December 24–25. Adults $1.00, students 50¢.* This brick dwelling was built in 1790 by John Marshall (1755–1835), who served as Chief Justice of the United States Supreme Court from

Houdon statue of George Washington, Capitol Rotunda, Richmond
(METROPOLITAN RICHMOND CHAMBER OF COMMERCE)

1801 to 1835. The small wing and three porches were added about 1805. The house, which contains the original floors and paneling, is furnished with many original pieces and family portraits.

Born in a log cabin on the Virginia frontier, Marshall left home as a young man to fight in the American Revolution. After serving in the Patriot forces that defeated the British at Great Bridge, Virginia (in December 1775), he was commissioned a lieutenant in the Third Virginia Continentals. By the time he retired from military service in 1781, he had seen action at Germantown, Monmouth, and Stony Point. Marshall then served as a member of the Virginia Assembly (1782–1797), as a member of the United States House of Representatives (1799–1800), and as a Secretary of State (1800–1801) in the cabinet of President John Adams.

During his tenure as Chief Justice of the Supreme Court he made landmark decisions in the case of *Marbury vs. Madison* (1803), which established the power of the Court to overrule acts of Congress or state legislatures that it considered unconstitutional, and in the case of *Gibbons vs. Ogden* (1824), which confirmed Congressional control of interstate and foreign commerce. Marshall also presided over the 1807 trial of Aaron Burr in Richmond.

ST. JOHN'S EPISCOPAL CHURCH *East Broad and 24th Streets. Open Monday through Saturday 10 A.M. to 4 P.M., on Sunday after services.* On March 23, 1775, Patrick Henry's famous words rang out here: "I know not what course others may take, but as for me, give me Liberty or give me Death!" His speech urging the colony into a state of defiance fell on the sympathetic ears of the Virginia burgesses, who were convening here because Royal Governor Dunmore had dissolved the legislature, depriving Virginians of their rights to representative government.

St. John's was the only church in Richmond until

1814. Built in 1740–1741, the original rectangular structure (which measured twenty-five feet by forty feet) was enlarged in 1772 by an extension on the north side and by the addition of a belfry. A chancel and vestry room were added to the south end in 1880, giving the church the cross shape it now has.

Visitors to St. John's may see the pew Patrick Henry stood in while delivering his speech and the baptismal font used to baptize the Indian princess Pocahontas. (It was moved here from a church that had fallen into disrepair and is no longer in use.)

In the churchyard are buried two distinguished men of the Revolutionary period: George Wythe (1726–1806), a member of the Virginia House of Burgesses and a signer of the Declaration of Independence, and Dr. James McClury (1746–1823), a physician who served during the War of Independence as director general of Virginia's military hospitals.

VIRGINIA HISTORICAL SOCIETY   *428 North Boulevard. Open Monday through Friday 9 A.M. to 5 P.M., Saturday and Sunday 2 P.M. to 5 P.M. Adults $1.00, children 50¢.*   This windowless white marble building, known as "Battle Abbey," houses military memorabilia, manuscripts, uniforms, weapons, and portraits. Of special interest to Revolutionary War buffs is the broadsword that Washington presented to Peter Francisco, the "giant" who ferociously attacked the British at Guilford Courthouse (March 15, 1781). Charles Willson Peale's portrait of Lafayette and Thomas Sully's painting of Pocahontas are also displayed here.

WILTON   *South end of Wilton Road off Cary Street Road. Open Tuesday through Saturday 10 A.M. to 4 P.M., Sunday 2:30 P.M. to 4:30 P.M. Closed national holidays and Sunday from July 1 through Labor Day. Fee $1.00.*   Wilton was built in the 1750s by William Randolf III, a member of the Virginia House of Burgesses. The design of this imposing Georgian mansion is attributed to

Richard Taliaferro, leading Williamsburg architect. The structure was originally located on a bluff overlooking the James River about ten miles east of Richmond. Here Randolf and his wife Anne (sister of Benjamin Harrison of Berkeley, a signer of the Declaration of Independence), lived with their seven children.

Thomas Jefferson (whose mother was a Randolf) and George Washington were frequent visitors to Wilton. On May 15, 1781, General Lafayette made his headquarters here but hastily departed five days later when Cornwallis crossed the James River in pursuit of him.

After Randolf's death, the estate passed through the hands of many owners. In 1933 the Colonial Dames of America, rescuing the mansion from destruction, moved it to its present site in Richmond.

Important Colonial Houses

AMPTHILL   *211 Ampthill Road. Not open to the public.* Built by Henry Cary, the architect of many of Williamsburg's public buildings, this elegant mansion was begun in 1732. The central court and dependencies were added in 1750. The house was moved to Richmond from its site in Cumberland County in 1929.

CRAIG HOUSE   *1812 East Grace Street. Not open to the public.*   Built between 1784 and 1787, this large two-story structure was the home of Adam Craig, clerk of the Richmond Hustings Court, the Henrico County Court, and the General Court.

HOPKINS-CALL HOUSE   *217 West Grace Street. Not open to the public.*   This dwelling, which was probably built in the mid-eighteenth century, was owned by John Hopkins (commissioner of loans), who rented it to Jean-Auguste-Marie Chevallié, an agent of Pierre Augustin Caron de Beaumarchais, the famous French playwright who furnished arms to the Patriots in 1776–1777 and who was instrumental in gaining French aid for the American colonies. The house was sold in 1798 to Daniel Call, a distinguished lawyer and brother-in-law of John Marshall.

Non-Revolutionary Sites of Interest

HOLLYWOOD CEMETERY *Cherry and Albemarle Streets. Open Monday through Saturday 7:30 A.M. to 5 P.M., Sunday 8 A.M. to 5 P.M.* Many distinguished leaders, including Presidents James Monroe (1758–1831) and John Tyler (1790–1862) and Confederate President Jefferson Davis (1808–1889), are interred here.

LEE HOUSE *707 East Franklin Street. Open Monday through Friday 10 A.M. to 4 P.M. September through May, Tuesday through Saturday 10 A.M. to 4 P.M. and Sunday 2 P.M. to 4 P.M. during the summer. Closed holidays. Adults 50¢, children 25¢.* Built in 1844, this Greek Revival three-story house was used by Confederate General Robert E. Lee in 1864–1865, during his Virginia campaign.

MONUMENT AVENUE *A boulevard running east-west from the terminus of Franklin Street at Lombardy Street to Horsepen Road* Five imposing monuments line this avenue:

J. E. B. STUART MONUMENT *Monument Avenue and Lombardy Street* The equestrian statue of the Confederate cavalry general was designed by Fred Moynihan and dedicated in May 1907.

ROBERT E. LEE MONUMENT *Monument Avenue and Allen Avenue* This statue of Robert E. Lee mounted on his beloved horse "Traveller" was the first to be raised on Monument Avenue. The work was executed by French sculptor Jean Antoine Mercie, and the unveiling took place on May 29, 1890.

JEFFERSON DAVIS MONUMENT *Monument Avenue and Davis Avenue* Honoring the President of the Confederacy, this monument consists of a statue of Davis at the foot of a soaring column topped by a female figure. A semicircular colonnade surrounds the shaft. The monument was designed by Edward Valentine and was unveiled in June 1907.

THOMAS J. "STONEWALL" JACKSON MONUMENT *Monument Avenue and Boulevard* This equestrian statue, which honors Confederate General "Stonewall" Jackson, was sculpted by F. William Sievers and dedicated in October 1919.

MATTHEW F. MAURY MONUMENT *Monument Avenue and Belmont Avenue* Designed by F. William Sievers and dedicated in November 1929, this monument honors Matthew F. Maury, Commodore of the Confederate Navy and an important oceanographer.

MUSEUM OF THE CONFEDERACY *Clay and 12th Streets. Open Monday through Saturday 9 A.M. to 5 P.M., Sunday 2 P.M. to 5 P.M. Closed holidays. Adults $1.00, children 50¢.* Designed by Robert Mills and constructed in 1818, this building is known as the White House of the Confederacy because it was the residence of President Jefferson Davis (1808–1889) for three and a half years during the Civil War, when Richmond was the capital of the Confederate States. It is now a museum displaying documents, weapons, uniforms, and memorabilia of the period.

POE MUSEUM   *1914 East Main Street. Open Tuesday through Saturday 10 A.M. to 4:30 P.M., Sunday and Monday 1:30 P.M. to 4:30 P.M. Closed December 25. Adults $1.00, college students 75¢, children 25¢.*   The Poe Museum—which displays memorabilia, including many of the writer's possessions—occupies Richmond's oldest house, a rough stone structure built in the late 1680s. Although Edgar Allan Poe (1809–1849) lived and worked in the area for twenty-six years, he probably did not reside in this building. The adjacent carriage house exhibits drawings based on his well-known poem "The Raven."

RICHMOND NATIONAL BATTLEFIELD SITE   *3215 East Broad Street (on Route 60), in Chimborazo Park. Visitors' Center is open daily 9 A.M. to 5 P.M. Closed December 25. Free.*   Two of the seven attempts to capture Richmond during the Civil War took place in this area. Visitors who follow the foot trail will see breastworks, fortifications, and other landmarks that remain from McClellan's attack (1862) and Grant's campaign (1864–1865).

ST. PAUL'S CHURCH   *Grace and 9th Streets. Open Monday through Saturday 10 A.M. to 4 P.M., Sunday 1 P.M. to 4 P.M.*   Confederate President Jefferson Davis and General Robert E. Lee frequently worshipped at this church (built in 1845). It was during services on Sunday morning, April 2, 1865, that President Davis received the tersely worded message from General Lee that the government must evacuate Richmond and that supplies must be destroyed so they would not fall into the hands of the approaching Union Army.

TOBACCO COMPANIES   Visitors to Richmond who wish to tour these industrial plants are advised to phone the companies to verify schedules and to ascertain whether reservations are necessary.

American Tobacco Company   *26th and Cary Streets* Tours offered Monday through Thursday 8 A.M. to 4

P.M. Closed first week in July and Christmas. Phone 643–5341.

Philip Morris Company *20th and Main Streets* Tours offered Monday at 1 P.M., Tuesday through Friday from 9 A.M. to 11 A.M. and from 1 P.M. to 2 P.M. Phone 275–8361.

VALENTINE MUSEUM COMPLEX *1015 East Clay Street. Open Tuesday through Saturday 10 A.M. to 4:45 P.M., Sunday 1:30 P.M. to 5 P.M. Adults $1.00, students 50¢, family rate $2.50*

Wickham-Valentine House, which is the main structure of this three-building complex, is a restored federal mansion. It was built in 1812 by John Wickham (1763–1839), one of the lawyers who successfully defended Aaron Burr in 1807 against charges of treason. On the death of the last occupant, Mann Valentine, in 1891 the house was converted into a museum.

Granville-Valentine Building adjoins the Wickham-Valentine House and contains permanent and rotating exhibitions of the history of Richmond.

Bransford Cecil House, built in 1840, was moved from 5th Street to this site in 1954.

Recommended Side Trips

Hanover

From Richmond take Route 301 north for about 18 miles.

HANOVER COURTHOUSE *On the main street* In this T-shaped brick courthouse (built in the 1730s) the twenty-seven-year-old Patrick Henry won fame in December 1763 in a case referred to as "The Parson's Cause." Henry argued that his client, Parson James Maury, and other clergymen had been harmed by the Two Penny Acts, which forced ministers to accept paper money of the colony (in the value of about £133) in lieu of their usual annual salary of 16,000 pounds of tobacco (£400 market value). While tobacco was a convenient medium of exchange, especially in England, the paper money forced upon the clergymen was a depreciated currency and almost worthless outside the colonies. After hearing Henry's arguments, the jury decided that Reverend Maury was entitled to damages.

HANOVER TAVERN   *Across the road from the courthouse. Open daily 10 A.M. to 5 P.M. Free.*   This structure (built about 1723) was acquired in 1760 by Patrick Henry's father-in-law John Shelton. Henry and his wife Sarah lived in the family quarters of the tavern for several years in the 1760s, and it is known that he frequently tended bar here. Cornwallis occupied rooms at the tavern briefly during the Virginia campaign of 1781. Today the building is used by the Barksdale Theater.

SITE OF PATRICK HENRY BIRTHPLACE   *About one and a half miles south on Route 301, in Studley*   A stone marker records the location of Henry's birthplace.

Plantation Houses

BERKELEY   *26 miles east of Richmond on Route 5. Open daily 8 A.M. to 5 P.M. Adults $1.50, children 75¢.*   Berkeley was the home of two Presidents: William Henry Harrison (1773–1841), ninth President of the United States, and his grandson, Benjamin Harrison (1833–1901), twenty-third President. Berkeley has the distinction of having been visited by every President from Washington to Buchanan (from 1789 to 1861). During the Civil War the mansion was seized by General McClellan for his headquarters.

SHIRLEY *25 miles east of Richmond on Route 5. Open daily 9 A.M. to 5 P.M. Adults $1.50, children 60¢.* This Georgian mansion—a three-story brick building with colonnaded porticoes—was begun about 1723 by Edward Hill III, whose daughter Elizabeth married John Carter, son of the wealthy and powerful Virginian Robert "King" Carter. Another member of the family who resided here was Anne Hill Carter, who married Henry ("Light-Horse Harry") Lee, the Revolutionary War cavalry officer. The Carters entertained George Washington, Thomas Jefferson, and many other distinguished leaders at Shirley.

Charlottesville

Revolutionary War History

When Cornwallis invaded Virginia in 1781, members of the Virginia government considered it unsafe to remain in Richmond. On May 10, 1781, the legislature adjourned with plans to meet again in Charlottesville on the 24th. Governor Thomas Jefferson returned to his home in Monticello near Charlottesville, and forty members of the legislature took quarters in the town. (Among them were four signers of the Declaration of Independence—Richard Henry Lee, Thomas Nelson, Jr., Benjamin Harrison, and Thomas Jefferson.)

Hoping to capture these prominent leaders, Cornwallis dispatched to the area Lieutenant Colonel Banastre Tarleton with a troop of 180 cavalry and 70 infantrymen. On the morning of June 3 they left the British encampment on the North Anna River (about twenty miles north of Richmond) and advanced swiftly toward Charlottesville. At 11 P.M. they reached Louisa Courthouse, fifty-five miles from their destination. Tarleton's forces rested there for three hours, then pushed on again through the night. As they passed the Cuckoo Tavern twelve miles down the road, Jack Jouett—a captain in the Virginia Militia and a resident of Charlottesville—observed the enemy's movements. He was spending the night at the tavern, according to some sources, after courting a local maiden. Aware of the imminent peril to the legislators in Charlottesville, he quickly saddled his mare and rode furiously toward the town. Hoping to reach his destination in time to sound the alarm, he followed an old Indian path known only to local residents.

At dawn he reached Milton (a short distance from Monticello) and roused the local inhabitants shouting: "The British are coming!" Gasping for air, he arrived ten minutes later at Monticello, awakening Jefferson and his household. After informing the governor of Tarleton's approach, Jouett rode into Charlottesville spreading the news.

When Tarleton reached the town, he could see that his mission had failed. Seven legislators who tarried in their flight were the only prisoners he could take. Enraged, he ordered his men to destroy property and seize military supplies. To the dismay of the citizens, the Redcoats carried the county records to the courthouse Green to destroy them in a fierce conflagration. On June 5, after receiving information that the local militia was organizing, Tarleton, with his prisoners, withdrew toward Tidewater.

Jouett's gallant action received official recognition from the Virginia Assembly in December 1786 when the grateful legislators introduced a resolution commending his courage and presented him with a handsome sword and a pair of pistols.

Monticello

From Interstate 64, traveling west, get off at the second Charlottesville Exit. Follow the signs to Monticello. From downtown Charlottesville take Route 250 East (traveling along West Main Street), 20 South (Monticello Avenue) to Route 53 East. Follow the signs to Monticello. After you have parked your automobile, walk to the Entrance Pavilion, where you can take a tram to the mansion. The ride is free and takes about four minutes.

Open daily 8 A.M. to 5 P.M. March through October, 9 A.M. to 4:30 P.M. November through February. Adults $2.00, children 50¢.

Monticello was the home of Thomas Jefferson (1743–1826), author of the Declaration of Independence (1776), governor of Virginia (1779–1781), Minister to France (1785–1789), Secretary of State (1790–1793), and third President of the United States (1800–1808).

Because Jefferson's estate is located on the crest of one of the highest hills in the area, he named it "Monticello," which means "little mountain" in Italian. He planned and supervised every stage of the building of his mansion. Construction began about 1769, but because of numerous alterations in the design, the house was not completed until 1809. Crowned by an octagonal dome, the structure is symmetrical in appearance and has two long L–shaped

Thomas Jefferson. *Painting by Thomas Sully.* (OFFICE OF THE ARCHITECT OF THE CAPITOL, WASHINGTON, D.C.)

balustraded terraces with pavilions at each end. These terraces served a special purpose—to roof and conceal small outbuildings such as a kitchen, dairy, smokehouse, and laundry. The small pavilion at the tip of the south terrace is known as the "Honeymoon Cottage" because in January 1772, with the main house still incomplete, Jefferson brought his bride, Martha Wayles Skelton, to live here.

When Jack Jouett brought news on the morning of June 4, 1781, of the approach of Tarleton's troops, Jefferson sent his wife and children fourteen miles away to Enniscorthy, the home of his friend Colonel Coles. While two trusted slaves concealed valuables under the floor of the portico at Monticello, Jefferson climbed a nearby hill with a telescope to view the terrain. Seeing the approach of the Redcoats, he swiftly departed to join his family. The property and the grounds received little damage at the hands of the British. Tarleton was so anxious to push on toward Charlottesville that he orderd his men to restrict their activity to raiding the wine cellar.

Although Jefferson's political career forced him to spend many years away from Monticello, he did retire here in 1809 after serving two terms as President.

In 1819 he encountered serious financial difficulties when a friend failed to cover a note Jefferson had endorsed. He was about to sell his lands when a sympathetic public rallied to his aid with voluntary contributions. One year after Jefferson's death, however, his heirs were forced to hold a public sale of furnishings. Two years later the estate was purchased for $7,000 by James T. Barclay, a Charlottesville apothecary. Monticello then passed through many hands until the Thomas Jefferson Memorial Foundation purchased it in 1923 for $500,000.

The house holds many attractions for visitors. For some persons, the chief interest lies in the beautiful interior decoration and furnishings; for others, the focus of attention is Jefferson's inventions.

He designed the time-keeping system in the **Entrance**

Monticello, near Charlottesville (ALPER)

Hall. The cannonballs on the right wall mark the day of the week and the time of day as they descend, controlled by eight weights (located on the left wall), which also regulate the gong on the roof. The busts near the entrance are of Voltaire, Turgot, and Hamilton.

The **Parlor** doors, operating by metal drums connected by a chain, open simultaneously when either is moved. The floor of this elegant room—squares of cherry with beechwood border—is thought to be the first parquet in America. The Louis XVI furniture is similar to the pieces Jefferson brought to Monticello from Paris in the late 1780s, and the harpsichord was made about 1800 in London for his daughter Martha.

On each side of the **Dining Room** mantel (which is decorated with unusual Wedgwood medallions) are dumbwaiters used to bring wine bottles from the cellar. The fine ormolu and marble clock on the mantel was purchased in France. The Chippendale dining table is believed to have been a wedding gift from George Wythe, Jefferson's friend and former law teacher. Prominent figures such as James

Monroe and James Madison were entertained here. During his visit to Monticello in November 1824, Lafayette dined here after being reunited with his friend in an emotional ceremony on the south lawn.

All the furniture in the **Master Bedroom** is original to the house. The unit comprising the chair, the table, and the long bench—forming a kind of chaise longue—was arranged by Jefferson in his later years so that he could write in a comfortable position. The profile of Jefferson was executed by artist Amos Doolittle, and the plaster bust of John Adams is a copy of the work by J. B. Binon. Jefferson died in this bed at the age of eighty-three on July 4, 1826— fifty years after signing the Declaration of Independence. He is buried in the family cemetery on the grounds of his beloved Monticello.

Other Sites near Monticello

ASH LAWN *Follow Route 53 East 2 miles past Monticello. Open daily 7 A.M. to 7 P.M. Adults $1.00, children 50¢.* Ash Lawn was the home of James Monroe (1758–1831). As a young man he fought in the American Revolution and was a delegate to the Continental Congress. Later, he served as United States Senator (1790–1794), Minister to France (1794–1796), governor of Virginia (1799–1802), and participated in the negotiations with France that led to the Louisiana Purchase (1802–1803). Monroe became Secretary of State (1811–1817) under James Madison and served two terms as the fifth President of the United States (1817–1825).

This house, built in 1799, was designed by Thomas

Jefferson, Monroe's friend and neighbor. The Monroes maintained this residence for twenty-one years before moving into their large home, "Oak Hill," near Leesburg, Virginia. In the 1860s several structural modifications were made by the new owners of Ash Lawn.

Many of the furnishings here once belonged to President Monroe: the Hepplewhite table and the Duncan Phyfe chairs in the dining room; the hand-carved mahogany bed and the medicine chest in the master bedroom; and the sofa and chairs (a gift of Napoleon I) in the drawing room.

In the boxwood gardens stands a marble statue of Monroe, unveiled here on the 100th anniversary of his death. The sculptor was Attilio Piccirilli.

MICHIE TAVERN *Located ½ mile before Monticello on Route 53 East. Open daily 9 A.M. to 5 P.M. Closed December 25 and January 1. Adults $1.00, children 75¢.* The oldest section of this elongated building (which dates from 1735) was originally located on the Back Mountain Road in North Albemarle and served as Patrick Henry's boyhood home. In 1746 the house was sold to John Michie, who enlarged it and established a tavern. Michie, a Scotsman, had come to Virginia after taking part in an abortive uprising against the Crown. He had been captured and sentenced to take part in a lottery to decide his fate—execution or exile. The condemned prisoners drew from a bag containing black and white beans. Those who drew black were shot; Michie drew white and was forced to bid farewell forever to his native land.

Many of the furnishings here are original. Among the rare items are a dulcimer, a "banister" chair, a clock with painted eagle and stars, a Chippendale blanket chest, and several hurricane sconces.

The taproom is the only original Colonial bar in existence in Virginia. According to tradition, the "round dance," or waltz, was introduced to America in the up-

*Ash Lawn, near
Charlottesville*
(ALPER)

stairs ballroom. (Some local historians speculate that it
was introduced by Jefferson's daughter, who had learned
the dance in France.)

In 1927 Michie Tavern was moved to its present site
and refurbished.

Downtown Charlottesville

GEORGE ROGERS CLARK MEMORIAL *West Main
Street near 12th Street* Born near Charlottesville,

George Rogers Clark (1752–1818, brother of explorer William Clark) fought the British and Indian forces in the Northwest Territory. In 1778 he persuaded Governor Patrick Henry to send an expedition against the British-held settlements of Kaskaskia, Cahokia, and Vincennes. Because of his success as a military strategist, he was sometimes called the "George Washington of the West."

The monument was created by sculptor Robert Ingersol Aitken and was unveiled January 6, 1922.

LEWIS AND CLARK MEMORIAL *Ridge and West Main Streets*   This memorial honors the Lewis and Clark expedition (1803–1806), approved by President Jefferson and the United States Congress. The purpose was to search out a route to the Pacific and to survey the lands newly acquired by the Louisiana Purchase.

The sculptor, Charles Keck, depicts Meriwether Lewis (1774–1809) and William Clark (1770–1838)—both born near Charlottesville—and the young Indian maiden who served as their guide, Sacajawea. The three-figure group was dedicated on November 21, 1919.

UNIVERSITY OF VIRGINIA *West Main Street. Free tours of the campus are offered during the academic year and originate at the Rotunda at 11 A.M., 2 P.M., and 4 P.M.*   Founded by Thomas Jefferson in 1819, the university opened for instruction in 1825. Jefferson also designed the eight original buildings on campus, including the imposing Rotunda at the north end of the quadrangle. Edgar Allan Poe and Woodrow Wilson were among the many distinguished persons who, as students, resided in the West Range. In 1974 almost 10,000 students were enrolled here.

Fredericksburg

Revolutionary War History

In 1727 the Virginia Assembly directed that fifty acres of "lease-land" be developed here as the town of Fredericksburg (named for Frederick Louis, Prince of Wales and grandson of George II). Throughout the eighteenth century Fredericksburg was an important port and center of political activity.

The town is well known for its association with George Washington and his family. He spent his boyhood at Ferry Farm across the Rappahannock River and attended school in Fredericksburg. For many years his mother and sister continued to reside here.

Six generals who fought in the Revolutionary War came from Fredericksburg and vicinity: George Washington, Hugh Mercer, George Weedon, William Woodford, Gustavus Wallace, and Thomas Posey. John Paul Jones, the Revolutionary War naval hero, also lived for a time in Fredericksburg.

During the Revolution arms for the Patriot cause were manufactured at the gunnery located here. Many important leaders of the period visited the town, including Thomas Jefferson, Patrick Henry, George Mason, George Wythe, and Edmund Pendleton. In 1780 Nathanael Greene passed through Fredericksburg on his way to assume command of the Southern forces. After the British surrender at Yorktown in October 1781, citizens of surrounding farms and villages converged on the town for a great celebration honoring the visiting heroes of the battle. A gala Peace Ball

VISITORS' CENTER   706 Caroline Street, phone 373–9391. Visitors to Fredericksburg may wish to stop here to obtain tour information and maps. A combination ticket may be purchased for admittance to the Mary Washington House, Rising Sun Tavern, Monroe Museum, Mercer Apothecary Shop, and Kenmore—adults $3.00, children and students $1.50.

PUBLIC TRANSPORTATION   At the present time, no bus service is provided in Fredericksburg. Plans are under way for the establishment of a public transportation system, possibly to be operated by the Colonial Transit Company, phone 373–1200.

TAXI SERVICE   Associated Cab, phone 373–3103; Blue Streak Cab, phone 371–5829; Richardson Taxi, phone 373–7575; Virginia Cab, phone 373–8555.

After stopping at the Visitors' Center, if you wish to start your tour at Kenmore, travel down Princess Anne Street until you come to Lewis Street, turn right and proceed to Washington Avenue. (Some sightseers may wish to start at the Mary Washington House.)

Driving Tour

Start on Washington Avenue between
Lewis and Fauquier Streets:

Kenmore

Mary Washington Monument

Mary Washington House

Rising Sun Tavern

Mercer Apothecary Shop

Monroe Museum

Masonic Lodge

End on Princess Anne Street near
Hanover Street.

held at the Rising Sun Tavern was the high point of the festivities.

Lafayette was a guest at the homes of several of Fredericksburg's leading citizens while he was touring the United States in 1824. During the official welcoming ceremonies the town's children—dressed in red, white, and blue—sang the *Marseillaise*. In the evening Lafayette attended a ball given in his honor.

Fredericksburg justly takes pride in the role it played in our nation's early history.

Colonial and Revolutionary War Sites

KENMORE *1201 Washington Avenue. Open daily 9 A.M. to 5 P.M. March 1 through November 15, 9 A.M. to 4:30 P.M. the remainder of the year. Closed December 25–26 and January 1–2. Adults $1.25, students 60¢, or admittance with combination ticket.* Construction of this brick Georgian mansion began in 1752, when Fielding Lewis married his nineteen-year-old sweetheart, Betty (the sister of George Washington). The estate, originally called Millbank, extended for 861 acres.

Fielding Lewis was elected to the Virginia House of Burgesses in 1760 and served on several of its important committees during the following years. But he is perhaps best remembered as a great Revolutionary War Patriot. He supervised the Fredericksburg Gunnery which manufactured armaments for the Continental Army, and when public funds were exhausted, he used his own money to keep it in operation. As chairman of the Virginia Committee of Safety, Lewis' responsibilities were varied: he was in charge of the purchase and the fitting of military vessels; he helped secure provisions for the troops; and he traveled extensively throughout the colony to inspire young men to bear arms for the Patriot cause.

During the Revolutionary period many famous leaders visited the Lewis home—Thomas Jefferson, Patrick Henry, George Mason, the Marquis de Lafayette, the Comte de Rochambeau, and John Paul Jones.

Washington's diaries record almost forty visits here. He frequently stopped on his way to Williamsburg, the Colonial capital, where he was a member of the House of Burgesses. During the week of celebration after the Battle of Yorktown, almost all the prominent officers were received by the Lewis family. Washington and Lafayette were overnight guests on that occasion.

Fielding Lewis died in 1782 leaving a debt amounting to $7,000 and a mortgage on Millbank, thus causing his wife to dismiss many servants and to sell parcels of the estate. After Mrs. Lewis' death in 1797, the property was sold, passing through many hands until the first decade of the nineteenth century when it came into possession of the Gordon family, who changed the name to Kenmore.

The house, designed by architect John Ariss, is noted for its exquisite interior. The outstanding feature of the **Dining Room** is the elaborate relief decoration on the ceiling—a rayed circle, perhaps a sun-god image, is surrounded by circular motifs and rosettes. The Queen Anne Virginia dining table stands in front of the fireplace, with its carved mantel bearing the Washington crest, the "Swan and Crown." On the Chippendale-design mahogany hunt board stands a silver triple urn that belonged to the Lewises. China and glassware once owned by the Lewis and Washington families are also on display.

The elegant **Great Room** is distinguished by its relief overmantel which depicts a scene from Aesop's fable, "The Fox and the Crow." This overmantel is thought to have been designed by George Washington (from European style books) and executed by two Hessian prisoners. A fine fire screen, once the possession of Lord Botetourt, a royal governor of Virginia, adorns the hearth. Nearby, John Wollaston's portraits of Betty and Fielding Lewis show the dignity and character of his subjects. The great room's extraordinary carved ceiling combines circular motifs with stylized leaf designs. Although the Chippendale sofa and chairs are not original to the house, they are similar to those used here.

The **Library** has walls painted pompeian red. Inspired by the frescoes in the ruins of Pompeii (which had been discovered in 1748), this color became popular in the last half of the eighteenth century. The highboy—a Philadelphia piece, *c.* 1750—is unusually attractive; it has a broken-arch pediment and finials.

Betty Lewis' bed (a four-poster Chippendale with blue-and-white hangings), her desk, and her trunk may be seen in the **Master Bedroom.**

MASONIC LODGE *803 Princess Anne Street. Open Monday through Friday 9 A.M. to 6 P.M. Donations accepted.* George Washington was initiated into Fredericksburg Lodge Number 4 on November 4, 1752, and was raised to a Master Mason on August 4, 1753. His initiation took place in Market Hall, which stood at the corner of Market Alley and Caroline Street. The building was torn down in 1812, and a new Masonic Hall was erected the next year here on Princess Anne Street.

Fielding Lewis, Washington's brother-in-law (the owner of Kenmore), was also a member of this Lodge. Lafayette was made an honorary member in 1824.

On display here are the Bible on which Washington was sworn, a lock of his hair, and a portrait of him by Gilbert Stuart.

MERCER APOTHECARY SHOP *Caroline and Amelia Streets. Open daily 9 A.M. to 5 P.M. March 1 through November 15, 9 A.M. to 4:30 P.M. the remainder of the year. Closed December 25–26 and January 1–2. Adults*

75¢, students 35¢, or admittance with combination ticket.
In this small building Dr. Hugh Mercer (1725–1777)
practiced medicine and operated an apothecary shop.

Born in Aberdeen, Scotland, he was graduated in
medicine from the University of Aberdeen in 1744. Two
years later, he left his homeland to settle in Pennsylvania. While serving as a captain (1754–1756) under
General Edward Braddock during the French and Indian Wars, he met young Colonel George Washington—
the beginning of a close and lasting friendship. After the
war, at Washington's suggestion, he settled in Fredericksburg, opened this shop, and married Isabel Gordon,
sister-in-law of George Weedon (innkeeper of the Rising
Sun Tavern). Washington, a frequent visitor here, sometimes used the library and office.

The Great Room, Kenmore, Fredericksburg (FREDERICKSBURG
VISITORS' CENTER)

Interior of the Mercer Apothecary Shop, Fredericksburg
(FREDERICKSBURG VISITORS' CENTER)

When the Revolutionary War began, Mercer closed his office and enlisted for military service. Because of his military experience, he was commissioned a brigadier general in the Continental Army in June 1776. Seven months later he was killed in the Battle of Princeton.

This shop—where medicines were mixed and sold—displays pillboxes, bottles, pap boats, carboys, and accessories such as mortars, pestles, lancets, and bleeding pans. When the shop was restored about 1930, a false partition was discovered behind which were stored many eighteenth-century bottles. (It is believed that Mercer had concealed his equipment before going off to war.) In the adjoining room Dr. Mercer examined patients and performed surgery.

MONROE MUSEUM *908 Charles Street. Open daily* 9 A.M. *to* 5 P.M. *Closed December 25, Adults 75¢, stu-*

dents 35¢, or admittance with combination ticket.
Dating from 1758, this brick building has changed little
since James Monroe (1758–1831) practiced law here
from 1786 to 1789. He shared a practice with Robert
Brooke and Bushrod Washington. (Brooke became a
governor of the state and Washington was later appointed an Associate Justice of the United States
Supreme Court.) Monroe served as the first district
attorney of this section of Virginia, and his political
career culminated when he was inaugurated the fifth
President of the United States in 1817.

This museum now contains personal belongings of
the Monroe family: the desk on which President Monroe
prepared the message to Congress (December 1823)
setting forth principles of the so-called Monroe Doc-
trine; a six-and-one-half-pound umbrella with whalebone
ribs presented to him in 1824 by the city of Boston; a
bust of Lafayette, which the Frenchman presented to
Monroe during his visit to the United States in 1824;
and several pieces of furniture used in the new White
House. (The White House was burned by the British
during the War of 1812; it was reconstructed several
years later in time for Monroe's occupancy in 1817.)

The gown Mrs. Monroe wore at the court of Napoleon
is on display, along with a topaz necklace and matching
earrings.

Of special interest are Rembrandt Peale's portrait of
Monroe (painted in the White House) and Benjamin
West's portrait of Mrs. Monroe.

RISING SUN TAVERN   *1306 Caroline Street. Open daily
9 A.M. to 5 P.M. March 1 through November 15, 9 A.M.
to 4:30 P.M. the remainder of the year. Closed December 25–26 and January 1–2. Adults 75¢, students 35¢,
or admittance with combination ticket.*   Located on the
route between Alexandria and Williamsburg, this popular tavern was built about 1760 by George Washington's
youngest brother, Charles.

As hostilities with England intensified in the 1770s, the innkeeper of the Rising Sun, George Weedon, was accused by Loyalists of "blowing the seeds of sedition." He not only wrote numerous fiery letters entreating his friends to defy the authority of the Crown, but he also urged open rebellion in 1775, when Royal Governor Dunmore seized the powder stored in the magazine at Williamsburg. The irate citizens of Fredericksburg who met here to organize a march to the capital were spurred to action by Weedon's impassioned words.

Among the Patriots who gathered here during the Revolution to discuss the course of affairs were George Washington, Patrick Henry, Thomas Jefferson, George Mason, John Marshall, and Hugh Mercer. In 1777 a committee of burgesses (Jefferson, Mason, Wythe, and Pendleton) met at the tavern to draft the "Bill for Establishing Religious Freedom" for presentation to the Virginia Assembly.

After affairs of state were attended to, the distinguished guests turned to relaxation. Describing an evening at the gaming table, George Washington wrote in his diary: "Evening at the Rising Sun. . . . Lost money as usual. The boys at Fredericksburg are too smart for me."

After the Yorktown victory Fredericksburg enjoyed a week of festivities. Visitors flocked to the town, and a Peace Ball was held in the assembly room of the tavern on November 11, 1781. Among the guests were George Washington and his mother, Colonel James Monroe, General Anthony Wayne, and the Marquis de Lafayette.

The Rising Sun Tavern is a two-and-a-half-story frame building with a steep gabled roof, narrow dormer windows, and built-in end chimneys. The eighteenth-century furnishings and accessories are of English and American origin. Noteworthy are the gaming table, the pewter collection, the spinet which once belonged to the Washington family, and the desk that was designed and owned by Jefferson.

Mary Washington House, Fredericksburg (FREDERICKSBURG VISITORS' CENTER)

MARY WASHINGTON HOUSE *1200 Charles Street, at Lewis Street. Open daily 9 A.M. to 5 P.M. March 1 through November 15, 9 A.M. to 4:30 P.M. the remainder of the year. Closed December 25–26 and January 1–2. Adults 75¢, students 35¢, or admittance with combination ticket.* George Washington's mother, who had resided for three decades at Ferry Farm across the Rappahannock River, moved to Fredericksburg in 1772 when her son purchased this small frame house for her. (The north wing is a later addition.) With her housekeeper Polly Skelton and two Negro servants, Mrs. Washington continued to live here for sixteen years—tending her garden, entertaining guests, and exchanging visits with her daughter, Betty Lewis (who resided at a nearby estate, Kenmore).

After the British defeat at Yorktown, the triumphant Washington came to visit his mother and sister. During the same week Lafayette arrived and blushed to hear Mrs. Washington remark, "It is strange to think of you as a general; you look just a boy."

Washington's last visit here was on April 12, 1789, when he knelt beside his mother's sickbed to receive her blessing before journeying to New York to be inaugurated as the first President. She died four months later.

The house contains many possessions of the Washington family, including a mirror, a waistcoat, several kitchen implements, and a Wedgwood china set. Among the noteworthy antiques are a secretary-desk, a pencil-post bed, an Oriental bird cage, and French silver chests. In the garden the same boxwoods Mary Washington planted two centuries ago may still be seen.

MARY WASHINGTON MONUMENT *On Washington Avenue at the end of Pitt Street* A large granite shaft marks the grave of George Washington's mother, Mary Ball Washington (1708–1789). When she died in 1789, her coffin was carried from the church on the shoulders of six Kenmore slaves and laid to rest here (on land originally part of the Kenmore estate).

In 1832 Silas E. Burroughs a wealthy New York merchant, donated money for the building of a monument to her. The following year President Andrew Jackson laid the cornerstone, but work was halted when Burroughs went bankrupt.

During the Civil War the half-completed monument was scarred by shells and defaced by vandals.

Enthusiasm for a new monument was generated in 1890, and money was successsfully raised by various organizations. In 1894 the ruined monument was removed and a shaft was erected. On May 10 crowds swarmed the streets and bands played as President Grover Cleveland and several Congressmen arrived in Fredericksburg for the dedication ceremonies. They reviewed a parade of marching Masons, fire companies, and military units before delivering appropriate speeches. The monument was then dedicated by the Grand Master of Masons of Virginia.

In the evening President Cleveland visited the Mary Washington House to meet descendants of the Washington and Ball families. That night an elaborate reception was held in his honor at the Opera House.

Important Colonial Houses

DICK HOUSE   *Princess Anne Street between Amelia and Lewis Streets. Not open to the public.*   This structure may be the oldest house standing in Fredericksburg. Charles Dick, the owner, was in partnership with Fielding Lewis at the gunnery, which manufactured armaments for the Patriot forces.

JOHN PAUL JONES HOUSE   *Corner of Caroline and Lafayette Streets. Not open to the public.*   This dwelling was bought in 1752 by John Paul Jones' older brother, William Paul. (John Paul Jones added the name "Jones" in 1775 to disguise his identity after he was involved in a murder in the West Indies.) This is the one house in America that the seafaring Jones considered his home.

Scottish-born John Paul Jones (1747–1792) entered the newly established Continental Navy in 1775. The next year, while commanding the sloop *Providence,* he captured sixteen British ships. Promoted to commodore, Jones was placed in command of a fleet of five vessels. He named his flagship the *Bonhomme Richard* in honor of the character created by Benjamin Franklin in *Poor Richard's Almanac.* On the night of September 23, 1779, the fleet encountered a convoy of merchant ships accompanied by two men-of-war, the *Countess of the Scarborough* and the *Serapis*. The *Countess* was captured by the American vessels, and Jones' flagship attacked the *Serapis*, forcing it to surrender.

MORTIMER HOUSE *218 Caroline Street. Not open to the public.* This two-story house (built in 1755) was the home of Dr. Charles Mortimer, Mary Washington's physician, and the first mayor of Fredericksburg. Many distinguished men were guests here: Washington, Lafayette, Rochambeau, and Henry Lee.

WEEDON HOUSE ("SENTRY BOX") *133 Caroline Street. Not open to the public.* General George Weedon (who commanded the Virginia troops during Yorktown) and his wife Isabella lived here after the Revolutionary War. The property had been owned previously by Hugh Mercer. The name "Sentry Box" was adopted by Weedon as a whimsical reference to his war service. The tradition that the house was used as a lookout during three wars is erroneous.

Non-Revolutionary Sites of Interest

FREDERICKSBURG AND SPOTSYLVANIA NATIONAL MILITARY PARK This park consists of four battlefields covering 3,600 acres. The four Civil War battles that occurred here were the Battle of Fredericksburg, the Battle of Chancellorsville, the Battle of the Wilderness, and the Battle of Spotsylvania Courthouse.

BATTLE OF FREDERICKSBURG (December 13, 1862) When General Ambrose Burnside moved his divisions along the north side of the Rappahannock River (opposite Fredericksburg), delay in bringing up pontoon bridges prevented him from crossing to the south bank and occupying a strategic position. This gave time to Generals Lee, Jackson, and Longstreet to prepare a strong defense. Union troops finally crossed the river, but they were unable to sustain an assault against the Confederate defenses. They lost more than 12,000 soldiers —a serious defeat for the North.

VISITORS' CENTER   Lafayette Boulevard (Route 1) and Sunken Road. The Information Center distributes maps for self-guided tours. On each of the battlefields narrative markers relate the events and identify the siege lines. Conducted tours of the Fredericksburg Battlefield are offered during the summer months.

BATTLE OF CHANCELLORSVILLE (May 2–4, 1863) Through a series of brilliant maneuvers, Robert E. Lee and Stonewall Jackson routed the Union forces under the command of Joseph Hooker at Chancellorsville (located about ten miles west of Fredericksburg).

BATTLE OF THE WILDERNESS (May–June 1864) The Confederate forces of Robert E. Lee and the Union army under Ulysses S. Grant attacked and counterattacked in a series of inconclusive battles in an area of dense forest about eleven miles west of Fredericksburg. Losses were extremely high on both sides.

BATTLE OF SPOTSYLVANIA COURTHOUSE (May 8–19, 1864) The fiercest fighting of the Wilderness campaign took place at Spotsylvania Courthouse, where Grant hammered away at Confederate lines. On May 12 the Union army attacked the center (the "Bloody Angle") of the Confederate line and was repulsed in a serious setback. In June the armies moved south toward Richmond, where Grant launched another unsuccessful assault and was finally forced to withdraw.

Recommended Side Trip

Wakefield
(George Washington's Birthplace)

From Fredericksburg travel on Route 3 East for about 37 miles. Just past the town of Oak Grove pick up Route 204 East and proceed 2 miles until you arrive at the obelisk at the site's entrance. The Washington plantation is located on Pope's Creek.

Wakefield is open daily 9 A.M. to 5 P.M. Closed December 25 and January 1. Fee 50¢ a person or $1.00 a car. Admission free from Labor Day to June 1.

George Washington's great-grandfather, John Washington, reached Virginia in 1657 on an English merchant ship. During a violent storm the vessel, which was attempting to sail up the Potomac River, floundered and ran aground. John Washington, second officer, decided to remain in the New World. When he married Anne Pope two years later, his bride's father presented him with land on Mattox Creek (near Wakefield) as a wedding gift. John attained influence and respect in the community: he was elected vestryman of the church and in 1662 was appointed justice of Westmoreland County Court.

His son, Lawrence, served in the Virginia Militia and, at the age of twenty-five, was elected to the House of Burgesses. In 1690 he married Mildred Warner, daughter of a prominent planter. Their son, Augustine, born 1694, was destined to become the father of our country's first President.

He married Jane Butler in 1715 and bought 150 acres here on Pope's Creek (which flows into the Potomac a half-mile away). Augustine, who had attended school in England, held several responsible positions: justice of Westmoreland County Court, sheriff of Westmoreland County, and captain in the militia. He also was co-owner of two iron furnaces.

On his property at Pope's Creek he built a fine brick house (1724–1726). The family was living here only three years when Jane fell ill and died, leaving Augustine to care for their three children. On March 6, 1731, he married a second time—to Mary Ball of Lancaster County, an orphan who had been living in the house of her guardian, George Eskridge. On February 22, 1732 (February 11 Old Style Calendar) their first son, George, was born here. He spent the first three years of his life at Wakefield until the family moved to a plantation fifty miles up the Potomac (now called Mount Vernon). The Pope's Creek house passed to George's older half-brother, Augustine, Jr. When George was six years old his father purchased 288 acres at Ferry Farm near Fredericksburg and relocated there.

FAMILY CEMETERY   Buried here are generations of the Washington family, including George Washington's great-grandfather (John), grandfather (Lawrence), and father (Augustine). The large tombstones were erected in 1930 by the Wakefield National Memorial Association.

KITCHEN OUTBUILDING   This outbuilding was reconstructed in the 1930s on its original foundations. The east room now contains cooking utensils and furniture of the

Family cemetery, Wakefield (ALPER)

early eighteenth century. The west room is used as a museum to exhibit Colonial artifacts uncovered in the area and to present displays relating the early history of the Washington family.

MEMORIAL HOUSE (WAKEFIELD MANSION) The Washington house at Pope's Creek (sometimes referred to as Wakefield Mansion) burned to the ground on Christmas Day 1779, probably as the result of sparks emitted from the chimney, which set the roof afire. Since no reliable information exists about the exact location and appearance of the house, this building—constructed in 1930–1931—represents a typical plantation house of the Colonial period. The bricks were handmade of native clay. Memorial House is today furnished with eighteenth-century antiques. The only piece of furniture surviving from the original dwelling is a tilt-top table that was salvaged after the 1799 fire.

SITE OF BUILDING "X" During excavations conducted on this site between 1930 and 1936, a brick foundation

Memorial House, Wakefield (ALPER)

almost seventy feet long was unearthed. It was named
Building "X" because nothing was known about its origin
and history. Still a mystery, the structure that once stood
here may have been the home in which Washington was
born—not the one thought to have been on the Memorial
House site sixty feet away.

WASHINGTON BIRTHPLACE MONUMENT The
United States War Department erected this granite shaft
in 1896 near the foundations of the house in which
George Washington is believed to have been born. In
1930 the monument, weighing almost fifty tons, was
moved to its present location. It is modeled to the scale
of one-tenth of the Washington Monument (completed
1884) in the District of Columbia.

Alexandria

Revolutionary War History

In 1732 a group of merchants decided to create a port at West's Point—at the junction of the Potomac River and Hunting Creek—in order to facilitate the export of Virginia tobacco to the European market. A community sprang up around the warehouses and docks and grew rapidly into a town, which in 1748 was incorporated. It was named Alexandria for John Alexander, wealthy owner of large tracts of land in the area.

Surveyor John West, Jr., and his young assistant George Washington were commissioned to survey the land and lay out a formal street plan with eighty-four half-acre lots. Among the first purchasers of these lots were Lawrence Washington, William Ramsay, and John Carlyle.

Alexandria became a bustling port, and with the construction of more houses and commercial buildings developed into a flourishing cosmopolitan city.

In early July 1774, after the British Parliament had passed legislation closing the port of Boston to commerce, the Patriots of Alexandria assembled at the courthouse. Fiery speeches protested the act, and the citizens decided to offer aid to the Bostonians. George Mason, a trustee of Alexandria, led the opposition against the repressive policies of the Crown. He also drafted several important documents defining the rights of the colonists. During the Revolutionary War, recruits from this area—forming the core of the Fairfax County militia—distinguished themselves in the Virginia campaign.

Colonial Alexandria was enriched by the presence of

VISITORS' CENTER The Alexandria Tourist Council, 221 King Street (in the Ramsay House), provides information, maps, and parking passes, phone 549–0205. A new Visitors' Center may be built for the Bicentennial.

PUBLIC TRANSPORTATION The Metro Transit Company of Washington, D.C., provides bus service in Alexandria and Arlington. Phone (202) 637–2437 for information and schedules.

TAXI SERVICE Yellow Cab, phone 549–2500; All American Cab, phone 549–3711.

It is recommended that visitors drive or take a bus to the Henry Lee House, the Friendship Fire Company, and the George Washington Masonic National Memorial. Most of the other sites can be seen by walking through the area bounded by Cameron Street on the north, Wolfe Street on the south, Union Street on the east, and Pitt Street on the west. (P indicates a historic Colonial house which is now a *private residence.*)

Walking Tour

Start at the corner of King and Fairfax Streets:

>Ramsay House
>
>Carlyle House
>
>Gadsby's Tavern
>
>Stabler-Leadbeater Apothecary Shop
>
>Gilpin House (P)
>
>Dick House (P)
>
>Captains' Row (P)
>
>Brown House (P)
>
>Presbyterian Meeting House

End on Fairfax Street near Wolfe Street.

George Washington, its most prominent citizen. Washington was a trustee of the town, a parishioner of Christ Church, an organizer of the Friendship Fire Company, and the first Worshipful Master of the Lodge of Masons.

Colonial and Revolutionary War Sites

CARLYLE HOUSE   *121 North Fairfax Street. Open daily 10 A.M. to 5 P.M. Closed Thanksgiving, December 25, and January 1. Fee 50¢. (Presently closed for renovations.)*   This mansion, built in 1752, was the home of John Carlyle (a wealthy merchant and shipowner) and his wife Sarah (daughter of Colonel William Fairfax, a close friend of George Washington).

Here in 1755 General Edward Braddock met with five royal governors (from Virginia, Massachusetts, New York, Maryland, and Pennsylvania) to discuss plans for waging and financing the French and Indian Wars. A letter was drawn up at that meeting urging the British government to tax the colonies. Carlyle was placed in charge of supplies for Braddock's expeditions.

The Carlyle house was the social center of Alexandria. It was always full of guests, among them Aaron Burr, John Marshall, John Paul Jones, George Washington, and Thomas Jefferson.

The house is noted for its exceptional woodwork, mantels, and paneling. The furnishings include Carlyle's writing desk and a small wooden coach that Washington had made for the Carlyle children. Presently closed for renovations, the building is scheduled to reopen in 1977.

CHRIST CHURCH *Cameron and Columbus Streets. Open Monday through Saturday 9 A.M. to 5 P.M., Sunday 2 P.M. to 5 P.M.* This handsome brick church was designed by James Wren in the 1760s. He also lettered the tablets of the Lord's Prayer and the Ten Commandments which are located on either side of the pulpit.

For the maintenance of the church, the vestry levied a tithe on each parishioner, who paid his tax in tobacco. The first rector of Christ Church, the Reverend Townsend Dade (1765–1778), received an annual salary of about 17,000 pounds of tobacco.

George Washington served as a vestryman here, and he purchased pew number 60 for £36 10s (an unusually high price). The pew is marked by a silver plate. The Reverend Thomas Davis, rector here from 1792 to 1806, officiated at Washington's funeral at Mount Vernon on December 18, 1799. The family Bible of Washington was presented to the parish in 1804 by George Washington Parke Custis (a grandson of Martha Washington).

Robert E. Lee, who was confirmed in this church, frequently worshipped here during his boyhood and in later years when he resided at Arlington. On Sunday, April 21, 1861—the day after he resigned his commission in the United States Army—Lee came to this church to seek divine guidance for the onerous task that awaited him. Two days later he assumed command of the Virginia military forces. A white tablet on the east wall honors the great general, and his pew, number 46, bears a silver plaque.

FRIENDSHIP FIRE COMPANY *107 South Alfred Street. Open Monday through Saturday 9:30 A.M. to 5 P.M. Closed holidays. Donations accepted.* The Friendship Fire Company was organized on August 5, 1774, as a volunteer firefighting unit. George Washington was one of its first members. While attending the Continental Congress in Philadelphia in 1775, he purchased a fire engine for £ 80 and had it transported to Alexandria by oxcart.

When the bell in the tower of the Friendship firehouse rang out a warning, local volunteers ran through the cobblestone streets to the firehouse, where they would break out the equipment (buckets, hooks, and ladders) and man the engine.

A replica of this company's first engine is on display here along with several other eighteenth- and nineteenth-century fire engines. Many paintings and prints depicting scenes from Washington's life adorn the wall. One engraving relates an often-repeated story about him. One day, as he was riding past a fire in Alexandria, he noticed that the fire engine was inadequately manned. Seeing several young gentlemen idly watching the struggling fire volunteers, Washington scolded them for not helping and, jumping from his horse, took charge of the engine himself.

The present brick fire station dates from the 1850s and has been renovated and enlarged.

GADSBY TAVERN   *Cameron and North Royal Streets. Open daily 10 A.M. to 5 P.M. Adults 50¢, children 25¢.* The older section of this two-part structure was erected in 1752 and was known as City Tavern. Forty years later, John Wise, proprietor of the tavern, built the three-story brick addition as a hotel. In 1794 an Englishman, John Gadsby, purchased the property.

On at least two occasions the young George Washington used this tavern as his headquarters. In 1754, when a lieutenant colonel in the Virginia Militia, he stayed here while recruiting and drilling two companies of Provincial troops to reinforce the Virginia frontier posts against attacks by the French and Indians. Again, the following year, he used the tavern as a base of operations while organizing militiamen to fight in General Edward Braddock's ill-fated campaign against Fort Duquesne. After the Revolutionary War, Washington was frequently

Gadsby Tavern,
Alexandria (ALPER)

feted here on his birthdays by the citizens of Alexandria.
On his way from Mount Vernon to his presidential
inauguration in New York in April 1789, he stopped at
Gadsby's and was honored at a gala reception.

Several colorful events of the Revolutionary period
took place here. A committee of Virginians (including
George Washington and George Mason) met at the
tavern in the summer of 1774 to prepare a preliminary
draft of the "Fairfax County Resolves" which set forth
demands for colonial rights. Here, in 1777, John Paul
Jones met Baron de Kalb and the Marquis de Lafayette,
who both had recently arrived from Europe to fight
for the Patriot cause. Many Revolutionary leaders—including Thomas Jefferson, Alexander Hamilton, Benjamin Franklin, and Henry Lee—rested and dined at this
tavern.

In February 1779 the large **Ballroom** was the setting
for a birthday celebration for George Washington. At

this elegant ball and elaborate supper honoring him, many of his friends were to see him for the last time. He died ten months later.

President John Adams attended a public dinner in the ballroom on June 11, 1800, and the newly elected President, Thomas Jefferson, was guest of honor at a banquet here on March 14, 1801. His arch rival, Aaron Burr, was present and, instead of paying tribute to Jefferson's victory, he offered his toast to "The memory of our departed chief, George Washington." In 1824 a reception was given here for Lafayette, who was touring the United States.

In one of the upstairs **Bedrooms** Anne Warren, celebrated English actress, died in 1808. While performing at Alexandria's new theater, Liberty Hall, she suddenly was seized by a severe pain and fell stricken. She was carried back to her room at the hotel where, after suffering horrible agonies, she expired. Miss Warren was buried in the cemetery of Christ Church.

In 1816 a woman who occupied one of the third-floor bedrooms died under mysterious circumstances. One day an elegantly dressed woman accompanied by a young man arrived by ship in Alexandria. As no servants attended them, local observers became curious. Upon arriving at the hotel here she collapsed, never to recover. Gossips speculated that the beautiful young lady was the daughter of a wealthy English family who, disobeying her parents' wishes, had married a man beneath her station. Fleeing to Virginia, she had become ill during the turbulent crossing. Her companion remained by her bedside throughout her illness, but when she died, he suddenly vanished. From that time on the unidentified lady has been known as "The Female Stranger."

HENRY LEE HOUSE *607 Oronoco Street. Open daily 9 A.M. to 5 P.M. Adults $1.00, children 35¢.* This house was occupied by the widow and children of the Virginia Patriot Henry ("Light-Horse Harry") Lee (1756–1818), the Revolutionary War cavalry officer who, after the war, was a member of Congress (1786–1788, 1799–1801) and governor of Virginia (1792–1795). He is also remembered for a phrase describing George Washington: "First in war, first in peace, and first in the hearts of his countrymen." Henry Lee's son, Robert E. Lee (1807–1870), gained immortality as commander of the Confederate armies in the Civil War.

This house was built in 1795 by John Potts, who sold it four years later to William Fitzhugh, a cousin of Mrs. Lee. While the Fitzhughs were prospering in Alexandria, the Lees were suffering misfortune at Stratford. Drought and increasing debts caused the Lee estate to fall into disrepair, and Henry was imprisoned for debt in 1808. Two years later, Mrs. Lee moved her children and their belongings to a house in Alexandria on Cameron Street. (After Lee was released from prison, he went to Baltimore and later to the West Indies, where he spent his final years.)

Soon after her husband's death in 1818, Mrs. Lee rented this house on Oronoco Street from William Fitzhugh, who had moved to his Ravensworth estate (near Annandale). The Lee family resided here for seven years.

This fifteen-room mansion has been restored and furnished with period pieces. Among the treasured items are an early-nineteenth-century piano by Albrecht (Philadelphia), a green brocade Sheraton sofa, a Duncan Phyfe sewing table, Davenport china, and a bedspread that belonged to Martha Washington. A letter from Lafayette, now framed and hanging in the hallway, is a memento of his visit to the Lees in 1824.

PRESBYTERIAN MEETING HOUSE   *321 South Fairfax Street. Open 9 A.M. to 4 P.M. Monday through Friday, 9 A.M. to noon Saturday. Services at 11 P.M. Sunday.* This meeting house was completed in 1774 under the supervision of John Carlyle. In 1835 it was partially destroyed by fire but was rebuilt two years later.

On December 14, 1799, when news arrived of George Washington's death, the meeting house bell—the only church bell in Alexandria—began to toll. Its knell was heard for four days until his body was laid to rest in the family vault at Mount Vernon. On December 29 special memorial services were held here under the auspices of the Washington Society and the local Masonic Lodge.

Many prominent Alexandrians are buried in the churchyard: John Carlyle (Commissary of Virginia forces under Braddock), Dr. James Craik (Surgeon-General of the Continental Army and Washington's personal physician), Colonel Dennis Ramsay (an officer in the Continental Army, later a mayor of Alexandria and one of the pallbearers at Washington's funeral). Here also lie the remains of an unidentified Continental soldier—in the Tomb of the Unknown Soldier of the Revolutionary War.

RAMSAY HOUSE *221 King Street. Open 10* A.M. *to 4:30* P.M. *Monday through Saturday. Closed Thanksgiving, December 25, and January 1. Free.* This dwelling was built about 1749 by William Ramsay, one of Alexandria's most prominent citizens. During his long public career he served as census-taker, postmaster,

Ramsay House,
Alexandria
(ALPER)

member of the Committee of Safety, town trustee, and adjustor of weights and seals. He has the distinction of having been Alexandria's first and only lord mayor.

Ramsay married Anne McCarty, a cousin of George Washington. Mrs. Ramsay was devoted to the cause of improving the welfare of the orphaned children of Revolutionary War soldiers.

Some architectural historians believe the Ramsay House may have been built at Dumfries (about twenty-five miles away) and moved here by barge; others claim the structure has always stood on its present location.

The present dwelling, however, is a reconstruction—not a restoration—as the house was almost totally destroyed by fire in 1942. Since Ramsay had a large family, it is probable that he resided elsewhere in Alexandria and merely used this small house as an office or warehouse.

On display here are blue Canton china once owned by Dr. James Craik (a friend of and physician to George Washington) and love letters written to Ramsay's daughter, Bess, by an officer in the Continental Army.

STABLER-LEADBEATER APOTHECARY SHOP AND MUSEUM *107 South Fairfax Street. Open daily 10 A.M. to 5 P.M. Closed December 25 and January 1. Donations accepted.* In 1792 Edward Stabler opened an apothecary shop in this building, which for over 140 years was a leading Alexandria establishment. Among the famous people who at one time patronized the shop were George Washington, Henry Lee, Daniel Webster, John C. Calhoun, and Robert E. Lee.

All the counters here are not only original but are also in their original locations. Many examples of eighteenth-century apothecary equipment are on display: mortars, pestles, lancets, scales, and jars. Of special interest are the tall tapered bottles with twelve sides that were designed by Stabler in 1796, the cobalt blue poison bottles, and the nursing bottles with glass nipples. The large "show-globes" in the front windows were used to identify apothecary shops. (According to tradition, a globe would be filled with red liquid during an outbreak of contagious disease, thereby warning strangers not to remain in the town.)

The large clock in the rear of the shop has been here since 1792. The black chair is said to have been a favorite of Robert E. Lee's when he visited the shop. Local historians believe that Lee was in this apothecary in October 1859 visiting with the proprietor, Mr. Leadbeater, when Lieutenant J. E. B. Stuart delivered orders from General Winfield Scott instructing Lee to proceed to Harpers Ferry to take command of defenses during John Brown's raid.

Much treasured are the extant records here. The documents include a note written by Martha Washington in 1802 for a quart of castor oil, an order for paint from George Washington Parke Custis, and a note from Nellie Custis (Mrs. Lawrence Lewis) requesting borax and pills.

The shop was in continuous use until 1933 when it was purchased by The Landmarks Society.

GEORGE WASHINGTON MASONIC NATIONAL ME-MORIAL *West end of King Street. Open daily* 9 A.M. *to* 5 P.M. *Closed Thanksgiving, December 25, January 1. Free.* This monument was built as a memorial to George Washington, who served as the first Worshipful Master of Alexandria Lodge Number 22. The 333-foot tower was designed by architect Harvey Wiley Corbett, who is said to have modeled it after a temple in Alexandria, Egypt. Construction was begun in 1923 on Shuter's Hill, one of the sites originally proposed for the United States Capitol Building. On May 12, 1932, this impressive Masonic temple was dedicated during ceremonies attended by President Herbert Hoover.

Memorial Hall—with its magnificent coffered ceiling and imposing marble colonnade—is dominated by a

*George Washington
Masonic National
Memorial,
Alexandria* (ALPER)

seventeen-foot bronze statue of George Washington executed in 1950 by sculptor Bryant Baker of New York. The two large murals, painted by Allyn Cox, show Washington presiding at ceremonies for the laying of the Capitol cornerstone and attending Christ Church in Philadelphia. Several stained-glass windows depict scenes in the lives of Benjamin Franklin, Dr. Joseph Warren, and the Marquis de Lafayette.

Elevators moving along slanted shafts carry visitors to the seven floors above Memorial Hall. The main rooms are: the **Washington Museum,** displaying memorabilia of the Washington family; the **Library** of 6,000 volumes primarily devoted to subjects associated with the Masonic Fraternity; the **Grotto Room,** decorated with Persian architectural elements; the **Royal Arch Room,** featuring paintings illustrating scenes from the Old Testament; the **Cryptic Room,** simulating the interior of the crypt reportedly built under King Solomon's Temple; the **Knights Templar Chapel,** dominated by the stained-glass window depicting the Ascension of Christ; and the **Observation Area,** offering a panoramic view of Alexandria.

This temple—built with the contributions of more than 3 million Masons—is the national home of Freemasonry. Each Grand Lodge is an active member of the George Washington Masonic National Memorial Association, and any Masonic body or individual Mason may become an honorary life member by contributing to the endowment fund.

Important Colonial Houses

BROWN HOUSE *212 South Fairfax Street. Not open to the public.* This two-story house, built in 1775, was the residence of Dr. William Brown, Physician-General of the Continental Army. His civic duties included service as the first president of the school known as the Alexandria Academy.

CAPTAINS' ROW *100 block of Prince Street. Not open to the public.* These charming eighteenth-century town houses were built by sea captains when Alexandria was a thriving port. According to local tradition, Hessian prisoners laid the cobblestones on this street.

CRAIK HOUSE *210 Duke Street. Not open to the public.* Built about 1790, this was the home and office of Dr. James Craik (1730–1814), Surgeon-General of the Continental Army and director of the hospital at Yorktown. As George Washington's attending physician, he was present at the President's deathbed.

DICK HOUSE *209 Prince Street. Not open to the public.* This three-story townhouse was owned by Dr. Elisha Cullen Dick, a prominent physician and health officer of Alexandria. He succeeded Washington as Worshipful Master of the Alexandria Lodge of Masons.

He was summoned by Dr. Craik to Mount Vernon for consultation at Washington's deathbed. According to tradition, Dick stopped the hands of the bedroom clock at the moment of Washington's death.

GILPIN HOUSE *206 King Street. Not open to the public.* Colonel George Gilpin, who had served as an aide to George Washington during the Revolutionary War, built this three-and-a-half story brick house in 1798. Active in the affairs of Alexandria, Gilpin was judge of the Orphans' Court, director of the Potomac Navigation Company, and postmaster. He served as a pallbearer at Washington's funeral.

LAFAYETTE HOUSE *301 St. Asaph Street. Not open to the public.* When Lafayette visited Alexandria in 1824, he was a guest at this fine town house, then owned by the Lawrison family.

Recommended Side Trips

Arlington

In Virginia Interstate 95 and Route 1 lead to Arlington. From the District of Columbia take the Arlington Memorial Bridge (near the Lincoln Memorial) across the Potomac River.

Arlington County was originally a part of the District of Columbia but was returned to Virginia in 1846. The area is heavily populated with government workers.

CUSTIS-LEE MANSION (ARLINGTON HOUSE) *Off Sherman Drive at the edge of Arlington National Cemetery. Open daily 9:30 A.M. to 6 P.M. April through September, daily 9:30 A.M. to 4:30 P.M. the remainder of the year. Fee 50¢.* This mansion was built between 1802 and 1817 by George Washington Parke Custis (Martha Washington's grandson). In 1831 his daughter Ann married Robert E. Lee (son of Henry Lee, the Revolutionary War cavalry officer), and in the succeeding thirty years they raised seven children here.

During the Civil War the Lees abandoned the mansion after removing most of the family possessions. It was occupied by Union soldiers because of its strategic position overlooking the Capital. In 1865, when Mrs. Lee did not pay the property taxes, the estate was confiscated by the federal government. At that time land was set aside for the establishment of a national cemetery.

The mansion—with its imposing grand portico of eight massive Doric columns—is an outstanding example of Greek Revival architecture. The design is attributed to George Hadfield, an Englishman who supervised work on the Capitol Building. Congress authorized the restoration and refurnishing of the Custis-Lee Mansion in 1925.

In front of the main portico is a granite monument marking the grave of Pierre Charles L'Enfant (1754–1825), an officer in the Continental Army who saw service at Valley Forge, Savannah, and Charleston, and who later drew up plans for the layout of the city of Washington, D.C.

ARLINGTON NATIONAL CEMETERY *Directly west of Memorial Bridge in Arlington. Open daily 8 A.M. to 5 P.M. October through March, daily 8 A.M. to 7 P.M. the remainder of the year. Free.* The largest burial ground in the United States, Arlington National Cemetery is a semicircular tract of about 500 acres with almost 143,000 graves of military personnel. Among the

famous persons buried here are George Washington
Parke Custis, William Jennings Bryan, William Howard
Taft, Oliver Wendell Holmes, General John J. Pershing,
John Foster Dulles, President John F. Kennedy, and
Senator Robert Kennedy.

VISITORS' CENTER   Since no automobiles are allowed
in the cemetery, persons wishing to tour the area may
take a guided tour by tram, which leaves from the
Visitors' Center on Arlington Ridge Road. Adults $1.25,
children 75¢.

The major monuments here include the Confederate
Memorial, the Marine Corps War Memorial, and the
Tomb of the Unknown Soldier.

CONFEDERATE MEMORIAL   *West side of Arlington National Cemetery off McPherson Drive*   In 1914 the
United Daughters of the Confederacy erected this imposing monument to honor those who sacrificed their
lives for the Confederate cause in the Civil War. The
graves of Confederate soldiers are arranged in concentric
circles around the monument.

MARINE CORPS WAR MEMORIAL (IWO JIMA STATUE)
Arlington Boulevard near Arlington Ridge Road   This
statue depicts the raising of the American flag on Mount
Suribachi, Iwo Jima, on February 23, 1945.

In February 1945, after seventy-two days of bombing,
the United States Marines stormed the island of Iwo
Jima, site of a Japanese air base. The Americans won the
battle, but at a high cost. During the attack Company E
of the 28th Regiment of the Fifth Division reached the
crest of Mount Suribachi (546 feet high), where several
men raised the American flag. Joseph Rosenthal, a pho-

tographer accompanying the troops, photographed this dramatic moment. (After the war it was disclosed that the stirring photograph was a reenactment of the flag-raising after the victory had been achieved.)

Sculptor Felix W. de Weldon was commissioned by the United States Marine Corps in the early 1950s to honor the event by creating a bronze sculpture based on Rosenthal's photograph. The work is the largest sculpture ever cast in bronze; it weighs 100 tons and each of the soldiers is almost 32 feet high. It was dedicated in 1954.

TOMB OF THE UNKNOWN SOLDIER   This gigantic block of white Colorado marble stands at the approximate center of the cemetery. On November 11, 1921, the remains of an unknown American soldier of World War I were entombed here beneath the inscription: "Here rests in honored glory an American soldier known but to God." On Memorial Day 1958 an unknown soldier killed in World War II and another who died in the Korean conflict were interred in the marked crypts at the head of the tomb. Sentries stand guard here twenty-four hours a day; the guard is changed every half-hour during the day and every two hours throughout the night.

Gunston Hall

From Alexandria travel about 16 miles south on Route 1, then 4 miles east on Route 242.

Gunston Hall is open daily 9:30 A.M. to 5 P.M. Closed December 25. Adults $1.50, children 50¢.

This house was built from 1755 to 1758 by George Mason (1725–1792), a member of the Virginia House of Burgesses and author of the Virginia Declaration of Rights (1776). Although he was a framer of the United States Constitution (1787), he refused to sign the document because it contained weak tariff provisions and failed to abolish slavery.

Four tall chimneys and a steep roof with dormers give this brick dwelling a dramatic appearance. The carved woodwork of the interior—the work of Englishman William Buckland—is among the finest found in this country. The Chinese Chippendale dining room he created here was the first of its kind in the colonies. The most important piece of furniture in the house is the writing table on which Mason drafted the Virginia Declaration of Rights.

Mason's nine children received their early education in the schoolhouse near the mansion. The schoolmaster lived in the loft above the classroom.

The sprawling boxwood gardens overlooking the Potomac are in the English manor house tradition. Both Mason and his wife Ann are buried in the family cemetery on this estate.

Woodlawn Plantation

From Alexandria take Route 1 South for about 7 miles.

Woodlawn Plantation is open daily 9:30 A.M. to 4:30 P.M. Closed December 25. Adults $2.00, students and servicemen 50¢.

In 1799 George Washington gave a tract of his Mount Vernon estate as a wedding gift to Eleanor Parke Custis (Martha Washington's granddaughter) on her marriage to Major Lawrence Lewis (Washington's nephew). On this site the Lewises built an imposing Georgian mansion. It was designed by William Thornton, an intimate friend of the Washington family and a designer of the United States Capitol. While Woodlawn was being built, the young couple resided at Mount Vernon.

The Lewises' son Lorenzo inherited Woodlawn in 1839

and sold the estate in 1846. The property then passed through many hands until it was purchased in 1948 by the Woodlawn Public Foundation. In 1957 the title was transferred to the National Trust for Historic Preservation.

The plan of this magnificent house—a wide central hallway with two rooms on either side—is typical of the period. The dining room, music room, parlor, and master bedroom are on the ground floor; the remaining bedrooms are located on the second floor.

Many of the furnishings here belonged to the Lewis family. Among the noteworthy pieces are a Hiram Powers bust of George Washington, a pianoforte, a Baltimore sideboard, Mrs. Lewis' four-poster bed, a painted Sheraton chair from Mount Vernon, and a marble and ormolu clock once owned by Lafayette (who visited this house in 1824). Examples of Mrs. Lewis' needlework are also on display.

Mount Vernon

Revolutionary War History

Mount Vernon, George Washington's estate on the Potomac River, is perhaps America's most cherished historical shrine.

In 1669 John Washington (George Washington's great-grandfather) and Nicholas Spenser applied for a royal grant of 5,000 acres. Washington's share of the land they acquired eventually passed to his grandson Augustine (1726). In 1735 he built a modest one-and-a-half-story house on this site and brought his wife and children from Wakefield. (George Washington was born at Wakefield in 1732.) When a fire destroyed the structure here in 1739, Augustine moved his family to an estate near Fredericksburg and gave this land to Lawrence, his oldest son (George's half-brother).

In 1743 Lawrence built a new house on this site, naming it "Mount Vernon" in honor of Admiral Edward Vernon under whom he had served in the West Indies. When Lawrence died in 1752, the property passed to the twenty-year-old George Washington, who made this his permanent residence.

In January 1759 Washington brought his bride Martha Dandridge Custis (a wealthy young widow) and her two children to live at Mount Vernon. The couple never had children of their own.

Wishing to enlarge the house, Washington made numerous architectural modifications: a second story was added (1758–1759), the length of the house was extended (1774, 1776), and a colonnaded porch was built (1780s). (During

George Washington. *Painting by Gilbert Stuart.* (OFFICE OF THE ARCHITECT OF THE CAPITOL, WASHINGTON, D.C.)

the Revolution a relative of Washington's managed the plantation and supervised the construction.) Washington increased the size of the estate from 2,126 acres to more than 8,000. Work on the plantation—which was comprised of farm land, orchards, workshops, mills, and distilleries— was done by several hundred slaves.

Washington died here in 1799 and was buried, as he had requested, on the estate grounds. When Martha died in 1802, Mount Vernon passed to George Washington's nephew, Bushrod Washington. After his death in 1829, the property passed through several hands until 1856, when it was purchased for $200,000 by the Mount Vernon Ladies Association. The Association is responsible for the restoration and maintenance of the estate.

Mount Vernon Mansion

Mount Vernon may be reached from Alexandria or Washington, D.C., by traveling south about 15 miles on the Mount Vernon Memorial Highway.

It is open daily 9 A.M. to 5 P.M. March through September, 9 A.M. to 4 P.M. the remainder of the year. Adults $1.50, children 75¢.

Meticulous care has gone into every detail of the restoration—from the copying of original draperies and bed coverings to the selecting of appropriate examples of eighteenth-century furniture.

The distinctive feature of the **Banquet Hall,** the first room one enters, is the Palladian window. To the left of the window stands a Hepplewhite sideboard, made in 1797 by John Aitken of Philadelphia. The marble mantel and the porcelain mantel vases were a gift of Washington's friend, Samuel Vaughan. Two engravings by John Trumbull, *The Death of General Montgomery* and *The Battle of Bunker's Hill*, adorn the walls.

In the **Central Hall** several items original to the house are displayed: a spyglass, a barometer, a lantern, a clock, and a key to the Bastille (a gift from General Lafayette in 1790).

The **Little Parlor** contains the harpsichord that Washington imported from London in 1793 for his ward Nellie Custis. One of the engravings above the harpsichord depicts the 1779 naval battle between John Paul Jones' *Bonhomme Richard* and the British ship *Serapis*. The three oval mezzotints are of Washington, Franklin, and Lafayette.

The **West Parlor** is noted for its handsome mantelpiece, fine paneling, denticulated molding, and decorated ceiling. The gaming table, made in England in the 1750s, is the work of cabinetmaker Philip Bell. Among the portraits are Charles Willson Peale's *George Washington*, James Sharples' *George Washington Lafayette* (Lafayette's son), and Robert Edge Pine's *Fanny Bassett* (Mrs. Washington's niece).

The elegant **Dining Room** is dominated by a Chippendale dining table on which is set a centerpiece, a mirrored plateau, which was a gift to Washington from Gouverneur Morris, a member of the Continental Congress and the Constitutional Convention. The ladder-back side chairs were made in Philadelphia in the early 1780s. The ornate mahogany Chippendale looking glass, with a scroll pediment and leaf motifs, belonged to Thomas Peter, who married Mrs. Washington's granddaughter, Martha Parke Custis. The Windsor high chair is said to have been used by children of the Custis family.

Five **Bedrooms** are located on the second floor. In **Washington's Bedroom** may be seen the portmanteau trunk acquired by the general in 1776 and used during the

*Tomb of George
Washington,
Mount Vernon*
(ALPER)

Revolutionary War. The shaving table and Mrs. Washington's desk are both French pieces, possibly purchased from the Comte de Moustier, the first Minister of France to the United States. The two portraits, by Robert Edge Pine, are of Mrs. Washington's granddaughters.

The four-poster canopied bed is the one in which President Washington died on December 14, 1799. Two days earlier, while inspecting his lands, he was caught in a snowstorm and returned home wet and chilled. Despite the admonitions of his wife, he spent the evening attending to correspondence. The next day Washington treated the resulting cold and sore throat with household remedies. Suddenly his condition began to deteriorate: breathing became difficult and pain racked his body.

On the 14th a slave was dispatched to Alexandria to fetch the family physician, James Craik. Alarmed at the condition of his friend, Dr. Craik called in Drs. Gustavus Brown and Elisha Dick for consultation. The only treatment they could agree on, bloodletting, further weakened their sixty-seven-year-old patient. Sensing that death was near, Washington gave his final instructions to his secretary, Tobias Lear. Several hours later, at 10:02 P.M., Washington died.

Washington's body was placed in a coffin bearing plates with the inscriptions *"Surge Ad Judicium"* (Rise for Judgment) and *"Glorio Deo"* (Thanks be to God). It was taken to the portico and set on a catafalque so that the crowds who had braved the bitter weather to come here could pay their respects.

On December 18, Washington was laid to rest in the family vault at Mount Vernon. As his coffin was carried by pallbearers to the vault, a military honor guard formed ranks at the gravesite, where the funeral service was performed. An artillery salute was fired from guns lining the river and from a warship anchored in the Potomac. As the sun was beginning to set, the heavy-hearted mourners turned homeward.

Thomas Jefferson spoke for the nation when he said of his fallen comrade: "His integrity was most pure, his justice the most inflexible I have ever known; no motives of interest, or consanguinity, or friendship, or hatred being able to bias his decision. He was indeed in every sense of the word, a wise, good and a great man."

Useful Facts

State Facts

SOUTH CAROLINA

DELEGATES TO THE FIRST CONTINENTAL CONGRESS (1774)	Christopher Gadsden Thomas Lynch, Sr. Henry Middleton Edward Rutledge John Rutledge
SIGNERS OF THE DECLARATION OF INDEPENDENCE (1776)	Thomas Heyward Thomas Lynch, Jr. Arthur Middleton Edward Rutledge
SIGNERS OF THE FEDERAL CONSTITUTION (1787)	Pierce Butler Charles Pinckney Charles Cotesworth Pinckney John Rutledge
STATEHOOD (DATE CONSTITUTION RATIFIED)	May 23, 1788 (8th)
POPULAR NAME	The Palmetto State
CAPITAL	Columbia
LARGEST CITY (POPULATION, 1970)	Columbia (113,542)
STATE POPULATION (1970 CENSUS)	2,589,891 (26th in rank)
STATE FLOWER	Yellow Jasmine
STATE TREE	Palmetto
STATE BIRD	Carolina Wren

NORTH CAROLINA

DELEGATES TO THE FIRST CONTINENTAL CONGRESS (1774)	Richard Caswell Joseph Hewes William Hooper

NORTH CAROLINA (Cont.)

SIGNERS OF THE DECLARATION OF INDEPENDENCE (1776)	Joseph Hewes William Hooper John Penn
SIGNERS OF THE FEDERAL CONSTITUTION (1787)	William Blount Richard Dobbs Spaight Hugh Williamson
STATEHOOD (DATE CONSTITUTION RATIFIED)	November 21, 1789 (12th)
POPULAR NAME	The Tarheel State
CAPITAL	Raleigh
LARGEST CITY (POPULATION, 1970)	Charlotte (241,178)
STATE POPULATION (1970 CENSUS)	5,082,059 (12th in rank)
STATE FLOWER	Dogwood
STATE TREE	Pine
STATE BIRD	Cardinal

VIRGINIA

DELEGATES TO THE FIRST CONTINENTAL CONGRESS (1774)	Richard Bland Benjamin Harrison Patrick Henry Richard Henry Lee Edmund Pendleton Peyton Randolph George Washington
SIGNERS OF THE DECLARATION OF INDEPENDENCE (1776)	Carter Braxton Benjamin Harrison Thomas Jefferson Francis Lightfoot Lee Richard Henry Lee Thomas Nelson George Wythe
SIGNERS OF THE FEDERAL CONSTITUTION (1787)	John Blair James Madison George Washington

VIRGINIA (Cont.)

STATEHOOD (DATE CONSTITUTION RATIFIED)	June 26, 1788 (10th)
POPULAR NAME	The Old Dominion
CAPITAL	Richmond
LARGEST CITY (POPULATION, 1970)	Norfolk (307,951)
STATE POPULATION (1970 CENSUS)	4,648,494 (14th in rank)
STATE FLOWER	Dogwood
STATE TREE	—
STATE BIRD	Cardinal

Motels and Hotels

Travelers who wish to make reservations at any of the motels and hotels listed below may use the appropriate toll-free telephone numbers. In order to guarantee reservations after 6 P.M. many establishments request a credit card number, thereby holding the prospective occupant responsible for payment. Resorts frequently demand a deposit in advance. If cancellation is necessary, always notify the reservation center or motel within the required time period.

BEST WESTERN MOTELS	800–528–1234 (In Arizona dial 800–352–1222)
HOLIDAY INNS	Contact your nearest Holiday Inn. Four major reservation centers accept toll-free calls. In most regions of the Northeast dial 800–243–2350; in most regions of the Midwest dial 800–323–9050; in most regions of the South dial 800–238–5400; in most regions of the West Coast dial 800–453–5555. If you are unable to reach these numbers, consult the Holiday Inn Directory for instructions.
HOWARD JOHNSON'S MOTOR LODGES	800–654–2000
MARRIOTT HOTELS AND MOTELS	800–228–9290
QUALITY INNS	800–323–5151 (In Hartford, Connecticut, and Philadelphia, Pennsylvania, dial 800–327–3384; in Illinois dial 800–942–8600).

RAMADA INNS	800–238–5800
SHERATON HOTELS AND MOTOR INNS	800–325–3535
TRAVELODGES	800–255–3050
TREADWAY INNS	800–631–0134
Persons with an American Express card may use the American Express Space Bank Reservation Center.	800–528–7700 (In Tennessee dial 800–542–5115)

(*Note:* In some areas it may be necessary to dial the digit 1 before 800.)

Motel and hotel prices are calculated according to the number of persons occupying a room as well as the size and location of the room. The base prices quoted below were in effect during 1974–1975 and are expected to rise. Prices do not include state, city, or local taxes (where applicable). Travelers should verify the exact rate before registering. Only a limited number of minimum-rate units are available. A few establishments permit pets; some city hotels and motor inns charge a fee for parking.

This compilation of motels and hotels is for the convenience of travelers and should not be considered a recommendation. The listing, furthermore, does not purport to be complete. Neither the author nor the publisher can be responsible for prices, procedures, accommodations, or services.

Since most rooms have telephones, televisions, and air-conditioning, these features are not mentioned in the entries below. The abbreviations used for credit cards are:

American Express	AX
Bank Americard	BA
Carte Blanche	CB

Diners Club	DC
Exxon	E
Gulf	G
Master Charge	MC
Mobil	M
Texaco	T

Motel and Hotel Listing

SOUTH CAROLINA

	PAGE
Camden	276
Charleston	274
Georgetown	275
Santee	275
Spartanburg	276

NORTH CAROLINA

Edenton	283
Greensboro	277
Hillsborough	281
New Bern	282
Wilmington	282
Winston-Salem	279

VIRGINIA

Alexandria	290
Charlottesville	288
Fredericksburg	289
Richmond	286
Williamsburg	283
Yorktown	285

SOUTH CAROLINA

CHARLESTON   (*Area Code 803*)

Dorchester Motor Lodge   4½ miles west on Route 26 at Dorchester Avenue. 747–0961. 199 rooms, 2 stories. Single $12 up; Double $15 up. Pool. Restaurant 5:30 A.M.–midnight. Checkout 1 P.M. AX, BA, CB, DC, MC.

Golden Eagle Motor Inn   157 Calhoun Street. (6 blocks south of Route 17.) 722–1621. 100 rooms, 6 stories. Elevator. Single $12 up; Double $14 up. Pool. Restaurant 6:30 A.M.– 10 P.M. Checkout 1 P.M. AX, BA, CB, DC, MC.

Golden Eagle Motor Inn   155 Meeting Street. (¾ mile south of Route 17.) 722–8411. 121 rooms, 2 stories. Single $11 up; Double $13 up. Pool. Restaurant 6:30 A.M.–10 P.M. Checkout 1 P.M. AX, BA, CB, DC, MC.

Holiday Inn–Airport   9 miles west on Route 26 at West Aviation Avenue. 744–1621. 207 rooms, 2 stories. Single $12 up; Double $17 up. Pool. Restaurant 6 A.M.–10 P.M. Checkout 2 P.M. AX, BA, DC, G, MC.

Holiday Inn–Riverview   1 mile south on Route 17 at Ashley River. 556–7100. 179 rooms, 13 stories. Elevator. Single $12 up; Double $18 up. Pool. Restaurant 6 A.M.–10 P.M. Checkout 1 P.M. AX, BA, DC, G, MC.

Holiday Inn–South   4 miles south on Route 17. 766–1651. 122 rooms, 2 stories. Single $13 up; Double $17 up. Pool. Restaurant 6 A.M.–10 P.M. Checkout 1 P.M. AX, BA, DC, G, MC.

Howard Johnson's   1540 Savannah Highway. (4 miles south on Route 17.) 766–8361. 38 rooms, 2 stories. Single $12.50 up; Double $16.50 up. Pool. Restaurant 6:30 A.M.–10 P.M. Checkout noon. AX, DC, E, MC, T.

Lord Ashley   1501 Savannah Highway South. (2½ miles south on Route 17.) 766–1611. 49 rooms. Single $10.50 up; Double $15 up. Pool. Restaurant open 24 hours. Checkout noon. AX, BA, CB, DC, MC.

Mills Hyatt House   Meeting and Queen Streets. 577–2400. 250 rooms, 7 stories. Elevator. Single $28 up; Double $36 up. Rooftop pool. Restaurant 7:30 A.M.–11 P.M. Checkout 1 P.M. AX, BA, CB, DC, MC.

Mt. Vernon 6 miles south on Route 17. 766–2361, 24 rooms, 1–2 stories. Single $10 up; Double $12 up. Pool. Restaurant opposite, 6 A.M.–10 P.M., weekends to 11 P.M. Checkout 11 A.M. AX, BA, DC, MC, M.

Sheraton Motor Inn 5981 Rivers Boulevard. 744–2501. 159 rooms, 7 stories. Elevator. Single $17 up; Double $24 up. Pool. Restaurant 7 A.M.–10 P.M. Checkout 1 P.M. AX, BA, CB, DC, MC.

GEORGETOWN (*Area Code 803*)

Deason's Church and St. James Streets. (6 blocks north on Route 17.) 546–4117. 22 rooms, 1 story. Single $8 up; Double $10 up. Restaurant 1 block, 6 A.M.–midnight. Checkout noon. AX, BA, MC, M.

Georgetonian 606 Church Street. (3 blocks north on Route 17.) 546–5111. 46 rooms, 1–2 stories. Single $10 up; Double $16 up. Pool. Restaurant 6:30 A.M.–10 P.M. Checkout noon. AX, BA, DC, MC.

Holiday Inn 1 mile north on Route 17. 546–6141. 119 rooms, 2 stories. Single $11 up; Double $15 up. Pool. Restaurant 6 A.M.–10 P.M. Checkout noon. AX, BA, DC, G, MC.

Quality Inn Carolinian 706 Church Street. (4 blocks north on Route 17.) 546–5191. 51 rooms, 1–2 stories. Single $8 up; Double $12 up. Pool. Restaurant 6 A.M.–10:30 P.M. Checkout noon. AX, BA, CB, DC.

Sea Gull Inn 9 miles north on Route 17. 237–4261. 100 rooms, 2 stories. Single $12 up; Double $16 up. Pool. Restaurant 7 A.M.–10 P.M. Checkout noon. AX, BA, CB, DC, MC.

SANTEE (*Area Code 803*)

Clover Inn On Routes 15, 301, just off Route 95. (½ mile south of junction of Route 6.) 854–2111. 40 rooms, 1-2 stories. Single $8 up; Double $9 up. Pool. Restaurant 6–11 P.M. Checkout noon. AX, BA, CB, DC, MC.

Gamecock On Routes 15, 301, just off Route 95. (1 mile south of junction of Route 6.) 854–2171. 29 rooms, 1 story. Single $8 up; Double $10 up. Pool. Restaurant 11 A.M.–9 P.M. Checkout 11 A.M. AX, BA, DC, MC, M.

Quality Inn Clark's On Routes 15, 301 at junction of Route 6. 854–2141. 100 rooms, 1–2 stories. Single $10 up; Double $12 up. Pool. Restaurant 6 A.M.–10:30 P.M. Checkout 1 P.M. AX, BA, DC, MC.

Royal Motor Lodge On Routes 15, 301 at junction of Route 6. 854–2107. 30 rooms, 1–2 stories. Single $10 up; Double $12 up. Pool. Restaurant adjacent, 5 A.M.–10 P.M. Checkout 11 A.M. AX, BA, CB, DC, MC.

CAMDEN　(*Area Code 803*)

Camden 1 mile north on Route 1. 432–7647. 14 rooms. Single $8 up; Double $9 up. Restaurant 1 block, 6:30 A.M.–11 P.M. Checkout noon. BA, MC.

Hampton Park DeKalb Street. (2 blocks north on Route 1, 2 blocks east of Routes 521, 601.) 432–2453. 35 rooms, 1–2 stories. Single $9 up; Double $10 up. Pool. Restaurant 6:30 A.M.–10:30 A.M., 6–10 P.M. Checkout noon. AX, BA, CB, DC, MC.

Holiday Inn 4 miles south on Routes 1, 601, 432–6131. 80 rooms, 2 stories. Single $10 up; Double $14 up. Pool. Restaurant 6 A.M.–10 P.M. Checkout 2 P.M. AX, BA, CB, G, MC.

Mona Lisa 3 blocks southwest on Routes 1, 601. 432–6093. 22 rooms. Single $7 up; Double $9 up. Pool. Restaurant 7 A.M.–2 P.M., 5–9:30 P.M. Checkout 11 A.M. BA, MC.

Parkview 1039 West DeKalb Street. (1 mile southwest on Routes 1, 601.) 432–7687. 20 rooms. Single $8 up; Double $8 up. Restaurant 6:30 A.M.–2 P.M., 5–8 P.M. Checkout 11 A.M. BA, MC.

SPARTANBURG　(*Area Code 803*)

El Dorado 1050 Greenville Highway. (2 miles west on Route 29.) 576–1660. 25 rooms. Single $7.50 up; Double $10 up. Restaurant 1 mile, 6 A.M.–midnight. Checkout 11 A.M.

Heart of Spartanburg 542 North Church Street. (6 blocks west on Routes 221, 56.) 585–4311. 79 rooms, 2 stories. Single $11 up; Double $13 up. Pool. Restaurant adjacent, 6 A.M.–11 P.M. Checkout noon. AX, BA, DC, MC.

Holiday Inn 5 miles west at junction of Routes 26, 85. 576–5220. 180 rooms, 2 stories. Single $11 up; Double $16 up.

Pool. Restaurant 6 A.M.–10 P.M. Checkout 2 P.M. AX, BA, DC, G, MC.

Howard Johnson's 3 miles northwest on Routes 29, 85 at junction of Route 176. 585–2241. 106 rooms, 2 stories. Single $12 up; Double $15 up. Pool. Restaurant 6:30 A.M.–10 P.M. Checkout noon. AX, BA, CB, DC, E, MC, T.

Main Street 700 West Main Street. (1 mile west on Route 29.) 583–8471. 30 rooms. Single $8 up; Double $10 up. Pool. Restaurant 3 blocks, 6 A.M.–midnight. Checkout 11 A.M. BA, MC.

Pine Street 150 Pine Street. (½ mile east on Routes 176, 9.) 582–5607. 68 rooms, 2 stories. Single $7 up; Double $10 up. Restaurant opposite, open 24 hours. Checkout 2 P.M.

Ramada Inn North Pine Street. (3 miles north on Route 85 at Route 585.) 585–4341. 141 rooms, 2 stories. Single $11.50 up; Double $14.50 up. Pool. Restaurant open 24 hours. Checkout 2 P.M. AX, BA, CB, DC, E, MC.

Scottish Inn Sigsbee Road. (5 miles west at junction of Routes 26, 85.) 576–7270. 100 rooms, 2 stories. Single $6 up; Double $9 up. Pool. Restaurant 6:30–9:30 A.M., 11:30 A.M.– 2 P.M., 5–9 P.M. Checkout noon. BA, MC.

Spartanburg TraveLodge 416 East Main Street. (½ mile east on Route 29 at junction of Route 176.) 585–6451. 40 rooms, 2 stories. Single $13 up; Double $15 up. Pool. Restaurant adjacent, open 24 hours. Checkout noon. AX, BA, CB, DC, MC, M.

NORTH CAROLINA

GREENSBORO (*Area Code* 919)

Albert Pick Motor Inn 10 miles west at junction of Routes 68, 40. 668–2431. 172 rooms, 2 stories. Single $18 up; Double $23 up. Pool. Restaurant 6:30 A.M.–10 P.M. Checkout noon. AX, BA, CB, DC, MC.

Americana 5½ miles southwest on Route 85. 299–6311. 60 rooms, 1–2 stories. Single $9 up; Double $11 up. Pool. Restaurant 5 P.M.–midnight. Checkout noon. AX, BA, DC, MC.

Coliseum 2428 High Point Road. (4 miles west on Routes 29A, 70A.) 292–1831. 72 rooms, 1–4 stories. Single $9.50 up;

Double $12 up. Pool. Restaurant 6:30 A.M.–2 P.M., Saturday, Sunday, 7–11 A.M. Checkout noon. AX, CB, DC, MC.

Diplomat   512 Farragut Street. (2 miles south on Route 220 at junction of Routes 29, 70, 40, 85.) 274–7656. 52 rooms, 1–2 stories. Single $10 up; Double $12 up. Pool. Restaurant 1 block, 6 A.M.–midnight, also adjacent 5 P.M.–midnight. Checkout noon. AX, CB, DC, MC.

Golden Eagle Motor Inn   201 East Market Street. 275–9481. 135 rooms, 4 stories. Elevator. Single $14.50 up; Double $19 up. Pool. Restaurant 9 A.M.–9 P.M. Checkout 1 P.M. AX, BA, CB, MC.

Greensboro TraveLodge   135 Summit Avenue. 273–5512. 55 rooms, 3 stories. Elevator. Single $13 up; Double $15 up. Pool. Restaurant 6 A.M.–9 P.M. Checkout noon. AX, BA, CB, DC, MC, M.

Happy Inn   2914 South Elm Street. (At Routes 85 South Elm Street Exit.) 275–9471. 97 rooms, 2 stories. Single $9 up; Double $12 up. Pool. Restaurant 6:30 A.M.–9 P.M. Checkout noon. AX, BA, MC.

Hilton Inn   830 West Market Street. (8 blocks west on Route 421.) 275–0811. 229 rooms, 10 stories. Elevators. Single $15.50 up; Double $18 up. Pool. Restaurant 6 A.M.–11 P.M. Checkout 2 P.M. AX, BA, CB, DC, MC.

Holiday Inn–Four Seasons   High Point Road. (5 miles southwest on Routes 29A, 70A at junction of Route 40.) 292–9161. 259 rooms, 5 stories. Elevator. Single $14 up; Double $16 up. Pool. Restaurant 6 A.M.–11 P.M. Checkout 2 P.M. AX, BA, G, MC.

Holiday Inn–North   3 miles north on Route 29 at 16th Street. 275–5371. 90 rooms, 2 stories. Single $12 up; Double $14 up. Pool. Restaurant 6 A.M.–10 P.M. Checkout noon. AX, BA, DC, G, MC.

Holiday Inn–South   Randelman Road. (2 miles south on Route 220 at junction of Routes 29, 70, 40, 85.) 273–5592. 195 rooms, 2–3 stories. Single $12 up; Double $14 up. Pool. Restaurant 6 A.M.–10 P.M. Checkout noon. AX, BA, DC, G, MC.

Howard Johnson's–North   South Elm Street. (1½ miles southeast on Route 85.) 275–9331. 136 rooms, 1–2 stories. Single $14 up; Double $15 up. Pool. Restaurant 6:30 A.M.–10 P.M. Checkout noon. AX, BA, DC, E, MC, T.

Howard Johnson's—West 5½ miles southwest on Routes 29, 70, 85 at Osborne Road Exit. 299–4612. 68 rooms, 2 stories. Single $13 up; Double $15 up. Pool. Restaurant 6:30 A.M.– 11 P.M. Checkout noon. AX, BA, DC, E, MC, T.

Journey's End Motel Court 2310 Battleground Avenue. (2½ miles north on Route 220.) 288–5611. 36 rooms, 1–2 stories. Single $12 up; Double $14 up. Pool. Restaurant open 24 hours. Checkout noon. AX, BA, MC.

Maplewood 2500 Battleground Avenue. (2½ miles north on Route 220.) 288–1022. 24 rooms. Single $9 up; Double $11 up. Pool. Restaurant 2 blocks, open 24 hours. Checkout 11 A.M. AX, BA, CB, DC, MC.

Oaks 1118 Summit Avenue. (1¼ miles north on Route 29A.) 272–0105. 88 rooms. Single $12 up; Double $14 up. Pool. Restaurant 7 A.M.–10 P.M. Checkout noon. AX, BA, DC, MC.

Quality Inn Central 1000 West Market Street. (10 blocks west on Routes 29A, 70A, 421.) 273–5503. 71 rooms, 2 stories. Single $13.50 up; Double $15.50 up. Pool. Restaurant 7 A.M.– 2:30 P.M., 5:30–10 P.M. Checkout 2 P.M. AX, BA, DC, MC.

Ramada Inn 120 Seneca Road. (Southwest of junction of Routes 29, 70, 421, 85.) 275–9571. 123 rooms, 2 stories. Single $13 up; Double $16 up. Pool. Restaurant 6 A.M.–10 P.M. Checkout 2 P.M. AX, BA, CB, DC, E, MC.

Shady Lawn 1020 West Market Street. 274–3211. 27 rooms, 2 stories. Single $8.50 up; Double $10 up. Restaurant adjacent, 7 A.M.–10 P.M. Checkout noon. AX, BA, MC.

Sheraton Motor Inn South Elm Street. (2 miles south at Route 85.) 275–0741. 128 rooms, 2 stories. Single 14 up; Double $16 up. Pool. Restaurant 6:30 A.M.–10 P.M. Checkout 2 P.M. AX, BA, CB, DC, MC.

Smith's Ranch 2210 Randleman Road. (On Route 220 ½ mile north of Routes 29, 70, 85.) 272–0182. 57 rooms. Single $8.50 up; Double $10 up. Pool. Restaurant 6 A.M.–11 P.M. Checkout noon. AX, BA, CB, DC, MC.

WINSTON-SALEM (*Area Code* 919)

Downtowner 128 Cherry Street at 2nd Street. (2 blocks north of Route 40, Cherry Street Exit.) 723–8861. 185 rooms,

7 stories. Elevator. Single $14 up; Double $17 up. Pool. Restaurant 6:30 A.M.–10:30 P.M. Checkout noon. AX, BA, CB, DC, MC.

Green Valley 4170 Patterson Avenue. (4½ miles north on Route 52 at Route 8.) 767–2900. 24 rooms, 1 story. Single $14 up; Double $16 up. Pool. Restaurant opposite, 6 A.M.–10 P.M. Checkout 11 A.M. AX, BA, DC, MC.

Hilton Inn Marshall and High Streets. (¼ mile south of Route 40, Cherry Street Exit.) 723–7911. 174 rooms, 7 stories. Elevators. Single 15.50 up; Double $18 up. Pool. Restaurant 6 A.M.–11 P.M. Checkout 2 P.M. AX, BA, CB, DC, MC.

Holiday Inn 127 South Cherry Street at Brookstown Avenue. (1 block south of Route 40, Cherry Street Exit.) 725–8561. 133 rooms, 2–3 stories. Single $12 up; Double $14 up. Pool. Restaurant 6 A.M.–10 P.M. Checkout 1 P.M. AX, BA, DC, G, MC.

Holiday Inn–North North Cherry–Marshall Expressway at 30th Street. 723–2911. 201 rooms, 4 stories. Elevator. Single $13.50 up; Double $18.50 up. Pool. Restaurant 6 A.M.–10 P.M. Checkout noon. AX, BA, DC, G, MC.

Holiday Inn–West 2008 South Hawthorne Road. (2 miles west, just off Silas Creek Parkway.) 765–6670. 162 rooms, 2 stories. Single $13.50 up; Double $18.50 up. Pool. Restaurant 6 A.M.–11 P.M. Checkout 1 P.M. AX, BA, DC, G, MC.

Howard Johnson's 150 South Stratford Road South West. (2½ miles west on Route 158 at Route 40, Stratford Road Exit.) 725–7501. 112 rooms, 1–2 stories. Single $13 up; Double $15 up. Pool. Restaurant 6:30 A.M.–9 P.M. Checkout noon. AX, BA, DC, E, MC, T.

Sheraton Motor Inn 380 Knollwood Street. (3 miles west on Route 40, Knollwood Street Exit.) 765–4321. 121 rooms, 2–3 stories. Single $14 up; Double $20 up. Pool. Restaurant 6–11 A.M., 5–11 P.M. Checkout 1 P.M. AX, BA, CB, DC, MC.

Travel Host of America North Patterson Avenue. (4½ miles north on Route 52N at exit to Route 8.) 767–1930. 56 rooms. Single $9 up; Double $14 up. Pool. Restaurant 6 A.M.–10 P.M. Checkout noon. AX, BA, CB, MC.

Winston Reidsville Road. (3 miles east on Route 158 at junction of Route 40.) 723–1878. 15 rooms. Double $12 up. Restaurant 1 mile, 6:30 A.M.–8:30 P.M. Checkout noon.

HILLSBOROUGH-DURHAM AREA *(Area Code 919)*

The following motels and hotels are located in or near Durham, Hillsborough's neighboring community.

Cavalier Inn 4026 Chapel Hill Boulevard. (3½ miles southwest, just east of junction of Routes 15, 501.) 489–9121. 60 rooms. Single $12 up; Double $14 up. Pool. Restaurant 5–10 P.M. Checkout noon. AX, BA, MC.

Downtowner 309 West Chapel Hill Street. 688–8221. 156 rooms, 5 stories. Elevator. Single $15.50 up; Double $19.75 up. Pool. Restaurant 6:30 A.M.–11 P.M. Checkout noon. AX, BA, CB, DC, MC.

Durham Corcoran and Chapel Hill Streets. 682–1101. 300 rooms. Single $11 up; Double $16 up. Pool. Restaurant 7 A.M.–2:30 P.M., 5:30–9 P.M. Checkout 3 P.M. AX, BA, CB, DC, MC.

Hilton 2424 Erwin Road. (¾ mile east of Routes 15, 501.) 286–7761. 137 rooms. Single $16 up; Double $20 up. Restaurant 7 A.M.–3 P.M., 5–9 P.M. Checkout 2 P.M. AX, BA, CB, DC, MC.

Holiday Inn–Downtown 605 West Chapel Hill. 682–5411. 132 rooms, 2–3 stories. Elevator. Single $13 up; Double $17 up. Pool. Restaurant 6 A.M.–10 P.M. Checkout noon. AX, BA, DC, G, MC.

Holiday Inn–West 3½ miles northwest at junction of Routes 15, 501. 383–1551. 143 rooms, 2 stories. Single $13 up; Double $17 up. Pool. Restaurant 6 A.M.–10 P.M. Checkout noon. AX, BA, DC, G, MC.

Homestead 3 miles southwest on Routes 15, 501. 489–9181. 25 rooms. Single $9 up; Double $11 up. Restaurant 1 block, 7 A.M.–10 P.M. Checkout noon. AX, BA, CB, DC, MC, M.

Howard Johnson's 3¼ miles northwest on Routes 15, 70, 501; on Route 85, Hillandale Exit. 477–7381. 64 rooms, 2 stories. Single $14 up; Double $16 up. Pool. Restaurant 6:30 A.M.–10:30 P.M., off-season to 10 P.M. Checkout noon. AX, BA, E, MC, T.

Ramada Inn 1900 west Route 85. (3 miles northwest on Routes 15, 70, 501; on Route 85, Guess Road Exit.) 477–7371. 100 rooms, 2 stories. Single $14 up; Double $19 up. Pool. Restaurant 6 A.M.–9:30 P.M. Checkout 2 P.M. AX, BA, CB, DC, E, MC.

WILMINGTON   *(Area Code 919)*

Americano   2929 Market Street. (2 miles northeast on Routes 17, 74.) 763–3318. 52 rooms. Single $9 up; Double $14 up. Pool. Restaurant opposite, 6:30–11:30 A.M., 5–11 P.M. Checkout noon. AX, BA, CB, DC, MC, M.

Carolinian   2916 Market Street. (2 miles northeast on Routes 17, 74.) 763–4653. 62 rooms, 1–2 stories. Single $13 up; Double $16 up. Pool. Restaurant adjacent, 6:30–11 A.M., 5–11 P.M. Checkout noon. AX, BA, DC, MC.

El Berta Motor Inn   4505 Market Street. (2¾ miles northeast on Routes 17, 74.) 799–1214. 82 rooms. Single $9 up; Double $12.50 up. Pool. Restaurant 5 A.M.–11 P.M. Checkout noon. AX, DC.

Golden Eagle Motor Inn   801 Market Street. 763–9851. 121 rooms, 2 stories. Single $11 up; Double $13 up. Pool. Restaurant 6 A.M.–10 P.M. Checkout 1 P.M. AX, BA, CB, DC, MC.

Heart of Wilmington   311 North 3rd Street. (On Routes 17, 74, 76, 117, 421.) 763–0121. 70 rooms, 3 stories. Elevator. Single $13 up; Double $16 up. Pool. Restaurant 6:30 A.M.–3 P.M., 4–11:30 P.M. Checkout noon. AX, BA, DC, MC.

Holiday Inn   4903 Market Street. (3 miles northeast on Routes 17, 74, 76.) 799–1440. 180 rooms, 2 stories. Single $13 up; Double $16 up. Pool. Restaurant 6 A.M.–10 P.M. Checkout noon. AX, BA, DC, G, MC.

Ramada Inn   5001 Market Street. (3¾ miles northeast on Route 17.) 799–1730. 100 rooms, 1–2 stories. Single $11 up; Double $16 up. Pool. Restaurant 6 A.M.–10 P.M. Checkout 1 P.M. AX, BA, CB, DC, E, MC.

Timme Plaza Motor Inn   On Water Street between Grace and Walnut Streets. 763–9881. 180 rooms. Single $15 up; Double $19 up. Pool. Restaurant 5:30 A.M.–10:30 P.M. Checkout 2 P.M. AX, BA, CB, DC, MC.

NEW BERN   *(Area Code 919)*

Carolina   3515 Carendon Boulevard. (3¾ miles south on Route 17.) 638–1184. 15 rooms. Single $8 up; Double $10 up. Pool. Restaurant 6–10 P.M. Checkout 11 A.M. BA, MC.

Holiday Inn 312 East Front Street. (Junction of Routes 17, 70.) 638–5111. 152 rooms, 2 stories. Single $11 up; Double $15.50 up. Pool. Restaurant 6:30 A.M.–10 P.M. Checkout noon. AX, BA, DC, G, MC.

Ramada Inn 925 Broad Street. (On Route 70 just north of junction of Route 17.) 638–3051. 112 rooms, 6 stories. Elevators. Single $11 up; Double $15 up. Pool. Restaurant 6 A.M.–10 P.M. Checkout noon. AX, BA, CB, DC, E, MC.

Ziegler 1914 Trent Boulevard. (1 block east of Route 17.) 637–4498. 18 rooms. Single $8 up; Double $9 up. Restaurant 2 blocks, 6 A.M.–9 P.M. Checkout noon. BA, MC.

EDENTON (*Area Code 919*)

Quality Inn–Eden On Route 17. 482–2107. 34 rooms, 1–2 stories. Single $8.50 up; Double $12 up. Pool. Restaurant 6:30–9 A.M., 11 A.M.–2 P.M., 5:30–9 P.M. Checkout noon. AX, BA, DC, MC.

Triangle Broad Street. (On Route 17 at junction of Route 32.) 482–2728. 13 rooms. Single $8 up; Double $10 up. Restaurant 1 block, 6–9:30 P.M. Checkout noon. MC.

VIRGINIA

WILLIAMSBURG (*Area Code 804*)

Colonial 1452 Richmond Road. (1¾ miles northwest on Route 60.) 229–3621. 30 rooms. Single $12 up; Double $12 up. Pool. Restaurant opposite, 7 A.M.–3 P.M., 5–10 P.M. Checkout 11 A.M. AX, BA, CB.

Commonwealth Inn 1233 Richmond Road. (1 mile northwest on Route 60.) 229–6922. 68 rooms, 3 stories. Elevator. Single $14 up; Double $16 up. Pool. Restaurant 1 block, 7 A.M.–11 P.M. Checkout noon. AX, BA, DC.

Governor Spotswood 1508 Richmond Road. (1½ miles northwest on Route 60.) 229–6444. 66 rooms. Single $14 up; Double $16 up. Pool. Restaurant opposite, 7 A.M.–3 P.M. Checkout noon. AX, BA, CB, DC, MC, M.

Heritage Inn   1324 Richmond Road. (1⅛ miles northwest on Route 60.) 229–6220. 54 rooms, 3 stories. Elevator. Single $14 up; Double $16 up. Pool. Restaurant 7–11 A.M., 5:30–9 P.M. Checkout noon. AX, BA, DC.

Hilton Inn   1600 Richmond Road. (1⅞ miles northwest on Route 60.) 229–1134. 180 rooms, 2–3 stories. Single $18 up; Double $23 up. Pool. Restaurant 7 A.M.–midnight. Checkout noon. AX, BA, CB, DC, MC.

Holiday Inn–East   814 Capitol Landing Road at Parkway Drive. (1½ miles east on Routes 5, 31.) 229–0200. 136 rooms, 3 stories. Elevators. Single $18 up; Double $27 up. Pool. Restaurant 6 A.M.–10 P.M. Checkout noon. AX, BA, DC, G, MC.

Howard Johnson's   Richmond Road. (2 miles northwest on Route 60.) 229–2781. 77 rooms, 2 stories. Single $22 up; Double $24 up. Pool. Restaurant 7 A.M.–11 P.M. Checkout noon. AX, BA, CB, DC, E, MC, T.

Lord Paget Motor Inn   901 Capitol Landing Road. (1½ miles northeast on Routes 5, 31; 1 block west of Route 143.) 229–4444. 86 rooms, 1–2 stories. Single $16 up; Double $18 up. Pool. Snack bar, 6:30 A.M.–11 P.M. Checkout 11 A.M. AX, BA, DC, MC.

Minuet Manor   1408 Richmond Road. (1½ miles northwest on Route 60.) 229–2981. 80 rooms, 1–3 stories. Elevator. Single $14 up; Double $16 up. Pool. Restaurant 7 A.M.–2:30 P.M., 4:30–11 P.M. Checkout noon. AX, BA, CB, DC, MC.

Motor House   1 mile southeast of Route 64. (Opposite Information Center.) 229–1700. 314 rooms, 1–2 stories. Single $25 up; Double $28 up. Pool. Cafeteria, 7 A.M.–8 P.M.; Dining Room 7:30–10 A.M., noon–5 P.M., 6–9 P.M. Checkout noon.

Princess Anne Motor Lodge   1350 Richmond Road. (1¼ miles northwest on Route 60.) 229–2455. 72 rooms. Single $14 up; Double $16 up. Pool. Restaurant adjacent, 7 A.M.–9 P.M. Checkout noon. AX, BA, DC, MC.

Quality Inn Colony   Page Street. (1 mile east on Route 60 at junction of Route 162.) 229–1855. 59 rooms. Single $16 up; Double $18 up. Closed December–January. Pool. Snack bar, 6 A.M.–midnight. Checkout 11 A.M. AX, BA, DC, MC.

Quality Inn Francis Nicholson   1½ miles northwest on Route 60. 229–6270. 115 rooms, 2 stories. Single $20 up; Double $22 up. Pool. Restaurant 7 A.M.–2:30 P.M., 5:30–9:30 P.M. Checkout noon. AX, BA, DC, MC.

Quality Inn Mount Vernon Richmond Road. (2 miles north-west on Route 60.) 229–2401. 65 rooms, 1–2 stories. Single $20 up; Double $22 up. Pool. Restaurant adjacent, 7 A.M.–11 P.M. Checkout noon. AX, BA, CB, DC, MC.

Ramada Inn 3 miles northwest on Route 60W. 229–0260. 98 rooms, 2–3 stories. Elevator. Single $18 up; Double $20 up. Pool. Restaurant 7 A.M.–10 P.M. Checkout 11 A.M. AX, BA, CB, DC, E, MC.

Rochambeau 929 Capitol Landing Road. (1¾ miles north-east on Routes 5, 31 at junction of Route 143.) 229–2851. 21 rooms. Single $14 up; Double $16 up. Pool. Restaurant 1 block, 7 A.M.–10 P.M. Checkout 11 A.M. AX, BA.

Sheraton Motor Inn 506 North Henry Street. (5 blocks north on Route 132.) 229–6605. 72 rooms, 3 stories. Elevator. Single $18 up; Double $20 up. Pool. Restaurant 7–11 A.M., 6–10 P.M. Checkout noon. AX, BA, CB, DC, MC.

Tioga Motor Court 906 Richmond Road. 229–4531. 25 rooms. Single $12.50 up; Double $14.50 up. Pool. Restaurant adjacent, 7 A.M.–9 P.M. Checkout 11 A.M. AX, BA, MC.

White Lion 912 Capitol Landing Road. (1¾ miles north-east on Routes 5, 31 at junction of Route 143.) 229–3931. 40 rooms, 1–3 stories. Single $16 up; Double $17 up. Pool. Restaurant 2 blocks, 7 A.M.–10 P.M. Checkout 11 A.M. AX, BA.

Williamsburg Colony 1½ miles northwest on Route 60. 229–7600. 202 rooms, 2–3 stories. Double $25 up. Pool. Restaurant 7 A.M.–10 P.M. Checkout 1 P.M. AX, BA, DC, MC.

Williamsburg Inn Francis Street. 229–1500. 145 rooms in inn, 79 rooms in Colonial houses. Single $25 up; Double $32 up. Pools. Restaurant 7:30–10 A.M., noon–2 P.M., 6–8:30 P.M., 9:30–11 P.M. Checkout 2 P.M.

Williamsburg Lodge South England Street. 229–1600. 199 rooms, 2 stories. Single $25 up; Double $29 up. Pool. Restaurant 7 A.M.–11:30 P.M. Checkout 2 P.M.

YORKTOWN (*Area Code 804*)

Duke of York Ballard Street. (On Route 238, 1 block east of bridge, off Route 17.) 887–2331. 25 rooms, 2 stories. Single $14 up; Double $16 up. Pool. Restaurant ½ block, 7 A.M.–9 P.M. Checkout noon.

Tidewater 4 miles north of bridge on Route 17. 642–2155.

21 rooms. Single $10 up; Double 12 up. Restaurant adjacent, 6 A.M.–10 P.M. Checkout noon. AX, BA, CB, DC, MC.

Yorktown Motor Lodge   3½ miles south on Route 17. 898–5451. 42 rooms. Single $11 up; Double $12 up. Pool. Restaurant adjacent, 7 A.M.–10 P.M. Checkout 11 A.M. AX, BA, MC.

RICHMOND   (*Area Code 804*)

Econo-Travel   6523 Midlothian Turnpike. (6 miles southwest on Route 60.) 276–8241. 48 rooms, 2 stories. Single $7.50 up; Double $10 up. Restaurant adjacent, open 24 hours. Checkout noon.

Executive   5215 West Broad Street. (5¼ miles northwest on Route 250.) 288–4011. 142 rooms, 3 stories. Elevator. Single $15.50 up; Double $19.50 up. Pool. Restaurant 6:30 A.M.–10 P.M. Checkout 3 P.M. AX, BA, CB, DC, MC.

Hanover House   10 miles north at Route 95 Atlee-Elmont Exit. 798–6045. 52 rooms, 2 stories. Single 12 up; Double $16 up. Pool. Restaurant open 24 hours; Dining Room 9:30 A.M.–9:30 P.M. Checkout noon. AX, BA, CB, DC, MC.

Holiday Inn–Central   1501 Robin Hood Road. (3 blocks south of Route 95, Exit 14.) 359–4011. 156 rooms, 2 stories. Single $15 up; Double $18 up. Pool. Restaurant 6:30 A.M.–10:30 P.M. Checkout noon. AX, BA, DC, G, MC.

Holiday Inn–Crossroads   2002 Staples Mill Road. (2½ miles west on Route 33, 6 blocks south of Route 64.) 359–6061. 247 rooms, 8 stories. Elevator. Single $15.50 up; Double $17.50 up. Pool. Restaurant 6 A.M.–10 P.M. Checkout noon. AX, BA, DC, MC.

Holiday Inn–Downtown   Franklin and Madison Streets. (8 blocks west on Routes 33, 250; 10 blocks west of Route 95, Exit 10.) 644–9871. 234 rooms, 16 stories. Elevator. Single $16.50 up; Double $20.50 up. Pool. Restaurant 6 A.M.–5 P.M.; Dining Room 5–10 P.M. Checkout noon. AX, BA, DC, G, MC.

Holiday Inn–South   6346 Midlothian Turnpike. (6 miles southwest on Route 60.) 276–6450. 167 rooms, 2 stories. Single $14.50 up; Double $18 up. Pool. Restaurant 6:30 A.M.–10:30 P.M. Checkout 1 P.M. AX, BA, DC, G, MC.

Holiday Inn–West   3200 West Broad Street. (2 miles northwest on Route 250, 1 mile south of Route 95, Exit 14.) 359–

4061. 200 rooms, 6 stories. Elevator. Single $16.50 up; Double $19.50 up. Pool. Restaurant 6 A.M.–10 P.M.; Dining Room 5 P.M.–midnight, Sunday 7 A.M.–10 P.M. Checkout noon. AX, BA, DC, G, MC.

Howard Johnson's–North 5½ miles north on Route 1 at Route 95, Parham Road Exit. 266–8753. 82 rooms, 2 stories. Elevator. Single $17 up; Double $24 up. Pool. Restaurant 6 A.M.–11 P.M. Checkout noon. AX, BA, DC, E, MC, T.

Jefferson Hotel Jefferson and Main Streets. (9 blocks southwest of Route 95, Exit 13.) 643–3411. 330 rooms. Single $12.50 up; Double $17.50 up. Restaurant 7–10.45 A.M., noon–2:30 P.M., 6–9 P.M. Checkout 2 P.M. BA, MC.

Lemon Tree Inn 2301 Willis Road. (2 blocks southeast of Routes 1, 301 at Route 95 Exit 6A.) 275–1408. 52 rooms. Single $12.25 up; Double $16.25 up. Pool. Restaurant 6 A.M.–10 P.M. Checkout noon. AX, BA, CB, DC, MC.

John Marshall Hotel Franklin and 5th Streets. (5 blocks south of Route 95, Exit 11.) 644–4661. 464 rooms, 12 stories. Elevator. Single $21 up; Double $27 up. Restaurant 7 A.M.–3 P.M.; Dining Room noon–11:30 P.M. Checkout 2 P.M. AX, BA, DC, MC.

Martha Kay 8811 Jefferson Davis Highway. (9 miles south on Routes 1, 301, ½ mile northwest of Route 95, Exit 6A.) 275–1421. 26 rooms. Single $12 up; Double $14 up. Pool. Restaurant adjacent, 7 A.M.–10 P.M. Checkout 11 A.M. AX, BA, CB, DC, MC, M.

Quality Inn Intown 1600 Robin Hood Road. (3 miles northwest on Route 95, Exit 14.) 353–1287. 103 rooms, 3 stories. Elevator. Single $16 up; Double $18 up. Pool. Restaurant 7 A.M.–10 P.M. Checkout noon. AX, BA, DC, MC.

Quality Inn Princess Lee 6 miles north on Route 1, ½ mile north of Route 95, Parham Road Exit. 266–2444. 64 rooms. Single $14 up; Double $18 up. Pool. Restaurant 7 A.M.–9 P.M. Checkout noon. AX, BA, DC, MC.

Red Carpet Inn 2302 Willis Road. (1 block east of Routes 1, 301 at Route 95, Exit 6A.) 275–1412. 70 rooms. Single $11 up; Double $14 up. Pool. Restaurant 6:30 P.M.–10 P.M. Checkout noon. AX, BA, CB, DC, MC.

Sheraton Motor Inn Franklin and Belvidere Streets (½ mile southwest of Route 95, Exit 13.) 643–2831. 194 rooms.

Single $16 up; Double $22 up. Pool. Restaurant 6:30 A.M.–10 P.M. Checkout noon. AX, BA, CB, DC, MC.

Virginia Inn   5700 Chamberlayne Road. (5 miles north on Route 301 at Route 95, Exit 17.) 266–7616. 200 rooms, 2 stories. Single $13.50 up; Double $16.50 up. Pool. Restaurant 7 A.M.–3 P.M.; Dining Room 3–11 P.M., Friday, Saturday to 1 A.M. Checkout noon. AX, BA, CB, DC, MC.

White House Motor Lodge   9401 Jefferson Davis Highway. (9 miles south on Route 301.) 275–2616. 50 rooms. Single $10 up; Double $12 up. Pool. Restaurant ½ mile, 7 A.M.–10 P.M. Checkout 11 A.M. AX, BA, CB, DC, MC.

CHARLOTTESVILLE   (*Area Code 804*)

Boar's Head Inn   Ivy Road. (4 miles west on Route 250, 2 miles west of junction Route 29.) 296–2181. 103 rooms. Single $20 up; Double $24 up. Pool. Restaurant 7:30–11 A.M., noon–2 P.M., 6–9:30 P.M. Checkout 2 P.M. AX, DC.

Cardinal   2 miles north on Route 29, 1 block north of Route 250. 293–6188. 22 rooms. Single $10 up; Double $14 up. Pool. Restaurant adjacent, 6 A.M.–9 P.M. Checkout 11 A.M. AX, CB, DC, MC, M.

Downtowner   2 miles west at junction of Routes 29, 250. 296–8111. 120 rooms, 5 stories. Elevator. Single $12 up; Double $15 up. Pool. Restaurant 7 A.M.–11 P.M. Checkout 1 P.M. AX, BA, CB, DC, MC.

Econo-Travel   2014 Holiday Drive. (2 miles north on Route 29 at junction Route 250.) 295–3185. 48 rooms, 2 stories. Single $7.50 up; Double $10 up. Restaurant adjacent, 7 A.M.–midnight. Checkout 11 A.M.

Executive Plaza   400 Emmett Street. (2 miles north on Route 29, 2 blocks north of Route 250.) 296–2104. 61 rooms, 2 stories. Single $12 up; Double $15 up. Pool. Restaurant 7 A.M.–10 P.M. Checkout 11 A.M. AX, BA, DC, MC.

Holiday Inn   2 miles north on Route 29 at junction of Route 250. 293–9111. 205 rooms, 2–3 stories. Elevator. Single $12 up; Double $16 up. Pool. Restaurant 6 A.M.–10:30 P.M. Checkout 1 P.M. AX, BA, DC, G, MC.

Howard Johnson's   13th and West Main Streets. (10 blocks west on Route 250E.) 296–8121. 126 rooms, 9 stories. Elevator.

Single $12.50 up; Double $18 up. Pool. Restaurant 7 A.M.– 11 P.M. Checkout noon. AX, BA, DC, E, MC, T.

FREDERICKSBURG   (*Area Code 703*)

George Washington   1320 Jefferson Davis Boulevard. (1¼ miles west on Route 1A, ¾ mile south of junction Routes 1, 17.) 373–5066. 35 rooms, 1–2 stories. Single $8 up; Double $10 up. Pool. Restaurant 3 blocks, 7 A.M.–11:30 P.M. Checkout 11 A.M. AX, BA, CB, DC, MC, M.

Holiday Inn   4 miles south at junction of Routes 1 and 95. 373–1102. 200 rooms, 2 stories. Single $12 up; Double $17 up. Pool. Restaurant 6 A.M.–10 P.M. Checkout noon. AX, BA, DC, G, MC.

Horne's   4 miles south at junction of Routes 1 and 95. 371–2800. 155 rooms, 2 stories. Single $10 up; Double $15 up. Pool. Restaurant 6 A.M.–10 P.M. Checkout noon. AX, BA, CB, DC, MC.

Howard Johnson's   5 miles south on Route 1, 4 blocks north of junction of Route 95. 371–1800. 140 rooms, 4 stories. Elevator. Single $13 up; Double $19 up. Pool. Restaurant 6:30 A.M.–midnight. Checkout noon. AX, BA, DC, E, MC, T.

Kaywood   3 miles northwest of Route 1 on Route 17, 2 blocks west of Route 95, Falmouth-Fredericksburg Exit. 373–0000. 87 rooms, 2 stories. Single $10 up; Double $13 up. Pool. Restaurant 6:30 A.M.–10 P.M. Checkout noon. AX, BA, CB, DC, MC.

Ramada Inn   3 miles west on Route 3 at junction of Route 95, Culpeper Exit. 786–8361. 130 rooms, 2 stories. Single $13 up; Double $17 up. Pool. Restaurant 6 A.M.–10 P.M. Checkout 1 P.M. AX, BA, CB, DC, E, MC.

Sheraton Motor Inn   3 miles west on Route 3 at junction of Route 95, Culpeper Exit. 786–8321. 200 rooms, 3 stories. Elevator. Single $15 up; Double $22 up. Pool. Restaurant 7 A.M.–10 P.M. Checkout 1 P.M. AX, BA, CB, DC, MC.

Twi-Lite   1209 Snowden Street. (1 mile south of Routes 1, 17.) 373–3510. 18 rooms, 2 stories. Single $11 up; Double $13 up. Restaurant adjacent, 6:30 A.M.–11 P.M. Checkout noon. AX, MC, M.

ALEXANDRIA   (*Area Code 703*)

Charter House   6461 Edsall Road. (5½ miles west at junction Routes 648, 95; 1 mile north of Route 495.) 354–4400. 213 rooms, 2–5 stories. Elevator. Single $16 up; Double $19 up. Pool. Restaurant 7 A.M.–10:30 P.M. Checkout noon. AX, BA, DC, MC.

Holiday Inn   6100 Richmond Highway. (2 miles south on Route 1, 1 mile south of Route 495, Exit 1S.) 765–0500. 108 rooms, 3 stories. Elevator. Single $14.50 up; Double $19.50 up. Pool. Restaurant 6 A.M.–10 P.M. Checkout noon. AX, BA, DC, G, MC.

Holiday Inn   2460 Eisenhower Drive. (Just off Route 495, Exit 2N.) 960–3400. 204 rooms, 10 stories. Elevator. Single $17.50 up; Double $20.75 up. Pool. Restaurant 6 A.M.–10 P.M. Checkout noon. AX, BA, DC, G, MC.

Howard Johnson's   5821 Richmond Highway. (Just off Route 495, Exit 1S.) 768–3300. 154 rooms, 7 stories. Elevator. Single $18 up; Double $24 up. Pool. Restaurant 6:30 A.M.–midnight. Checkout noon. AX, DC, E, MC, T.

Mt. Vee   8173 Richmond Highway. (6 miles south on Route 1.) 780–5290. 37 rooms, 1–2 stories. Single $12 up; Double $16 up. Pool. Restaurant 1 mile, 7 A.M.–midnight. Checkout 11:30 A.M. AX, BA, CB, DC, MC, M.

Quality Inn Olde Colony   First and North Washington Streets. (18 blocks north of Route 495, Exits 1E, 1N.) 548–6300. 151 rooms, 2 stories. Single $17 up; Double $21 up. Pool. Restaurant opposite, 7 A.M.–midnight. Checkout noon. AX, BA, DC, MC.

Towne   808 North Washington Street. (8 blocks north on Route 1A, 1 mile north of Route 495, Exit 1.) 548–3500. 25 rooms, 2 stories. Single $18 up; Double $20 up. Restaurant adjacent, open 24 hours. Checkout 11 A.M. AX, BA, DC, MC.

Travelers   5916 Richmond Highway. (1½ miles south on Route 1 at Route 495.) 768–2510. 30 rooms, 1 story. Single $17 up; Double $20 up. Pool. Restaurant 2 blocks, 6:30 A.M.–midnight. Checkout 11 A.M. AX, BA, CB, MC, M.

Wagon Wheel   7212 Richmond Highway. (4 miles south on Route 1, 2½ miles south of Route 495, Exit 1S.) 765–9000. 130 rooms, 1–2 stories. Single $13 up; Double $17 up. Pool.

Restaurant 7 A.M.–2 P.M., 5–10 P.M., Sunday 7 A.M.–1 P.M. Checkout noon. AX, BA, CB, DC, MC.

Thanks are due to the many regional Visitors' Centers and Chambers of Commerce for the motel and hotel information in this section.

Car Rentals

Rates vary from area to area and depend on the size of the car you require. Besides the standard daily rates—which range from approximately $11 to $24 plus a mileage charge—most companies have special weekly and weekend rates. Modest insurance fees are sometimes charged. Customers usually pay for the gasoline. Major credit cards are honored by the companies listed below.

Travelers who wish further information or need reservations for automobile rentals may use the following toll-free numbers:

AMERICAN INTERNATIONAL RENT-A-CAR	800–527–6346
AVIS RENT-A-CAR	800–231–6000
BUDGET RENT-A-CAR	800–228–9650
ECONO-CAR RENTAL	800–874–5000
HERTZ RENT-A-CAR	800–654–3131
NATIONAL RENT-A-CAR	800–328–4567
THRIFTY RENT-A-CAR	800–331–4200

(*Note:* In some areas it may be necessary to dial the digit 1 before 800.)

If you wish to contact a local office of any of the above car rental agencies, consult an appropriate telephone directory of the region.

Information for International Visitors

"Visit U.S.A." Program

Under the "Visit U.S.A." Program international travelers are entitled to transportation discounts. Visitors are advised to contact travel agents abroad, preferably in their country of residence. Completing arrangements before arriving in the United States will simplify procedures. An international traveler is one who lives more than 100 miles from the United States border and who arrives by commercial ship or airplane. All the information discussed below is subject to change. The prices quoted were in effect during 1974–1975 and are expected to rise.

Airplanes Several domestic airlines (including American, Braniff, Continental, Delta, Eastern, National, Northwest, TWA, and United) offer 25 percent discount on first-class and standard air fares within the forty-eight contiguous states providing the traveler remains in the U.S. thirteen to forty-five days. A twenty-one-day unlimited air travel ticket permits international visitors to take an unlimited number of flights on the combined routes of nine regional airlines. (Fare applies only when two or more transportation carriers are participating in this special program.) The cost for the twenty-one-day ticket is $200 plus $16 tax. For passengers two through twenty-one years old who are accompanied by parents or guardians, the price is $100 plus $8 tax.

The baggage allowance is usually sixty-six pounds. If a discount ticket is purchased in the United States, strict time requirements govern the period of purchase and use.

Trains An Amerail Discount of 25 percent is offered

to international travelers (except those from Canada and Mexico) who purchase train tickets from Amtrak-appointed travel agents overseas or from Amtrak representatives in the United States. Tickets are limited to sixty days from date of sale. This program does not apply to Metro-Liner service (a special commuter train) between Boston–New Haven–New York–Washington, although discount tickets are accepted on other trains along this route. Discounts are not granted for sleeper or parlor car accommodations.

Buses   A "See the U.S.A." bus fare is offered by the Greyhound Bus Company and the Continental Trailways Bus Company. (Buses are equipped with small rest rooms and air conditioning.) International visitors are permitted unlimited travel and stopover privileges. The price is $99 for fifteen days (only when ticket is purchased overseas), $165 for one month, and $220 for two months.

Car Rentals   Several automobile rental companies have special "packages" for persons from other countries who are over twenty-one years old and present appropriate credentials (including a certified driver's license).

Hertz Rent-A-Car offers several plans. A one-day rental for a Ford Pinto (or similar car) costs $8.59 plus a mileage charge. Customers must pay for the gasoline and must return the car to the city of origination. The Weekend or Holiday Plans cost $11.47 per day plus a mileage charge and gasoline. Discount rates on the Weekend Plan require a minimum two-day rental; discount rates on the Holiday Plan require a minimum seven-day rental. Hertz has other discount programs available and also extends a 10 percent discount to visitors from countries outside the Western Hemisphere (which does not apply to the special rates listed above).

National Rent-A-Car has a "See the U.S.A." discount for persons who make reservations prior to arrival in America. The "Circle Tour" Plan, which costs $108, permits a seven- or eight-day rental of a Chevrolet Vega (or similar car) with 1,000 free miles. For each day extra there is an added charge of $16. Customers wishing a larger car, such as a Chevrolet Impala, may take advantage of the "Vacation Special" Discount—$118 for a seven- or eight-day rental with 1,000 free miles. These discount prices are available only in the following cities: Atlanta, Boston, Chicago, Dallas, Miami, Minneapolis, New York, Orlando, Los Angeles, Philadelphia, Portland, San Francisco, Seattle, and Washington, D.C.

Budget Rent-A-Car has Chevrolet Vegas (or similar cars) at $11.95 a day and no mileage charge. Customers are expected to pay for gasoline. Larger automobiles are also available at special rates.

Travelers are advised to verify all rates and requirements before signing any agreements. The author and the publisher cannot be responsible for changes in programs or errors in information—nor for prices, procedures, accommodations, or services.

Aid for Travelers

The United States Travel Service (Washington, D.C., 202–967–3195) has instituted a program of placing multilingual receptionists at major United States airports. These receptionists are presently on duty in New York (Kennedy Airport), Seattle, Philadelphia, Boston, Bangor, and Washington, D.C. (Dulles International Airport). By 1976 similar services will exist in Los Angeles and San Francisco. These multilingual information specialists are usually located at Information Booths near customs desks or currency exchange centers.

Offices of the Travelers' Aid Society—an organization devoted to assisting visitors—are located throughout the United States. Listed below are offices in the South:

COLUMBIA, SOUTH CAROLINA.	1845 Assembly Street, (803) 779-3250.
SPARTANBURG, SOUTH CAROLINA.	168 Oakland Avenue, (803) 582-5590.
GREENSBORO, NORTH CAROLINA.	1301 North Elm Street, (919) 273-3691.
CHARLOTTE, NORTH CAROLINA.	301 South Brevard Street, (704) 372-7170.
RALEIGH, NORTH CAROLINA.	1330 St. Mary's Street, (919) 834-6264.
WILMINGTON, NORTH CAROLINA.	201 North Front Street, (919) 763-5189 or (919) 763-7239.
NORFOLK, VIRGINIA.	1309 Granby Street, (804) 622-7017 or (804) 399-6393.
RICHMOND, VIRGINIA.	515 East Main Street, (804) 643-0279 or (804) 648-1767.
ALEXANDRIA AREA, VIRGINIA.	Washington National Airport, (703) 684-3472; Dulles International Airport, (703) 661-8836.

(*Note:* Dial the area code, the number in parentheses, only when you are located outside the region or state.)

The National Council for Community Services to International Visitors (referred to as COSERV) operates a program for the benefit of businessmen and persons in government service who are traveling in America. COSERV staffs help schedule appointments, conferences, and consultations as well as arrange sightseeing tours. International visitors requesting assistance must notify COSERV at least forty-eight hours in advance, carry health and accident insurance during travel, be short-term visitors in the community, and require no financial aid. Travelers with the appropriate credentials may contact the following offices located in the South:

COLUMBIA, SOUTH CAROLINA.	Columbia Council for Internationals, (803) 256-1445 or (803) 252-1850.
ATLANTA, GEORGIA.	Atlanta Council for International Visitors, (404) 577-2248.
NORFOLK—VIRGINIA BEACH, VIRGINIA.	Committee for International Visitors, (804) 481-0814.

More information may be obtained by writing the National Council for Community Services to International Visitors, 1630 Crescent Place N.W., Washington, D.C. 20009.

Another excellent program for overseas travelers has been established by the International Visitors Service Council (referred to as IVIS), which provides general information and arranges home hospitality for visitors to the Washington, D.C. area. Anyone who wishes to meet Americans in their homes (the "Americans at Home" Program) must file an application and appear for a personal meeting at the International Visitors Service Council, 801 19th Street N.W., Washington, D.C. IVIS also has bilingual volunteers available for assistance at international conferences. To learn more about these programs, telephone (202) 872-8747.

Home hospitality is also arranged by the U.S. SERVAS Committee, P.O. Box 790, Old Chelsea Station, New York, New York 10011. Persons wishing to meet Americans in their homes must submit an application and appear for an interview. SERVAS suggests a $25 donation for their services.

Travelers under the age of thirty may wish to take advantage of the series of newly created Vacation Accommodations Centers sponsored by the British Student Travel Center. Approximately twenty centers are operational in New York, Chicago, San Francisco, and Washington, D.C. Several affiliate hotels across the United States are also participating in the program. The rates for rooms are quite reasonable. For information and an application for a VAC Card contact Vacation Accommodations Centers, 700 Eighth Avenue, New York, New York 10036, or phone (212) 354–1210. Since this program is still in its infancy, accommodations are limited.

International travelers who need general information or assistance may also phone from 7 A.M. to 11 P.M. a toll-free number, 800–255–3050. Ask to speak to one of the multilingual receptionists (French, German, Spanish, and Japanese) at the U.S.A. Desk. This service is provided by TraveLodge.

Visitors from abroad may find the staffs of local American Express offices very helpful. Government tourist agencies, of course, also specialize in aiding travelers. The following offices are all located in New York City.

AUSTRIAN NATIONAL TOURIST OFFICE.	545 Fifth Avenue, (212) 697–0651.
BRITISH TOURIST AUTHORITY.	680 Fifth Avenue, (212) 581–4700.
CANADIAN GOVERNMENT TRAVEL BUREAU.	680 Fifth Avenue, (212) 757–4917.
FINNISH NATIONAL TRAVEL OFFICE.	505 Fifth Avenue, (212) 524–0763.
FRENCH GOVERNMENT TOURIST OFFICE.	610 Fifth Avenue, (212) 757–1125.

GERMAN NATIONAL TOURIST OFFICE.	630 Fifth Avenue, (212) 757–8570.
GREEK NATIONAL TOURIST OFFICE.	601 Fifth Avenue, (212) 421–5777.
INDIA GOVERNMENT TOURIST OFFICE.	19 East 49th Street, (212) 688–2245.
IRAN NATIONAL TOURIST OFFICE.	630 Fifth Avenue, (212) 757–1945.
IRISH TOURIST BOARD.	590 Fifth Avenue, (212) 246–7400.
ISRAEL GOVERNMENT TOURIST OFFICE.	488 Madison Avenue, (212) 593–1685.
ITALIAN GOVERNMENT TRAVEL OFFICE.	630 Fifth Avenue, (212) 245–4822.
JAPAN NATIONAL TOURIST ORGANIZATION.	45 Rockefeller Plaza, (212) 757–5640.
NETHERLANDS NATIONAL TOURIST OFFICE.	576 Fifth Avenue, (212) 245–5320.
PUERTO RICO GOVERNMENT TOURIST CENTER.	8 West 51st Street, (212) 245–8512.
SCANDINAVIA NATIONAL TOURIST OFFICE.	505 Fifth Avenue, (212) 687–5605.
SPANISH NATIONAL TOURIST OFFICE.	589 Fifth Avenue, (212) 759–3842.
SWISS NATIONAL TOURIST OFFICE.	608 Fifth Avenue, (212) 757–5944.

(*Note:* When calling from New York City, do not dial the area code 212.)

Anyone encountering serious difficulties should contact a nearby consulate or an embassy in Washington, D.C.

Miscellaneous Information

To find the telephone number of a person or an institution in a distant region of the United States, dial the area code, then 555–1212. Ask the operator for the information you need, then dial the call directly. Area codes of major cities are listed below.

ATLANTA	404	MILWAUKFE	414
BOSTON	617	MINNEAPOLIS	612
CHARLESTON	803	NEW ORLEANS	504
CHICAGO	312	NEW YORK	212
CLEVELAND	216	OMAHA	402
DALLAS	214	PHILADELPHIA	215
DETROIT	313	ST. LOUIS	314
HOUSTON	713	SAN FRANCISCO	415
LOS ANGELES	213	SEATTLE	206
MIAMI	305	WASHINGTON, D.C.	202

Shoppers who plan to purchase clothing in the United States should be aware of the differences in designating sizes.

WOMEN'S SWEATERS AND BLOUSES

Continent	U.S. / England
38	32
40	34
42	36
44	38
46	40
48	42

WOMEN'S DRESSES AND SUITS

Continent	U.S.	England
42	12	34
44	14	36
46	16	38
48	18	40
50	20	42

WOMEN'S SHOES

Continent	U.S. / England
36	4
37	5
38	6
39	7
40	8

MEN'S SHIRTS

Continent	U.S. / England
36	14
37	14½
38	15
39	15½
41	16
42	16½

MEN'S SUITS

Continent	U.S. / England
44	34
46	36
48	38
50	40
52	42
54	44

MEN'S SHOES

Continent	U.S. / England
39	7
40	8
41	9
42	10
43	11
44	12

Anyone driving an automobile in the United States should be familiar with the following measurement equivalents.

DISTANCE

Kilometers	Miles
1	⅝
2	1¼
3	1⅞
4	2½
5	3⅛
10	6¼

GASOLINE

Liters	Imperial (Brit.) Gallons	U.S. Gallons
1	0.22	0.26
5	1.10	1.32
10	2.20	2.64
20	4.40	5.28

Enjoy your visit here and return soon!

Index

Abercrombie, Lieutenant
    Colonel, 182–83
Adams, John, 217, 245
Agnes of Glasgow, 60
Aitken, John, 260
Aitken, Robert Ingersol, 220
Alamance, Battle of, 98–103
Alexander, Isaac, 61
Alexander, John, 239
Alexander, Margaret, 72
Alexandria, Virginia, 239–57
    Colonial and Revolutionary
        War sites, 241–51
        Carlyle House, 241
        Christ Church, 242
        Friendship Fire Com-
            pany, 242–43
        Gadsby Tavern, 243–45
        Henry Lee House, 245–46
        Presbyterian Meeting
            House, 246–47
        Ramsay House, 247–48
        Stabler-Leadbeater
            Apothecary Shop and
            Museum, 248–49
        Washington (George)
            Masonic National
            Memorial, 250–51
    colonial houses, 251–52
        Brown House, 251
        Captain's Row, 251
        Craik House, 251
        Dick House, 251–52
        Gilpin House, 252
        Lafayette House, 252

    motels, hotels, and inns,
        290–91
    Revolutionary War history,
        239, 241
    side trips, recommended,
        252–57
        Arlington, 252–55
        Gunston Hall, 255–56
        Woodlawn Plantation,
            256–57
    taxi service, 240
    transportation, public, 240
    Visitors' Center, 240
    Walking tour, 240
Allen, Amy. See Husband,
    Amy Allen
Allen, John, 100
Allston, Benjamin, 45
Allston, Washington, 29
Alston, Joseph, 24
Alston, Robert F. W., 32
Alston, Theodosia Burr, 24
Ambler, Richard, 189
Anderson, Robert, 37, 38
Anne, Queen of England, 140
Arbuthnot, Marriot, 3, 36
Archer, Abraham, 189
Area codes, telephone, of
        major U. S. cities, 300
Ariss, John, 224
Arlington, Virginia, 252–55
Arlington National Cemetery
        (Virginia), 253–55
Arnold, Benedict, 198

Arthur, Chester A., 192
Aust, Gottfried, 113

Bacon, Nathanael, 161, 193
Baker, Bryant, 250
Ball, Mary. *See* Washington,
    Mary Ball
Barclay, Captain, 119
Barclay, James T., 215
Barker, Penelope, 148, 150,
    153
Barker, Thomas, 150
Barras, Admiral de, 187
Barry, Kate Moore, 82, 83
Bassett, Fanny, 261
Bee, Thomas, 24
Bell, Philip, 261
Bennett, Lydia, 157
Bennett, William, 157
Benzien, Ludwig, 106
Berkeley, Norborne, 170
Bethea, Lieutenant Governor
    (South Carolina), 94
Binon, J. B., 217
Blair, Jean, 148
Blair, John, 268
Blake, Daniel, 27
Bland, Richard, 268
Blount, William, 268
Blum, Jacob, 110
Boney, James, 125
Bonn, Jacob, 104
Bonnet, Stede, 9–10, 23
Boone, John, 33
Boone Hall Plantation (South
    Carolina), 33
Booth, Edwin, 8
Booth, Junius Brutus, 8
Botetourt, Baron de, 170, 174,
    225
Boyd, John, 72

Braddock, Edward, 226, 241,
    243
Bratton, Christina Winn, 64
Bratton, William, 64
Braxton, Carter, 268
Bretigny, Marquis de, 91
Brewton, Miles, 25
Brooke, John Mercer, 23
Brooke, Robert, 228
Brown, Gustavus, 263
Brown, John, 249
Brown, William, 251
Brumidi, Constantino, 183
Brunswick Town (North
    Carolina), 126–31
  Revolutionary War history,
    126–27
  sites of interest, 128–31
  Visitors' Center, 127
Brush, John, 165
Bryan, William Jennings, 254
Buchanan, James, 38, 211
Buchanan, John, 65
Buckland, William, 256
Burgwin, George, 119
Burgwin, John, 121
Burke, Thomas, 116–17
Burling, Thomas, 144
Burnside, Ambrose, 233–34
Burr, Aaron, 24, 201, 203, 209,
    241, 245
Burr, Theodosia. *See* Alston,
    Theodosia Burr
Burroughs, Silas E., 231
Burwell, Carter, 179
Butler, Jane. *See* Washington,
    Jane Butler
Butler, Pierre, 267
Butler, William, 115
Byrd, William, II, 198

Calhoun, John C., 16, 20, 24, 248
Call, Daniel, 206
Camden, South Carolina, 52–68
  Colonial and Revolutionary War Sites, 54–62
    Bethesda Presbyterian Church and De Kalb Monument, 54–55, 56
    Camden battlefield site, 55–56
    Central Square, 62
    Historic Camden, 56–59, 60, 61, 62
    Hobkirk's Hill battle site, 59
    Quaker Cemetery, 59–61
    Revolutionary War jail site, 62
  colonial houses, 61–62
    Blue House site, 61
    Carter-Lafayette House site, 61
    Washington House, 62
  motels, hotels, and inns, 276
  non-Revolutionary sites of interest, 62–63
    Confederate Generals' Memorial (The Pantheon), 62–63
    Confederate Monument, 63
    King Haiglar Weather Vane, 63
    Springdale Race Course, 63
  Revolutionary War history, 54
  side trips, recommended, 64–68
    Ninety-Six, 65–68
    Winnsboro, 64–65
  taxi service, 54
  transportation, public, 54
  Visitors' Center, 54
Campbell, Sally Izard, 26
Campbell, William, 11, 26, 27, 66, 69, 70, 72
Cantey, James, 63
Cantey, Zachariah, 58
Car rentals, 292, 294–95
Cardy, Samuel, 18
Carlyle, John, 239, 241, 246, 247
Carlyle, Sarah Fairfax, 241
Carter, Anne Hill. *See* Lee, Anne Carter
Carter, Elizabeth Hill, 211
Carter, John, 61, 211
Carter, Robert ("King"), 179, 211
Carter's Grove Plantation (Virginia), 179
Cary, Henry, 166, 170, 174, 205
Caswell, Richard, 133, 135, 138, 267
Chancellorsville, Battle of, 233, 234
Charles Towne Landing Park (South Carolina), 34–35
Charles II, King of England, 152
Charleston, South Carolina, 3–42
  Colonial and Revolutionary War Sites, 7–23
    Dock Street Theater, 7–8, 9
    Elfe House, 8

Charleston, South Carolina
(*Cont.*)
    Exchange Building and
       Provost Dungeon, 8–12
    Heyward-Washington
       House, 12–16
    Marion Square, 16–17
    Powder Magazine, 17–18
    St. Michael's Church,
       18–19
    St. Philip's Church, 19–
       20, 21
    Unitarian Church, 20, 22
    Washington Square, 22
    White Point Gardens
       (The Battery), 22–23
  colonial houses, 24–28
    Bee House, 24
    Brewton House, 25
    British Staff Quarters, 25
    Gibbes House, 25
    Izard House, 25–26
    Pink House, The, 26
    Rainbow Row, 26
    Ramsay House, 26–27
    Royal Governor's Resi-
       dence (Daniel Huger
       House), 27
    Rutledge House, 27
    Washington House, 27–
       28
  guided tours, 4–5
  motels, hotels, and inns,
    274–275
  non-Revolutionary sites of
    interest, 28–33
  walking tours, 5–6
    Cabbage Row, 28
    Charleston Museum, The,
      28
    City Hall, 28–29
    Gibbes Art Gallery, 29

    Huguenot Church, 29–30
    Hunley Museum, 30
    Kahal Kadosh Beth
      Elohim, 30
    Manigault House, 30–31
    Market Hall, 31
    Old Slave Market, 31–32
    Russell House, 32
    United States Naval Base,
      32–33
  Revolutionary War history,
    3–4
  side trips, recommended,
    33–42
    Boone Hall Plantation, 33
    Charles Towne Landing
      Park, 34–35
    Fort Moultrie, 36–37, 38
    Fort Sumter, 37–40
    Magnolia Gardens, 40–41
    Middleton Place Gardens,
      41–42
    Sullivan's Island, 35–37
  taxi service, 5
  transportation, public, 5
  Visitors' Center, 4
  walking tours, 5–6
Charlotte, Queen of England,
    140, 171
Charlottesville, Virginia,
    212–20
  Ash Lawn, 217–18, 219
  downtown, 219–20
    George Rogers Clark
      Memorial, 219–20
    Lewis and Clark
      Memorial, 220
    University of Virginia,
      220
  Michie Tavern, 218–19
  Monticello, 213–17

motels, hotels, and inns,
    288–89
Revolutionary War history,
    212–13
Charlton, Abigail, 148, 157
Charlton, Jasper, 157
Chestnut, James, 62
Chevallié, Jean-Auguste-
    Marie, 206
Childs, Thomas, 157
Christ, Rudolf, 113
Chronicle, William, 69, 72
Clark, George Rogers, 220
Clark, William, 220
Clay, Charles, 140
Clay, Henry, 178
Cleveland, Grover, 231–32
Clinton, Henry, 3, 4, 25, 127,
    181, 183, 186
Clothing, equivalent sizes in
    Europe and the U. S.,
    300–302
Coffin, John, 48
Cogdell, Ann. *See* Stanly,
    Ann Cogdell
Coker, Thomas, 26
Coles, Colonel, 215
Colonial Dames of America,
    122, 194, 205
Connelly, Henry, 122
Conrad, Judge, 94
Cook, Thomas, 174
Cook, William, 124
Corbett, Harvey Wiley, 249
Corbin, Francis, 152
Cornwallis, Charles, 18, 25,
    41, 53, 57, 64, 69, 75,
    87, 88, 104–105, 116,
    117, 119, 120, 121,
    123, 180–84, 186, 188,
    190, 191, 193, 199,
    205, 210, 212

Couper, William, 195
Cowpens, Battle of, 75–78,
    79, 82, 87, 96
Cox, Allyn, 250
Craig, Adam, 205
Craig, H., 119, 120
Craik, James, 247, 248, 251,
    252, 262–63
Craven, John, 58
Crawford, Thomas, 202
Creacy, Elizabeth, 148
Cunningham, William
    ("Bloody Bill"), 83
Currie, North Carolina,
    132–37
Custis, Ann. *See* Lee, Ann
    Custis
Custis, George Washington
    Parke, 242, 249, 253,
    254
Custis, Martha Dandridge.
    See Washington,
    Martha
Custis, Martha Parke. *See*
    Peter, Martha Custis
Custis, Nellie. *See* Lewis,
    Nellie Custis

Dade, Townsend, 242
Daughters of the American
    Revolution, 12, 50, 65,
    78, 98, 155
Daves, Edward, 94
Davis, Jefferson, 206, 207, 208
Davis, Justina. *See* Russell,
    Justina Davis
Deane, Silas, 151
Deas, Zack C., 63
De Kalb, Johann, 52, 53, 54,
    55, 56, 61, 244
De la Warr, Lord, 192
Deux Ponts, Guillaume de, 182

Dick, Charles, 232
Dick, Elisha Cullen, 251–52,
    263
Dickinson, Samuel, 152, 153,
    154
Digges, Dudley, 190
Dinwiddie, Robert, 170, 177
Dobbs, Arthur, 121, 122, 130,
    131, 146
Doolittle, Amos, 217
Doubleday, Abner, 40
Drakeford, Richard, 57
Drayton, John, 41
Drayton, William, 41
Drayton, William Henry, 40–
    41
Dry, William, 130
Drysdale, Hugh, 170
Dudley, Edward Bishop, 125
Duesbury, William, 145
Dulles, John Foster, 254
Dundas, Thomas, 186
Dunmore, Lord. *See* Murray,
    John

Eddy, Mary Baker, 123
Eden, Charles, 156
Edenton, North Carolina,
    148–57
  Colonial and Revolutionary
    War Sites, 150–56
    Barker House, 150
    Chowan County Court-
      house, 150–51, 153
    Chowan County Jail, 151
    Courthouse Green, 151,
      152
    Cupola House, 151–54
    Iredell House, 154–55
    St. Paul's Episcopal
      Church, 155–56

colonial houses, 157–58
  Charlton House, 157
  Leigh-Bennett House,
    157
  Millen House, 157
  Paxton-McCulloch House,
    157
  Pembroke Hall, 157–58
  Wessington-Everard
    House, 158
guided tour, 149
motels, hotels, and inns, 283
Revolutionary War history,
  148–50
Visitors' Center, 149
Elfe, Thomas, 8, 16, 30
Elliott, Jane. *See* Washington,
  Jane Elliott
Eskridge, George, 236
Espry, James, 128
Eutaw Springs battlefield
  site, 48–51
Everard, Sir Richard, 158
Everard, Thomas, 165

Fairfax, Sarah. *See* Carlyle,
  Sarah Fairfax
Fairfax, William, 241
Fanning, David, 116
Fanning, Edmund, 99, 115,
  117
Fauquier, Francis, 170
Ferguson, Patrick, 69–70,
  72–74
Fitzhugh, William, 246
Fort Holmes (South Caro-
  lina), 65, 66, 68
Fort Moultrie (South Caro-
  lina), 36–37, 38
Fort Sumter National Monu-

ment (South Carolina),
37–40
Fort Watson (South Caro-
lina), 50–51
Fortune, Pompey, 65
Francisco, Peter, 91, 92, 204
Franklin, Benjamin, 16, 151,
232, 244, 250, 261
Franklin, Jesse, 98
Fraser, Charles, 29
Frederick Louis, Prince of
Wales, 221
Fredericksburg, Battle of,
233–34.
Fredericksburg, Virginia,
221–38
Colonial and Revolutionary
War Sites, 223–32
Kenmore, 223–25
Mary Washington House,
229–31
Mary Washington Monu-
ment, 231–32
Masonic Lodge, 225
Mercer Apothecary Shop,
225–27
Monroe Museum, 227–28
Rising Sun Tavern, 228–
29
colonial houses, 232–33
Dick House, 232
John Paul Jones House,
232–33
Mortimer House, 233
Weedon House ("Sentry
Box"), 233
driving tour, 222
motels, hotels, and inns, 289
non-Revolutionary sites
Fredericksburg and

Spotsylvania National
Military Park, 233–35
Revolutionary War history,
221, 223
side trip, recommended
Wakefield, 235–38
taxi service, 222
transportation, public, 222
Visitors' Center, 222
Fullerton, John, 25

Gadsby, John, 243–45
Gadsden, Christopher, 10, 20,
29, 267
Garfield, James, 80
Gasoline, 302
Gaston, Alexander, 147
Gaston, William, 147
Gates, Horatio, 52–53, 54,
69, 75, 92, 116
Geddy, James, 169
Geddy, James, II, 169
George II, King of England,
45, 46, 145, 221
George III, King of England,
18, 131, 140, 141, 171
Georgetown, South Carolina,
43–47
Colonial and Revolutionary
War Sites, 44–46
Belle Island Gardens, 44
Bolen-Bellume House, 44
Hopsewee Plantation, 44–
45
Kaminski House, 45
Masonic Temple, 45
Pawley-Parker House, 45
Prince George Winyah
Church, 45–46
Rice Museum, 46

Georgetown, South Carolina (*Cont.*)
   Winyah Indigo Society, 46
   colonial houses, 46–47
   guided tours, 43
   motels, hotels, and inns, 275
   Revolutionary War history, 43–44
   Visitors' Center, 43
Gershwin, George, 28
Gibbes, William, 25
Gilpin, George, 252
Gist, Mordecai, 53
Glen, James, 25
Glover, George W., 123
Godfrey, Thomas, 123
Gooch, William, 166, 170
Goodwin, W. A. R., 162
Gordon, Isabel. *See* Mercer, Isabel Gordon
Gordon family, 224
Grady, John, 133, 135
Graffenreid, Baron Christopher de, 140
Grant, Ulysses S., 208, 234–35
Grasse, Comte de, 180–81
Graves, Admiral, 180
Graves, Calvin, 94
Green, Valentine, 67
Greene, Nathanael, 23, 48, 59, 65, 66, 67, 68, 75, 87, 88, 91–94, 95, 98, 104, 144, 146, 221
Greensboro Area, North Carolina, 87–103
   Alamance, 98–103
     Allen House, 100–101
     Battle Monument, 101
     Battleground State Historic Site, 100–103

     Hunter Monument, 101–102
     Pugh's Rock, 102–103
     Revolutionary War history, 98–100
     Visitors' Center, 100
   driving tour, 90
   Guilford Courthouse, 87–98
     Delaware Monument, 90–91
     Francisco Monument, 91, 92
     Greene Monument, 91–94
     Maryland Monument, 94
     No North-No South Stone, 94–95
     Revolutionary War history, 87–88
     Signers' Monument, 95
     Stewart Monument, 95–96
     Third Line Monument, 96
     Turner Monument, 96–97
     Visitors' Center, 90
     Winston-Franklin Graves, 98
     Winston Monument, 96, 97–98
   motels, hotels, and inns, 277–79
Grimké-Drayton, John, 41
Grunewald, Gustavus, 113
Guilford Courthouse (North Carolina), 87–98
Gunston Hall (Virginia), 255–56
Gurney, Richard, 174

Hadfield, George, 253
Hagood, Governor (South Carolina), 80

Haidt, John Valentine, 113
Haiglar, King, 63
Hamilton, Alexander, 182, 216, 244
Hampton, Senator (South Carolina), 80
Hanover, Virginia, 209–210
Hansen, Oskar J. W., 192
Harnett, Cornelius, 122, 123, 126
Harrison, Anne. *See* Taliaferro, Anne Harrison
Harrison, Benjamin, 173, 198, 205, 210, 212, 268
Harrison, Elizabeth. *See* Randolph, Elizabeth Harrison
Harrison, William Henry, 210
Hatch, General, 25
Hawks, Francis, 147
Hawks, John, 138, 142, 147, 150, 151
Hayne, Robert, 24
Henry, Patrick, 162, 166, 168, 171, 174, 190, 198, 199, 202, 203, 204, 210, 218, 220, 221, 224, 229, 268
Henry, Sarah Shelton, 210
Hepburn, Charles, 128
Hewes, Joseph, 95, 148–49, 156, 267, 268
Heyward, Daniel, 12, 15
Heyward, DuBose, 28
Heyward, Mary Miles, 15
Heyward, Thomas, 12–13, 267
Heyward, Thomas, Jr., 15, 16, 18
Hill, Edward, III, 211
Hill, Elizabeth. *See* Carter, Elizabeth Hill
Hill, Frederick, 132

Hillsborough, North Carolina, 115–18
  motels, hotels, and inns, 281
  Revolutionary War history, 115–16
  sites of interest
    Thomas Burke Grave, 116–17
    Colonial Inn, 117
    Fanning House site, 117
    Hooper House, 117
    Orange County Historical Museum, 117
    Presbyterian Church Cemetery, 117–18
    Regulator Marker, 118
    Tryon's Military Camp site, 118
Hilton, Richard Hobson, 61
Himley, John James, 16
Hodgson, Thomas, 153
Holmes, Isaac, 14
Holmes, John Bee, 13, 16
Holmes, Oliver Wendell, 254
Hood, Admiral, 180
Hooker, Joseph, 234
Hooper, William, 95, 115, 117, 118, 124, 267, 268
Hoover, Herbert, 74, 249
Hopkins, John, 206
Hotels, 270–91
  North Carolina, 277–83
  South Carolina, 274–77
  Virginia, 283–91
Houdon, Jean Antoine, 201
Houston, William, 119
Howard, Martin, 147
Howe, Robert, 131
Hudson, Charles, 36
Huger, John, 29
Hunt, R. M., 191
Hunt, Robert, 194

Hunter, James, 101–102
Hus, Jan, 104
Husband, Amy Allen, 100
Husband, Herman, 100, 115

Inns, 270–91
    North Carolina, 277–83
    South Carolina, 274–77
    Virginia, 283–91
International visitors, information for, 293–302
Iredell, Hannah Johnston, 154, 155
Iredell, James, 149, 154–55, 156, 157
Izard, Polly. *See* Middleton, Polly Izard
Izard, Ralph, 26
Izard, Sally. *See* Campbell, Sally Izard
Izard, Walter, 26

Jackson, Andrew, 24, 29, 62, 231
Jackson, Thomas J. ("Stonewall"), 207, 234
James Fort (Virginia), 195–96, 197
Jamestown, Virginia, 192–97
Jasper, William, 23
Jefferson, Martha, 216, 219
Jefferson, Martha Skelton, 215
Jefferson, Peter, 176
Jefferson, Thomas, 162, 165, 166, 171, 173, 174, 176, 178, 179, 190, 198, 201, 202, 205, 212, 213–19, 220, 221, 224, 229, 241, 244, 245, 263, 268
Jenner, Edward, 149

Jobson family, 128
Johnson, Robert, 20
Johnston, Anne, 148
Johnston, Hannah. *See* Iredell, Hannah Johnston
Johnston, Samuel, 116, 156
Jones, John Paul, 221, 224, 232–33, 241, 244, 261
Jouett, Jack, 212–13, 215

Kaminski, Mrs. Harold, 45
Keck, Charles, 220
Kelley, Eunice, 141
Kennedy, John D., 61, 63
Kennedy, John F., 254
Kennedy, Robert, 254
Kershaw, Joseph, 57
Kershaw, Joseph Brevard, 61, 62
Kilometers, conversion into miles, 302
King, Mrs. Elizabeth, 151
King's Mountain National Military Park (South Carolina), 71–75
Kirkland, Richard, 61
Kirkwood, Robert, 91
Kneller, Godfrey, 140
Krauss, John, 108

Lafayette, George Washington, 261
Lafayette, Marquis de, 29, 43, 55, 61, 65, 173, 175, 180, 181, 191, 193, 198, 201, 204, 205, 217, 223, 224, 225, 228, 229, 231, 233, 244, 245, 246, 250, 252, 257, 261

Lami, Louis Eugene, 182
La Pierre, John, 123
Laurens, Henry, 11, 18
Laurens, John, 186
Lawrison family, 252
Leach, James, 128
Lear, Tobias, 263
Lee, Ann Custis, 253
Lee, Anne Carter, 245, 246
Lee, Arthur, 151
Lee, Francis D., 20
Lee, Francis Lightfoot, 268
Lee, Henry ("Light-Horse
        Harry"), 43, 48, 51,
        65, 66, 211, 233, 244,
        245–46, 248, 253
Lee, Richard Henry, 212, 268
Lee, Robert E., 19, 206, 207,
        208, 234, 242, 246,
        248, 249, 253
Leicht, Johann Simon, 111
Leinbach, Henry, 111
L'Enfant, Pierre Charles, 253
Lewis, Betty Washington,
        122, 223, 224, 225,
        230, 231
Lewis, Fielding, 223–25, 232
Lewis, Lawrence, 256
Lewis, Nellie Custis, 249,
        256, 257, 261
Lewis, Lorenzo, 256–57
Lewis, Meriwether, 220
Lillington, Alexander, 133
Lillington, Arthur, 135
Lincoln, Abraham, 38, 39, 61
Lincoln, Benjamin, 3–4, 184,
        188
Littledale, Mary, 158
Littlejohn, Sarah, 148
Littlejohn, William, 148
Lobb, Jacob, 126

Longstreet, James, 234
Lord, William, 128
Lorrain, Claude, 141
Lukeman, Augustus, 93
Luyten, William, 19
Lynch, Thomas, Jr., 45, 267
Lynch, Thomas, Sr., 10, 18,
        44–45, 46, 267

McCarty, Anne. *See* Ramsay,
        Anne McCarty
McClellan, George, 208, 211
McCulloch, Henry Eustace,
        157
McDonald, Adam, 27
McDonald, Donald, 132–33
McDowell, John, 130, 131
McLean, William, 72
McLeoad, Donald, 133
McNeill, Hector, 116
Madison, James, 166, 217, 268
Magnolia Gardens (South
        Carolina), 40–41
Maham, Hezekiah, 51
Manigault, Gabriel, 28, 30–31
Manigault, Joseph, 30–31
Manigault, Mrs. Peter, 31
Marion, Francis, 16, 18, 23,
        43–44, 48, 51
Marion, Robert, 18
Marjoribanks, John, 48, 49, 50
Marshall, John, 178, 202–203,
        206, 229, 241
Martin, James, 61
Martin, Josiah, 116, 132, 138,
        143, 145
Mason, Ann, 256
Mason, George, 168, 198,
        221, 224, 229, 239,
        244, 255–56
Matear, Robert, 118

Mathieu, J. B., 63
Mattocks, John, 72
Maury, James, 210
Maury, Matthew F., 207
Meade, George C., 25
Mercer, Hugh, 221, 226–27,
    229, 233
Mercer, Isabel Gordon, 226
Mercie, Jean Antoine, 207
Merrill, Benjamin, 118
Meyer, Dorothea, 110
Meyer, Jacob, 109, 110
Michie, John, 218
Middleton, Arthur, 18, 26, 42,
    267
Middleton, Henry, 10, 42, 267
Middleton, Polly Izard, 26
Middleton Place Gardens
    (South Carolina), 41–
    42
Miksch, Johann Matthew, 108
Miles, conversion into kilo-
    meters, 302
Miles, Mary. *See* Heyward,
    Mary Miles
Millen, Quentin, 157
Mills, Robert, 55, 207
Monk, George, Duke of
    Albemarle, 34
Monroe, James, 20, 29, 151,
    166, 206, 216–18,
    227–28, 229
Montgomery, Richard, 261
Monticello (Virginia), 212,
    213–17
Moore, Andrew, 82
Moore, Augustine, 186
Moore, Augustus, 150
Moore, Charles, 81, 82, 83
Moore, James, 132, 133
Moore, James Fulton, 135

Moore, Kate. *See* Barry, Kate
    Moore
Moore, Lucy, 186
Moore, Mary, 81, 82
Moore, Maurice, 126, 128,
    129, 131, 132
Moore, Nathaniel, 128–29
Moore, Roger, 129, 132
Moore, Thomas, 82
Moore's Creek National
    Military Park (North
    Carolina), 132–37
Moravians, 104–14
Morehead, James, 97
Morgan, Daniel, 75–76, 79,
    80, 82, 87
Morris, Gouverneur, 261
Morse, Samuel F. B., 16, 29
Mortimer, Charles, 233
Motels, 270–91
    North Carolina, 277–83
    South Carolina, 274–77
    Virginia, 283–91
Motte, Rebecca, 25
Moultrie, William, 11, 36, 50
Mount Vernon (George
    Washington's estate),
    236, 242, 247, 252,
    256, 257, 258–263
Moustier, Comte de, 262
Moynihan, Fred, 207
Mullins, W. H., 97
Murray, John, Earl of
    Dunmore, 170, 171,
    172, 198, 203, 229

Napoleon I, 218, 228
Nelson, Thomas ("Scotch
    Tom"), 191
Nelson, Thomas, Jr., 190, 191,
    202, 212, 268

New Bern, North Carolina,
138–47
  Colonial and Revolutionary
    War Sites, 139–46
    Christ Episcopal Church,
      145–46
    Clermont Cemetery, 146
    Cypress Tree, 146
    Lady Blessington
      Cannon, 146
    Tryon Palace Complex,
      139–45
  colonial houses, 146–47
    Gaston Office, 147
    Hawks-Lasitter House,
      146–47
    Howard House, 147
    Masonic Meeting Hall,
      147
  motels, hotels, and inns,
    282–83
  Revolutionary War history,
    138–39
Newman, Stephen, 129
Ninety-Six, South Carolina,
  65–68
North Carolina, 87–157
  Edenton, 148–57
    Colonial and Revolution-
      ary War Sites, 150–56
    colonial houses, 157
    Revolutionary War his-
      tory, 148–50
  Greensboro area, 87–103
    Alamance, 98–103
    Guilford Courthouse,
      87–98
    Revolutionary War his-
      tory, 87–88, 98–100
  Hillsborough, 115–18

    Revolutionary War his-
      tory, 115–16
    sites, 116–18
    motels, hotels, and inns,
      277–83
  New Bern, 138–47
    Colonial and Revolution-
      ary War Sites, 139–46
    colonial houses, 146–47
    Revolutionary War his-
      tory, 138–39
  State Facts, 267–68
  Wilmington area, 119–37
    Brunswick Town, 126–31
    Colonial and Revolution-
      ary War Sites, 120–23
    colonial houses, 123–24
    Currie (Moore's Creek),
      132–37
    non-Revolutionary sites
      of interest, 125–26
    Orton Plantation, 131–32
    Revolutionary War his-
      tory, 119–20
  Winston-Salem, 104–14
    Old Salem sites, 108–14
    Revolutionary War his-
      tory, 104–108
  See also individual names
    of cities and towns
Noailles, Viscount de, 186
Noland, William C., 102

O'Hara, Charles, 184, 188
Orton Plantation (North
  Carolina), 131–32
Osceola, 37
Overman, Lee, 93

Pacheo (Spanish artist), 123
Packer, Francis, 93, 125

Page, John, 176
Parker, Peter, 36
Parks, William, 162
Partridge, William Ordway, 194
Paul, John. *See* Jones, John Paul
Paul, William, 232
Peale, Charles Willson, 29, 204, 261
Peale, Rembrandt, 29, 228
Pelzer, A., 95
Pendleton, Edmund, 168, 221, 229, 268
Penn, John, 95, 268
Pennington, William, 126
Pershing, John J., 254
Person, Ogden, 94
Pescud, Peter Francisco, 91
Peter, Martha Custis, 261
Peter, Thomas, 261
Pettygrove, Charles, 153
Peyster, Abraham de, 70
Phillips, General, 88
Piccirilli, Attilio, 218
Pickens, Andrew, 48
Pickens, F. W., 38
Pinckney, Charles, 14, 267
Pinckney, Charles Cotesworth, 13, 19, 31, 267
Pinckney, Eliza Lucas, 15, 18
Pine, Robert Edge, 261, 262
Pitt, William, 22
Pocahontas, 192, 194–95, 204
Poe, Edgar Allan, 207–208, 220
Pollock, Thomas, 156
Pope, Anne. *See* Washington, Anne Pope
Posey, Thomas, 221
Potts, John, 246

Powers, Hiram, 257
Powhatan, Indian Chief, 194, 196
Pratt, Charles, Earl of Camden, 57
Pratt, Matthew, 174
Preston, William, 105
Pugh, James, 102–103, 118

Queen Anne's Town. *See* Edenton, North Carolina
Quince, Mrs. John, 124
Quince, Richard, 130, 132

Rabb, William, 72
Raleigh, Sir Walter, 174
Ramsay, Anne McCarty, 248
Ramsay, Bess, 248
Ramsay, David, 26–27
Ramsay, Dennis, 247
Ramsay, William, 239, 247–48
Ramsey, Allan, 171
Randolf, William, III, 204–205
Randolph, Elizabeth Harrison, 173
Randolph, Peyton, 162, 172–74, 175, 268
Randolph, William, 176
Rawdon, Francis, 25, 53, 54, 57, 59, 66, 68
Reonalds, George, 128
Reynolds, Joshua, 140
Rhett, William, 10, 20
Richmond, Virginia, 198–211
   Colonial and Revolutionary War Sites, 201–205
   Capitol, The, 201
   Capitol Square, 201–202

Marshall House, 202–203
St. John's Episcopal
  Church, 203–204
Virginia Historical
  Society, 204
Wilton, 204–205
colonial houses
  Ampthill, 205
  Craig House, 205
  Hopkins-Call House,
    205–206
driving tour, 200
motels, hotels, and inns,
  286–88
non-Revolutionary sites of
  interest, 206–209
  Hollywood Cemetery, 206
  Lee House, 206
  Monument Avenue,
    206–207
  Museum of the Con-
    federacy, 207
  Poe Museum, 207–208
  Richmond National
    Battlefield site, 208
  St. Paul's Church, 208
  tobacco companies,
    208–209
  Valentine Museum
    Complex, 209
Revolutionary War history,
  198–99
side trips, recommended,
  209–11
  Hanover, 209–210
  Plantation House, 210–11
taxi service, 199
transportation, public, 199
Visitors' Center, 199
walking tours, 199–200
Rochambeau, Comte de, 178,
  180, 181, 187, 188,
  224, 233
Rockefeller, John D., Jr., 162
Roebling, Mrs. Washington
  A., 25
Rolfe, John, 192, 194
Rosenthal, Joseph, 254–55
Ross, Alexander, 186
Russell, George, 158
Russell, John, 130
Russell, Justina Davis, 130
Russell, Nathaniel, 32
Rutledge, Governor John
  (South Carolina), 4
Rutledge, Edward, 10, 13, 18,
  20, 267
Rutledge, John, 10, 11, 19,
  267

Sacajawea, 220
Sanderson, Richard, 151
Santee, South Carolina, 48–51
  Colonial and Revolutionary
    War Sites, 49–51
    Eutaw Springs battlefield
      site, 49–50
    Fort Watson site, 50–51
  motels, hotels, and inns,
    275–76
  non-Revolutionary site of
    interest, 51
    Wings and Wheels
      Museum, 51
  Revolutionary War history,
    48–49
Savage, Edward, 29, 144
Savage, Thomas, 28
Savery, William, 144
Schanck, Garrett, 45
Schenck, David, 89, 91
Schenck, Paul, 93

Scott, Winfield, 249
Sevier, John, 69, 70, 72
Sharples, James, 261
Sheeter, Charles, 151
Shelby, Isaac, 69, 70, 72
Shelton, John, 210
Shelton, Sarah. *See* Henry,
    Sarah Shelton
Sherman, William T., 18, 39,
    42, 63
Sievers, F. William, 207
Simcoe, John G., 198
Simms, William Gilmore, 23
Sitgreaves, John, 143
Skelton, Martha Wayles. *See*
    Jefferson, Martha
    Skelton
Skelton, Polly, 230
Slocomb, Ezekiel, 135–36
Slocomb, Mary, 135–36, 137
Smith, Benjamin, 132
Smith, C. Alphonso, 94
Smith, Captain John (c. 1579–
    1631), 194, 195
Smith, Captain John (Mary-
    land), 96
Smith, Robert, 20
Smith, Sarah Moore, 25
South Carolina, 3–84
    Camden, 52–68
        Colonial and Revolution-
            ary War Sites, 54–62
        colonial houses, 61–62
        non-Revolutionary sites
            of interest, 62–63
        Revolutionary War his-
            tory, 52–54
        side trips, recommended,
            64–68
    Charleston, 3–42
        Colonial and Revolution-
            ary War Sites, 7–23

        colonial houses, 24–28
        non-Revolutionary sites
            of interest, 28–33
        Revolutionary War his-
            tory, 3–4
        side trips, recommended,
            33–42
    Georgetown, 43–47
        Colonial and Revolution-
            ary War Sites, 44–46
        colonial houses, 46–47
        Revolutionary War his-
            tory, 43–44
        motels, hotels, and inns,
            274–77
    Santee, 48–51
        Colonial and Revolution-
            ary War Sites, 49–51
        non-Revolutionary sites
            of interest, 51
        Revolutionary War his-
            tory, 48–49
    Spartanburg Area, 69–84
        Cowpens, 75–78
        King's Mountain, 69–75
        Revolutionary War his-
            tory, 69–71, 75–77
        side trips, recommended,
            81–84
    State Facts, 267
    See also individual names
        of cities and towns
Spaight, Elizabeth Wilson,
    146
Spaight, Richard, 146
Spaight, Richard Dobbs, 139,
    146, 268
Spartanburg Area, South
    Carolina, 69–84
    Cowpens, 75–78, 79
    downtown area, 78–80

Morgan Statue, 78–80
Spartanburg Regional
   Museum, 80
King's Mountain, 69–75
motels, hotels, and inns,
   276–77
Revolutionary War history,
   69–71, 75–77
side trip, recommended,
   81–84
   Walnut Grove Plantation,
      81–84
Spenser, Nicholas, 258
Spotswood, Alexander, 166,
   170, 172
Spotsylvania Courthouse,
   Battle of, 233, 234–35
Sprunt family, 132
Stabler, Edward, 248
Stanly, Ann Cogdell, 143,
   144, 145
Stanly, John Wright, 142–45,
   146
Steadman, Captain, 82–83
Steadman, Charles, 93
Stevenson, Captain, 145
Stewart, Alexander, 48
Stewart, James, 95–96
Stuart, Gilbert, 15, 29, 225,
   259
Stuart, J. E. B., 206–207, 249
Sullivan's Island (South
   Carolina), 35–37
Sully, Thomas, 113, 204, 214
Sumter, Thomas, 38
Sweeney, George, 178
Symonds, Thomas, 186

Taft, William Howard, 254
Taliaferro, Elizabeth. *See*
   Wythe, Elizabeth
   Taliaferro

Taliaferro, Richard, 177, 205
Taliaferro, Anne Harrison, 205
Tannenburg, Daniel, 112
Tarleton, Banastre, 53, 54,
   75, 76, 98, 179, 212,
   213, 215
Tarpley, James, 166
Taylor, N., 129
Taylor, Zachary, 202
Teach, Edward ("Black-
   beard"), 9, 23
Theus, Jeremiah, 15, 16, 31
Thornton, William, 256
Timrod, Henry, 22
Todd, George, 61
Trumbull, John, 29, 79, 190,
   261
Tryon, Charles, 142
Tryon, Margaret, 130, 138
Tryon, William, 99, 101, 102,
   103, 118, 126, 130,
   131, 138, 139–45
Turgot, 216
Turner, Mrs. Kerrenhappuck,
   96–97
Tyler, John, 206

United Daughters of the Confederacy, 31, 254

Vail, Mary. *See* Wilson,
   Mary Vail
Valentine, E., 22, 207
Valentine, Mann, 209
Van Brunt, H., 191
Vanderlyn, John, 29
Vaughan, Samuel, 261
Vernon, Edward, 258
Vile, William, 141
Villepigue, John B., 63

Villepigue, John Cantey, 61
Virginia, 161–263
  Alexandria, 239–57
    Colonial and Revolution-
      ary War Sites, 241–51
    colonial houses, 251–52
    Revolutionary War his-
      tory, 239, 241
    side trips, recommended,
      252–57
  Charlottesville, 212–20
    downtown, 219–20
    Monticello, 213–17
    Revolutionary War his-
      tory, 212–13
    sites near Monticello,
      217–19
  Fredericksburg, 221–38
    Colonial and Revolution-
      ary War Sites, 223–32
    colonial houses, 232–33
    non-Revolutionary sites
      of interest, 233–35
    Revolutionary War his-
      tory, 221–23
    side trip, recommended,
      235–38
    motels, hotels and inns,
      283–91
  Richmond, 198–211
    Colonial and Revolution-
      ary War Sites, 201–205
    colonial houses, 205–206
    non-Revolutionary sites
      of interest, 206–209
    Revolutionary War his-
      tory, 198–199
    side trips, recommended,
      209–211
  State Facts, 268–69
  Williamsburg, 161–79

    Revolutionary War his-
      tory, 161–65
    side trip, recommended,
      178–79
    sites of interest, 165–78
  Yorktown, 180–97
    battlefield site, 184–86
    Revolutionary War his-
      tory, 180–84
    side trip, recommended,
      192–97
    sites of interest, 188–92
  See also individual names
    of cities and towns
Virginia, University of, 220
"Visit U.S.A." Program,
  293–95
Vogler, Christina, 112, 113
Vogler, John, 112–13
Voltaire, 216

Waddell, Hugh, 99
Waite, Ezra, 25
Wakefield (Washington's
  birthplace), 235–38
Walker, Henderson, 156
Walker, Robert, 14
Wallace, Gustavus, 221
Walnut Grove Plantation
  (South Carolina), 81–
  84
Ward, J. Q. A., 78, 191
Warner, Mildred. *See* Wash-
  ington, Mrs. Lawrence
Warren, Anne, 245
Warren, Joseph, 250
Warren, Russell, 32
Washington, Anne Pope, 235
Washington, Augustine, 236,
  258

Washington, Augustine, Jr., 236

Washington, Betty. *See* Lewis, Betty Washington

Washington, Bushrod, 228, 260

Washington, Charles, 228

Washington, George, 8, 12, 13–14, 15, 19, 22, 24, 36, 45, 62, 92, 95, 107, 110, 124, 132, 139, 140, 141, 144, 146, 147, 154, 155, 166, 177, 178, 179, 180, 181, 184, 186, 187, 188, 198, 204, 205, 211, 221, 223, 224, 225, 226, 228, 229, 230, 231, 233, 239, 241, 242–45, 246, 247, 248, 249, 251, 252, 256, 268
    birthplace, 235–38, 258
    busts of, 16, 257
    estate of. *See* Mount Vernon
    paintings of, 29, 259
    portraits of, 15, 225, 261
    statues of, 201, 202, 250

Washington, Jane Butler, 236

Washington, Jane Elliot, 28

Washington, John, 235, 236, 258

Washington, Lawrence (George's grandfather), 236, 239

Washington, Lawrence (George's half-brother), 258

Washington, Martha, 242, 246, 249, 253, 256, 258, 260, 261, 262

Washington, Mildred, 236

Washington, Mary Ball, 229–32, 236, 258

Washington, William, 16, 27–28, 48, 49, 76, 77, 88, 91, 122

Wayne, Anthony, 193, 229

Webster, Daniel, 248

Weedon, George, 221, 226, 228, 233

Weedon, Isabella, 233

Weldon, Felix W. de, 255

Wesley, John, 19

West, Benjamin, 29, 228

West, John, Jr., 239

Wetherburn, Henry, 175–76

Whedbee, Joseph, 155

Whistler, Anna, 125–26

Whistler, James Abbott McNeill, 125–26

White, E. B., 29

Wickham, John, 209

Wilderness, Battle of the, 233, 234

Wilkens, John, 131

William and Mary, College of, 161, 173, 178

William III, King of England, 161

Williams, John, 69, 115

Williamsburg, Virginia, 161–79
    Brush-Everard House, 165
    Bruton Parish Church, 165–66, 167
    Capitol, 166, 168–69
    Courthouse, 169
    Geddy House, 169–70
    Governor's Palace, 170–72
    guided tours, 163–64
    Magazine, 172

Williamsburg, Virginia (*Cont.*)
  motels, hotels, and inns,
    283–85
  Public Gaol, 174
  Raleigh Tavern, 174–75
  Randolph House, 172–74
  Revolutionary War history,
    161–62, 165
  side trip, recommended
    Carter's Grove Plantation,
      178–79
  Visitors' Center, 163
  walking tours, 164
  Wetherburn's Tavern,
    175–77
  Wythe House, 177–78
Williamson, Hugh, 149–50,
  268
Wills, Robert, 191
Wilmington Area, North
    Carolina, 119–37
  Revolutionary War history,
    119–120
  Colonial and Revolutionary
      War Sites, 120–23
    Cornwallis House
      (Burgwin-Wright
      House), 120–22
    Harnett Monument, 122
    St. James Episcopal
      Church, 122–23, 124
    Stamp Act Defiance
      Monument, 123
  colonial houses, 123–24
    Captain Cook House,
      123–24
    Hooper House site, 124
    Quince-Washington
      House, 124
  Brunswick Town, 126–31

  Revolutionary War his-
      tory, 126–27
  Currie (Moore's Creek),
      132–37
    Revolutionary War his-
        tory, 132–33
  motels, hotels, and inns, 282
  non-Revolutionary sites of
      interest, 125–26
    Confederate Monument,
      125
    Dudley Mansion, 125
    National Cemetery, 125
    U.S.S. *North Carolina*
      Battleship Memorial,
      125
    Whistler House site,
      125–26
  Orton Plantation, 131–32
    Revolutionary War history,
      119–20
  taxi service, 120
  transportation, public, 120
  Visitors' Center, 120
Wilson, Alexander, 82
Wilson, Elizabeth. *See*
    Spaight, Elizabeth
    Wilson
Wilson, James, 149
Wilson, Mary Vail, 146
Wilson, William, 146
Wilson, Woodrow, 220
Wilton, Joseph, 22
Winkler, John C., 113–14
Winn, Christina. *See* Bratton,
    Christina Winn
Winn, Richard, 64
Winnsboro, South Carolina,
    64–65
Winston, Joseph, 69, 97–98

Winston-Salem, North Carolina, 98, 104–14
  motels, hotels, and inns, 279–80
  Old Salem sites, 108–14
    Miksch Tobacco Shop, 108
    Museum of Early Southern Decorative Arts, 108–109
    Salem Tavern, 109–10
    Single Brothers' House, 110–12
    Vogler House, 112–13
    Wachovia Museum (Boys' School), 113
    Winkler Bakery, 113–14
  Revolutionary War history, 104–108
  Visitors' Center, 105
  walking tour, 105
Wise, John, 243
Witherspoon, John Knox, 118
Wollaston, John, 153, 225
Woodford, William, 221
Woodlawn Plantation (Virginia), 256–57

Wragg, Samuel, 10
Wren, James, 242
Wright, Joshua, 121
Wythe, George, 177–78, 198, 204, 216, 221, 229, 268
Wythe, Elizabeth Taliaferro, 177

Yolin, F. C., 71
Yorktown, Virginia, 180–97
  Archer Cottage, 189
  battlefield site, 184–88
  Custom House, 189
  Digges House, 190
  driving tour, 185
  Grace Church, 190
  motels, hotels, and inns, 285–86
  Nelson House, 190–91
  Revolutionary War history, 180–84
  side trip, recommended Jamestown, 192–97
  Swan Tavern, 191
  Victory Monument, 191–92
  Visitors' Center, 185